Backcountry
Skiing

D1011971

BACKCOUNTRY SKIING

The Sierra Club Guide to Skiing off the Beaten Track

Lito Tejada-Flores

SIERRA CLUB BOOKS   SAN FRANCISCO

The Sierra Club, founded in 1892 by John Muir, has devoted itself to the study and protection of the earth's scenic and ecological resources—mountains, wetlands, woodlands, wild shores and rivers, deserts and plains. The publishing program of the Sierra Club offers books to the public as a nonprofit educational service in the hope that they may enlarge the public's understanding of the Club's basic concerns. The point of view expressed in each book, however, does not necessarily represent that of the Club. The Sierra Club has some fifty chapters coast to coast, in Canada, Hawaii, and Alaska. For information about how you may participate in its programs to preserve wilderness and the quality of life, please address inquiries to Sierra Club, 530 Bush Street, San Francisco, CA 94108.

Library of Congress Cataloging in Publication Data

Tejada-Flores, Lito.
BACKCOUNTRY SKIING.

Bibliography: p. 297
Includes index.
1. Cross-country skiing.   2. Skis and skiing.
I. Title.
GV855.3.T44   796.93   81-8958
ISBN 0-87156-287-1 (pbk.)   AACR2

Cover design by Pushpin Studios
Book design by Jon Goodchild
Illustrations by Lito Tejada-Flores

Printed in the United States of America

10   9   8   7   6   5   4   3   2   1

*Pour Linda, avec qui
j'ai redécouvert le ski*

Contents

Introduction

***B**ackcountry skiing is not new.* No more than skiing itself. In fact, what I think of as backcountry skiing—skiing away from ski areas, off the beaten track, far from the crowd—has much more in common with early skiing than with today's prepackaged, high-priced versions of the sport. You don't need a lift ticket or a trail pass to go backcountry skiing. You don't have to join a ski club or wear the right clothes in the right colors. You don't even have to use a certain type of skis or a particular technique. Simply skiing into the winter landscape, away from prepared terrain, on your own or with friends—that's what I'm talking about and what this book is about.

Backcountry skiing, like the backcountry, has a lot to do with one's state of mind. The backcountry does not begin 3.7 kilometers or a two-day walk from the roadhead. Rather we feel ourselves in the backcountry when a mantle of overcivilized responses slips away, when a peculiarly urban weight lifts from the spirit, and the landscape seems to promise adventure, or at least the possibility of adventure.

So with backcountry skiing. It is not synonymous

with arduous expeditions in remote regions, though they are definitely a part of backcountry skiing. It is not a sport reserved for superathletes, though they will find it endlessly challenging. Backcountry skiing is accessible to families, to children, to those who have spent their whole lives skiing and to those who never saw a ski before the age of forty. The essence of backcountry skiing is skiing on your own. You and winter. Your skis and untracked, unprepared snow. It is definitely a state of mind you put on, much as you put on your skis and boots. It's a state of mind composed of audacity and prudence, a love of winter and of effort, of graceful movement, and of exploration. In this overexplored world of ours, the winter backcountry is always fresh and unexplored because it's always changing; each storm, each shift in temperature creates new terrain. The backcountry—mountains, forests, high plateaus—has been renewing itself every winter beyond all memory. And as long as I can remember, skiers too have been renewing themselves in this challenging, white environment.

Backcountry skiing isn't new, but it is changing. Hence this book. In 1972, Allen Steck and I wrote *Wilderness Skiing* for the Sierra Club. We were talking about the very same sport, and it still doesn't matter whether you call it ski touring, wilderness skiing, cross-country skiing, ski mountaineering or, as I do here, backcountry skiing. The focus is the same: getting away from it all on skis.

But our skis and the rest of our equipment have changed over the years; classic skiing techniques have evolved and been perfected, and new techniques have emerged. Learning to ski is easier today; the equipment is better, true, but we also know more about the motor skills involved in skiing and about the way people learn. Most exciting, many of the traditional limits of backcountry skiing have disappeared as adventurous skiers have sought to utilize ever-lighter ski equipment in ever more remote and challenging situations, combining the

2

techniques and strategies of different styles of skiing. This new synthesis of equipment and technique demanded a new handbook, and here it is.

But this book, I hope, is far more than just an update of *Wilderness Skiing*. Both format and organization are different, reflecting a very practical focus on the skiing skills needed to handle the full spectrum of backcountry conditions, the challenging terrain and challenging snow, found far from lift-served slopes and packed cross-country trails.

In the eight years since *Wilderness Skiing* first appeared, I have spent each winter as a ski teacher and tourer, each spring touring for my own pleasure. My own skiing in backcountry situations has become more efficient, more sophisticated, more carefree. Through continuous teaching I have developed new approaches for mastering ever more effective techniques for ungroomed snow. More than half of this new book is devoted to ski technique—justifiably so. Backcountry skiing is first and foremost a question of attitude, of freeing oneself from the confines of the beaten track; but this freedom quickly proves to be an illusion if the skier seeks new horizons without adequate technique. Contemporary backcountry ski techniques as well as a new presentation of classic ski techniques, then, constitute the backbone of this book. New tools for a new generation of backcountry skiers.

One thing, however, hasn't changed: my conviction that there is no one right way to ski. My own skiing experience has been enriched by my willingness and ability to use all kinds of equipment in all terrain, to use and mix eclectically different kinds of ski techniques to achieve a perfect run or a delightful tour. There is no inherent virtue in a certain ski, a certain binding, a certain turn. The complete backcountry skier makes them all his own, and ultimately sees both equipment and technique as means to an end—that old white magic.

This is what backcountry skiing is all about. Freedom, easy, graceful movement in a seemingly surreal world where most people don't belong; a universe where the skier, touched by a special grace, not only fits in but dances, as though the winter landscape were the friendliest environment on earth. In fact, it can be, but only the backcountry skier knows this. Only the backcountry skier can tap into the full magic of the winter wilderness. Other travelers in this white world—the winter alpinist, the snowshoer—seem hobbled, crippled by the slowness of their pace; the snowmobiler, on the other hand, is so addicted to speed that he destroys the stillness of winter in his attempt to enjoy it. The skier has it all: rhythmic movement, rapid pace, ecstatic descents, access to a world so potentially difficult to penetrate that it really doesn't need wilderness designation to preserve its wilderness character—uncrowded, snowbound, mysterious landscapes of peaks and passes, forests and fields before summer unlocks them to the masses, all this and a solitude deep as winter, companionship as joyous as spring. Yes, the backcountry skier has it all.

Unfortunately, you can't become a backcountry skier simply by reading this or any book. Skiing can only be learned by skiing; ski touring experience can only be gained on actual ski tours. So what can this book do? It can save you time, speeding your apprenticeship, orienting you, pointing you in the right direction. Learning to ski, much less to handle the varied and ofttimes tricky snow conditions found off the beaten track, is quite challenging enough even with the help of experienced friends or instructor/guides; by yourself it can be a real bear. But it can be done. Indeed, many folks actually taught themselves to ski from reading *Wilderness Skiing*; knowing this, I have tried to make this book an even more appropriate tool for the self-taught skier. It may take more than one season to master all the advanced Nordic and Alpine touring techniques described in this book (it's taken me closer to fifteen) but it will be well worth the effort. The learning, with all its attendant spills and crashes, is really just as much fun as expert performance. And no one ever claimed you must be an expert skier to enjoy backcountry skiing. Most ski tourers definitely aren't. From your first steps away from the practice trail or slope, backcountry skiing will be a delight. Good skiing!

Part One

LEARNING TO DO IT: TECHNIQUE AND GEAR

Snow
  rock
    sky
breathe deep then ski

Sky
  snow
    rock
stand dumb & look

Rock
  sky
    snow
only tracks to show

1

Ski Touring Options

How to begin? I know you're eager to put on your skis, to get down to the nuts and bolts of climbing, turning, striding—to delve into the mysteries of deep powder. But there are a few questions to tackle first. Which style of backcountry skiing will you be doing, Nordic or Alpine? If you don't already ski, how can you speed your initial steps? And if you do have some skiing experience, how can you use it to best advantage in off-trail touring?

Broadly speaking there are two styles of skiing, Nordic and Alpine, often called "cross-country" and "downhill," respectively. The Nordic branch of the sport is often held to be synonymous with ski touring while Alpine skiing is thought of only in the mechanized, flash-and-dash context of downhill ski resorts. Not necessarily! Both styles relate to skiing in the backcountry, although the Nordic style is generally more useful and more used. In fact, if you're not already a skier, my advice is *learn Nordic, cross-country skiing first.*

The difference between Nordic and Alpine skiing is primarily one of equipment; other distinctions—styles of movement, types of turns, suitability of terrain—derive from the difference in equipment. Nordic equipment is light (even ultra-light!) and flexible; it permits the skier to cover ground, lots of it, with minimum effort and fatigue. Nordic skis are long and thin; the boots light and relatively low-cut; and the binding, that all-important connection between ski and skier, is of a marvelous simplicity, holding only the toe of the boot to the ski. This combination is ideal for the free-striding motion on which almost all Nordic technique is based. Alpine gear is a good deal heavier, awkward on the flat by comparison but offering great control in steep, icy, or similarly desperate situations.

Alpine skis are wider than cross-country skis and all have steel edges; the boots are heavier, taller and more rigid. The bindings are designed to hold the whole foot flat on the ski (although Alpine touring bindings do permit heel lift in their uphill walking mode).

It comes down to a choice between rapid, efficient skiing on flat, rolling, or moderately inclined terrain; or greater security on steep terrain—an awkward choice for the backcountry skier who would like the advantages of both styles, but there you are. In recent years we have begun to see some equipment that combines some of the possibilities of Nordic and Alpine skiing—but it's just a start. The fusion of these two styles is a real but elusive goal for the expert backcountry skier (I'll cover this in Chapter 7, "The Best of Both Worlds"). But for the present, backcountry skiing implies a choice of one style or the other. It's interesting to see how this state of affairs came about.

Nordic skiing, obviously, is the style of skiing originally developed and still preferred in Norway, Sweden, and Finland. Broad, open, flat or gently rolling country is the characteristic landscape, and the Nordic style suits it perfectly. This is where skiing first appeared; originally, all skiing was Nordic skiing, period. (The oldest existing skis are literally prehistoric; the first written descriptions of

1. *An early backcountry skier in Lapland, from* Opera Laponia, *1673.*

Norwegian and Lapp skiers date from the 1600s; but recognizably "modern" skis didn't appear until the nineteenth century.) Such early skiing, of course, was for transportation rather than sport, getting from point A to point B in winter.

But even in Scandinavia, despite a skiing history based on striding and gliding in a straight line across the countryside, the most enjoyable moments have always been the downhill runs. All of us, not just Scandinavians, feel something akin to a child's dream of flight as we whoosh downhill on skis. So around 1850, skiers from two Norwegian towns invented two different styles of turns in order to control the downhill rush of their skis. The men from Telemark evolved a graceful arcing turn with one foot and ski thrust far ahead of the other. Those of Christiania (today's Oslo) developed a turn in which both skis skidded sideways together. The Telemark turn remains today a Nordic specialty, while the Christiania (or christy) became the basis for a whole new "parallel" style, now known as Alpine skiing.

12

Once again, the name tells all. Alpine skiing developed when Norwegian ski running was transplanted to the Austrian Alps and adapted to slopes far steeper than those in Scandinavia. This development, starting in the early days of the twentieth century, was to be crucial for skiing in general. As skiing in the Alps became a romantic and popular pastime, as winter tourism grew,

2. *A backcountry skier long before the days of fiberglass and Gore-Tex.*

Praktische Anleitung
zur
Erlernung des Schneeschuh-
(Ski-) Laufens
für Touristen, Jäger, Forstleute und Militärs.

→ Mit 33 Illustrationen. ←

Herausgegeben von Theodor Neumayer, München

Schneeschuhfabrikant und Armeelieferant.

Hamburg 1893.

Verlagsanstalt und Druckerei A.-G. (vormals J. F. Richter).
Königl. Schwedisch-Norwegische   Hofdruckerei und Verlagshandlung.

3. Ski instruction books and telemarks have both been around for some time. This book was published in Hamburg in 1893.

innovations in technique and technology came faster and faster.

The commercial development of Alpine skiing totally transformed the sport. Ski lifts, new equipment made of new materials, competition tied to advertising and tourism—all produced a new sport concerned only with skiing *down*, not up or across, mountains. Ease and efficiency of downhill turning was achieved at the expense of mobility and freedom on the level and uphill—and eventually Alpine skiers entrusted this part of their ski experience to machines: lifts and cable cars.

But today, the technological innovation that's characterized Alpine skiing for so long has spilled back over into the world of cross-country Nordic skiing. Sensing new commercial possibilities, the major Alpine ski manufacturers have, in the last ten years, transformed cross-country skiing with new high-technology fiberglass skis and other products. In North America, cross-country skiing seems to have come of age. The Nordic alternative is increasingly attractive in the face of rising costs and rising crowds at downhill resorts. In fact, it's estimated that sometime in the mid-1980s there will be more Nordic than Alpine skiers in this country. Here, too, commercial response to this new market has created a new phenomenon, the Nordic resort. Instead of lift-served slopes, these feature networks of packed trails; and consequently most Nordic skiing takes place not in virgin backcountry snow, but in narrow, ski-width tracks. These resorts are actually a plus for the wilderness skier, not a complaint; for in addition to providing great non-wilderness skiing in their own right, ski resorts, both Alpine and Nordic, are the ideal training grounds for developing backcountry technique.

And that's how it happened: the evolution of two separate styles of skiing. But what do they mean to the backcountry skier? Until very recently, the choice went like this: for winter travel, for the skier's equivalent of summer backpacking, choose Nordic gear hands down; if the goal was climbing to some high peak or pass to enjoy a thrilling downhill run, then Alpine equipment and technique would be preferable. But this generalization is no longer accurate. Improvements in Nordic equipment plus a veritable revolution in Nordic downhill technique (especially the rediscovery and refinement of the venerable Telemark turn) have made the Nordic style both practical and enjoyable for a lot of downhill skiing. In short, lightweight "skinny skis" are today more versatile touring tools than ever.

Then why bother with Alpine touring at all? For several reasons. First, of course, for extreme situations: extremely steep, extremely icy, extremely awkward or dangerous snow; for real ski mountaineering situations where you will already be wearing heavier mountaineering boots for climbing. Then, too, for the particularly dynamic sensation of linked short-radius turns in situations where the Nordic skier would have to use different techniques. Also for the simple ease of handling long descents; although Nordic skiers have expanded their downhill repertoire, downhill techniques on skinny skis are neither easy nor completely reliable. In almost all situations downhill skiing will be easier with Alpine rather than Nordic gear, requiring less strength, balance, and skill. (Dave Beck, author of *Ski Touring in California*, recognizing this fact, grades many of the tours in his book "advanced Nordic, intermediate Alpine," i.e., more skill required on Nordic skis due to the steepness of the terrain.) And finally, Alpine skiing should not be neglected by even the most fanatic Nordic tourer; there are a number of powerful parallel techniques that can be used effectively on Nordic skis but which can be learned much more easily on Alpine skis.

The next five chapters on basic and advanced touring techniques are almost evenly divided between Nordic and Alpine skiing. Personally, I love both styles; I enjoy tailoring both equipment and technique to the tour at hand, and mixing the two

4.   *Turn-of-the-century skiing was synonymous with what we think of today as backcountry skiing or ski touring: no lifts, no packed slopes, and, of course, free-heel bindings.*

styles whenever appropriate (the subject of Chapter 7). Almost all the really expert backcountry skiers I know are proficient at both styles, although they often have a favorite. In general, you will find more backcountry touring situations suitable for Nordic than for Alpine gear. This is especially true if you live in the East or Midwest, and still true to some extent in the Rockies, the Sierra Nevada, or the Pacific Northwest. Big peaks and volcanos, as well as steep chutes and couloirs under harder spring-snow conditions, are the most typically appropriate situations for Alpine touring.

But as I said before: *learn Nordic skiing first*. Not only is it more useful to the backcountry touring skier, it's also a good deal easier to learn. The first steps on the level, at least, are very easy indeed. And this is perhaps a good point at which to stress that you don't need to master advanced skiing skills before venturing into the backcountry in winter. Minimal skills plus a little craftiness will see you through many tours. After your first day on Nordic skis you should possess the basics for getting from here to there on the flat. You may lack the grace, efficiency and maneuverability of more experienced skiers, but who cares? Don't worry too much about downhilling on Nordic skis. At first, you will "fudge" your way past the downhill sections on cross-country skis and still have a great time.

One further point underlines the choice of Nordic skiing to get into backcountry touring—it's cheaper. Outfitting yourself with Nordic touring gear will cost less than half what you would pay for equivalent Alpine touring equipment. And Nordic ski lessons, too, usually cost much less than Alpine ski lessons at a downhill area. This brings us to an important consideration.

Should you take ski lessons? You bet. Although I would love to assure you that this book is all you need to become a hot backcountry skier, I know it's not true. Efficient learning of motor skills—learning to ski for example—depends in large measure on visual images and on imitation. To become an expert skier someday, you'll have to ski with and imitate expert skiers. What a ski instructor does, more than anything else, is give you a good image to copy. If your instructor is a gifted communicator and really concerned about your progress, so much the better (there are, alas, a lot of indifferent, unmotivated ski instructors, Alpine *and* Nordic). In any case, as a long-time ski instructor, I can guarantee you that lessons, while not absolutely necessary, will save you a lot of time, a lot of trial and error. Fortunately, the emergence of Nordic resorts nationwide has made good cross-country instruction much more available now than it was five years ago. So if you find good instruction nearby, do take advantage of it. Failing that, try to enlist the help of skiing friends— preferably patient ones—who can show you what they've learned to do and provide that all-important visual model. The technique chapters that follow will help you to identify and understand what other skiers are doing. But, knowing that all too often the would-be ski tourer is on his or her own, I've written about ski technique in a way that should also let you go out and learn on your own, although perhaps a bit more slowly.

If you are already an expert, or even a moderately competent downhill or cross-country skier, then acquiring the special skills for untracked backcountry snow should be relatively easy. If coping with steeper slopes and powder are your immediate goals, you can take special classes at downhill ski areas. The application to touring is obvious. And remember, there is a great crossover of skills from Nordic skiing to Alpine and vice versa. Any one thing you learn to do on skis will help everything else you try to learn on skis. There is no contradiction or interference between one type of skiing and another, one type of turn and another. The better you get at one style of skiing, the more interested you should be in mastering the other.

But enough of this general advice—it's time to get down to specifics. Let's get our equipment and go.

2

The meadow at dawn:
frozen heart
silent glide
squeak of snow

The meadow at dawn:
wax holds
kick explodes
pole flies out

In the meadow at dawn
two thin tracks
stretch up to a hill:
the hour is for repose
not acts,
even the skier
now stands still

Above the meadow at dawn
you wonder: is it
a new day or
a new skier
waiting
to be born?

2
Nordic
Paraphernalia

B **ravo!** You've taken my advice to learn Nordic skiing first. (If you're already an experienced cross-country skier you may want to skip ahead and use this and the next chapter for reference only, or perhaps for information on how to get a friend started.) In a few days on snow you will have lost all the awkwardness of a beginner; you'll be a real skier, if not yet a backcountry skier. But your long-term goal—skiing away from the beaten path—will definitely influence your first steps. In particular it will help you sort out a veritable jungle of Nordic cross-country ski gear, since a lot of cross-country gear isn't really suitable for off-trail use. The backcountry skier has very special equipment needs: your gear must be strong, light, and, above all, suitable for skiing unpacked, deep, and often difficult snow.

Personally, I hate talking about equipment. At least I hate the obsessive fascination with equipment that so many skiers, backpackers, climbers, and other outdoor people fall prey to. It's easy to become an equipment freak, spending more time thinking and talking about ski gear than actually skiing. An adventurous spirit, not the latest hot gear, is the key to backcountry skiing. But you can't ski without skis on your feet, so with the above caveat firmly in mind, let's see what you'll need. As a Nordic beginner you won't necessarily want the most sophisticated gear, and a great strategy to get started is simply to rent the basic equipment until you're a little more sure of what you want.

Skis

More than any other article of Nordic touring gear, cross-country skis have changed in the last few years. The wooden ski, a beautiful, often hand-crafted object, is dead; the synthetic (or fiberglass-reinforced plastic) ski is here to stay. This is a mixed blessing: Fiberglass skis do ski better and are tougher (a real plus in the backcountry), but they also cost somewhat more than wooden skis ever did. To understand how and why skis have changed, let's look first at the whole range of Nordic skis.

A bewildering array of models has typically been divided into several main categories: racing skis, light touring skis, general touring skis, and mountain touring skis. All Nordic skis are long and narrow; racing skis are the narrowest of all. These are thoroughbreds—special-purpose skis designed for maximum speed in a packed track. Avoid them like the plague for backcountry use. They are really difficult for a beginner or novice to ski on, bloody hard to turn, and a real pain in deep or difficult snow. They are, however, a fertile testing ground for new ski manufacturing concepts, and most recent advances in ski design and construction have originated with racing skis. And of course, the experienced Nordic skier, in a track, finds them a delight. I should explain here that a packed track is the Nordic equivalent of the downhill skier's packed slope. It is a parallel set of ski tracks that determines the direction in which one skis, so that the skier need concentrate only on speed and efficiency of movement—great for practice, highly pleasurable,

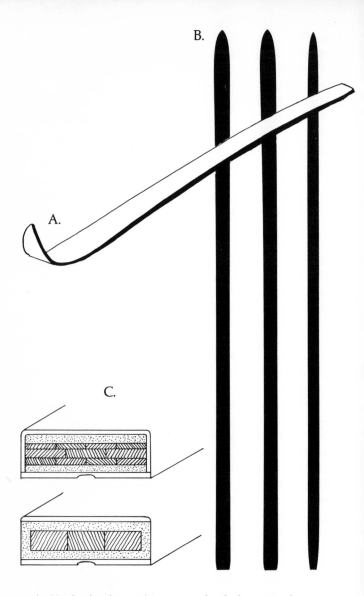

5. **A.** Nordic skis: long and narrow, with a high center arch, or camber. **B.** From left to right: the relative proportions of a mountain touring ski, a so-called light touring ski, and a slender cross-country racing ski. **C.** Two typical cross-sections indicate the complexity of modern fiberglass ski construction.

and sometimes challenging, but not exactly the road to backcountry freedom we're looking for!

Next come the so-called light touring skis, but the "touring" referred to is not what you might think. These skis, while not as fast or as difficult to handle as racing models, are nonetheless designed for "touring" primarily in packed trails or tracks. Light touring skis too are very narrow, although perhaps a smidgen wider than racing skis (46 to 52 mm at the waist or center of the ski, compared with 44 to 48 for racing skis). Unlike racing skis, which are straight-sided, many light touring skis have some degree of sidecut. *Sidecut* is the waisted or concave curve of the ski's sides (widest at the tip, narrowest near the center and somewhat wider again at the tail) which greatly facilitates downhill turning. We'll see why later. I should tell you, too, that a few expert backcountry ski tourers prefer light touring skis— primarily, of course, for their lightness—but these skis demand a high level of technical competence once you take them out of a packed track. More suitable both for learning and for off-track skiing is the general-purpose or plain touring ski.

Touring skis are not as narrow as light touring models (they range from around 50 to 55 mm at the waist), and they generally have a more pronounced sidecut for ease of turning. This is also the case with mountain touring skis, which can be even wider, but are really distinguished from plain touring skis by their metal edges—a must if you hope to cope with steeper icier slopes on Nordic gear. But even the widest of these mountain touring skis are a far cry from conventional Alpine skis; they are much lighter and not nearly as wide (seldom more than 60 mm at the waist). But aside from their dimensions, what are some of the important characteristics of various cross-country skis?

Camber is the upward-arched shape of the ski— like the arch of your foot—that actually lifts the middle of the ski off the snow when there is no weight on it. All skis have camber. It acts like a leaf spring, distributing the skier's weight more evenly toward the tip and tail of the ski. But the camber of modern cross-country skis, particularly racing skis, does something else. If racing skis have just the right amount of camber, it is possible to wax the center section of the ski exclusively for gripping, and to use a faster "speed wax" on the tip and tail sections. When the skier stands with weight equally on both skis—gliding downhill for example—the camber should be strong enough to keep the center "grippy" sections of the ski bases off the snow, for maximum glide. On the other hand, when only one ski is weighted (i.e., double the weight on that ski) then the camber should flatten out, bringing the gripping wax, or "kicker," into contact with the snow for maximum purchase.

More than any other factor, it was the ability of manufacturers to control and adjust the camber of fiberglass skis that led to the demise of traditional wooden skis in racing (although synthetic skis do have at least two other potential advantages: greater strength and lighter weight).

Camber control has been pushed to its limit and beyond in today's racing skis, in which the camber is so stiff that even resting all one's weight on one ski won't flatten it into contact with the snow; an explosive downward kick, characteristic of modern racing technique, is necessary to do the job. The result is an extremely fast ski that, however, tends to slip hopelessly on uphill stretches unless skied vigorously and perfectly. Obviously such stiffly cambered (or "double-cambered") skis are hopeless for general touring. In general, the move to stiff camber has been greatly overdone. For backcountry skiing especially, and for most relaxed cross-country skiing anywhere, soft cambered skis are desirable.

This brings us to the point of it all: choosing the right ski (right camber, length, type, base, brand, etc.). I've already recommended renting skis for the first few days; so, put yourself in the hands of the local sport shop rental department and wait until you're sure you enjoy Nordic skiing before buying anything. As a first trial pair, renting no-wax skis— skis that have textured bases which slide forward easily but grip to resist sliding backwards—will prevent some confusion and let you devote your full energies to learning ski technique. Whether or not to buy no-wax skis or conventional, waxable-base skis—when you do get around to buying your own skis—is another story. Suffice it to say that the same type of ski generally is available with either waxable and no-wax bases, and the pros and cons of each are more logically explained in the upcoming section on wax and waxing. For other considerations, here are some practical guidelines:

The traditional method of measuring ski length is still valid for Nordic skis. The ski's tip should reach about the middle of your palm as you stand next to it with your arm fully upraised. There is no great advantage to learning on a shorter ski, as there is with Alpine skis. As to the kind of ski, let yourself be guided by the sort of terrain you plan (or hope) to ski. If you live in the West and you're bound and determined to ski on higher, steeper slopes—say above timberline—then go ahead and buy a pair of Nordic skis with continuous metal edges. You will anyway, sooner or later. (Metal edges are also an advantage in the icy East.) If you plan to spend a lot of your time touring in more modest, less frankly mountainous surroundings (the western slopes of California's Sierra Nevada, for example, as opposed to the Sierra Crest), then get a pair of classic, general-purpose touring skis without metal edges. There is no precise dividing line between touring and light touring skis, but as a beginner avoid the narrowest of the latter, which will be tippy and hard to learn on. And whatever kind of ski you choose, check to make sure it doesn't have too much camber. The camber can be excessive in two different ways: too high an arch or too "stiff," that is, too hard to flatten out. In recent years, too many skis have been sold that were too stiff and with too much camber, and then skiers wondered why they could never grip going uphill. Don't let it happen to you. Expert advice about the flex and camber of a pair of skis is invaluable, but all too few ski shops employ salespeople who are also expert skiers. At any rate, the ski companies have wised up to this problem and have been softening and reducing the camber of non-racing skis. The simplest test is to squeeze the camber out of a pair of skis placed base to base. If the skis "close" easily, they are soft. If you can't squeeze the camber flat, look out!

At the risk of leaving out a few great skis, I have some definite thoughts on different brands. The original breakthroughs in synthetic ski technology occurred with Alpine, not Nordic, skis. Years after metal, fiberglass, and hybrid skis had become the norm on downhill slopes everywhere, Nordic skiers, racers and ski tourers alike, were still skiing on traditional wooden skis. Finally, in 1974, two Austrian ski companies, Kneissel and Fischer, produced fiberglass cross-country racing skis that were faster than Scandinavian wooden ones, and Nordic skis have never been the same. Naturally, the Scandinavian ski manufacturers scrambled to regain their lead, but the leading Alpine-ski manufacturers had too many years' head start in working with fiberglass technology. Companies like Fischer, Kästle and Rossignol have made major commitments not just to Nordic skiing but to off-track, wilderness skiing as well. Two Scandinavian manufacturers with great reputations for reliable backcountry skis are Epoke and Karhu. A popular Japanese ski for the backcountry is the Kazama. And there are dozens and dozens of small and medium sized manufacturers whose skis vary from great to terrible. Stick to the major brands unless you get a particularly good deal on a lesser-known ski (these are expensive times!).

Boots

Finding a good pair of Nordic ski boots is a much harder task for the backcountry skier than finding good skis. Yet in many ways, boots are more important. There are fewer boots than skis in the shops, and furthermore most Nordic boots are seriously inadequate for off-track skiing. The situation unfolds like this:

Nordic boots fall into categories much like those of Nordic skis (actually "boot" is something of a misnomer, as most Nordic ski boots tend to resemble lightweight running shoes). The lightest,

6. *Three types of Nordic boots, top to bottom: (1) common low-cut touring boots with an injection-molded sole, inadequate for serious touring and downhill control; (2) a quality low-cut boot with a torsionally rigid, hand-welted leather sole, excellent for all-around backcountry skiing; (3) a higher-cut version, sometimes preferred for high-country touring and telemarking.*

predictably, are for racing, with sturdier models toward the touring and mountain touring end of the spectrum. None of these boots are as high-cut or heavy as even a pair of medium-weight hiking boots, and they don't need to be. The skiing qualities we're interested in are determined by something else: the *torsional rigidity* of the sole. This is a fancy expression for the boot's resistance to twisting around its long (front-to-back) axis. Grab a ski boot in both hands and try to wring it as you would a dish towel. If the sole twists around, this boot will not give you much control on steep traverses or downhill turns. If the sole of the boot resists deforming, it will provide excellent edging, which is just what you want.

A word of explanation: the sole of the boot is your link to the ski. The protruding front of the sole engages the binding (which we'll learn more about in the next section), and nowadays the soles of Nordic boots have standard dimensions to insure compatibility with specific binding systems. The sole must flex forward smoothly as the skier walks or strides, allowing the heel to lift freely off the ski. But the torsional rigidity assures that when the boot is tilted sideways, or twisted in a new direction, the ski too will twist (edge) and turn. Unfortunately, the soles of most touring boots don't have enough torsional rigidity to do the job.

There are several standard sizes of Nordic ski-boot soles. The most important for our purposes is the so-called *Nordic Norm* sole, 75 mm across and 12 mm thick in front of the toe, where you'll also find three small holes on the underside to fit the three pins of the common Nordic ski binding. Only the dimensions are standardized, not the materials. There's the rub, for most touring boots have soft rubber, injection-molded soles with little or no torsional rigidity. The best boots for off-track Nordic skiing have traditional leather welted (sewn-on) soles. This construction is a good deal more expensive, which explains why such boots are so rare. But they ski so much better that they are worth looking for and well worth the extra money you'll have to pay. You will eventually get such boots anyway, so why not do it right away (after your rental experience has convinced you that Nordic skiing is really worth it)?

The other common soles are designed for ultra-light racing shoes: the *Norm 38* sole has a tiny 38-mm snout that projects forward into a tiny binding clip; and the *Racing Norm* sole has a somewhat more conventional toe section but is only 50 mm wide and 7 mm thick. These special racing soles, which are made of stiff plastic or nylon, not rubber, have great torsional stiffness and thus offer great control. But most of them are still not suitable for off-track skiing because the sole itself is so thin (7 mm) and the shoes so light and low-cut that they tend to be very cold, as well as devilishly slippery and awkward to walk around in off skis. Enthusiasts of ultra-light touring gear will welcome the appearance of another 50-mm binding–sole combination, the so-called *Touring Norm*, identical to the Racing Norm except for a thicker sole (12 mm). This combination permits the skilled backcountry skier to pare the weight of boots, skis, and bindings to an absolute minimum, with some loss of stability (and flotation in deep snow); but I don't recommend any of these super-light set-ups for the beginner.

Stick with the basic touring shoe, and look for good-quality leather uppers and a sturdy Norwegian welted leather sole (the stitches should be visible), which resists twisting around its long axis when you are holding the toe and heel. The height of your boot is a matter of personal preference. Many touring boots are cut just over the ankle bone and others just below it. In the backcountry, you'll want as much lateral support as you can get, so don't choose an exaggeratedly low-cut model; but the only advantage of the very high-topped boots is protecting your ankles from brush while you're hiking up to the snow. Unlike Alpine boots, where support comes from the high stiff sides, a Nordic ski boot gives you support through a good wrapping fit around the foot and a good sole. The standard in quality touring boots is the hand-sewn Norrona from Norway; other high-quality boots for serious backcountry skiing are the French Galibier and the Austrian Kastinger boots, and the American Vasque models. Italian backcountry boots by Fabiano and Asolo have just become available in the United States, and they are excellent.

If you plan only a little skiing away from trails and tracks, and very little on steeper slopes, then you can safely buy just about any touring boot that fits and not worry about leather soles and the like. Then too, things may change. I'm hoping that the boot situation will improve in a few years through increased use of plastics and synthetics. Who knows? —by the time this book is ready for revision, we may all be skiing in pure plastic cross-country shoes. This has already happened in Alpine touring boots, and such boots are virtually maintenance-free. Not so your Nordic touring shoes—once you've taken the trouble to find a really good pair, don't be sparing with the Sno-seal, Biwell, or other water-poofing and leather protecting compounds. There's nothing worse than spring touring with soggy feet; and it doesn't have to happen if you start taking care of your boots as soon as you get them.

Bindings

These cunning devices are really almost a footnote on the boot story because, as I've pointed out, boot soles and bindings are manufactured to the same compatible standards. Cross-country, or three-pin bindings, as they are commonly called, are also one of the last bargains in skiing. God knows, the ski companies have tried to spiffy up this simple device in order to come up with a higher-ticket item, but it hasn't worked. There's only so much you can do to such a simple binding—a piece of metal bent up at either side to hold and stabilize the toe of the boot, three small pins sticking out to mate with the

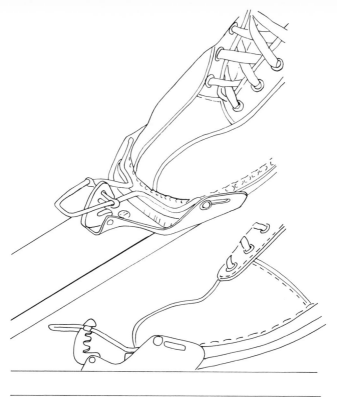

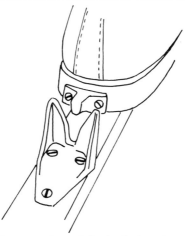

7. Nordic bindings: two views of the classic three-pin toe binding, plus one of the increasingly popular heel-locator units that can be used with pin bindings.

three holes in the ski boot sole, and a piece of wire, called a "bail," which catches and presses the protruding welt of the boot down onto those pins. Simplicity itself. The absolute fanciest are three-pin bindings on which the small catch that holds down the wire toe bail can be activated with a ski pole tip, both for engaging and releasing the binding, so that the skier doesn't even have to bend over. This is the Nordic equivalent of the Alpine skier's "step-in" binding. They cost a few dollars more than the simplest models but are perhaps a little more likely to break. Furthermore, most Nordic skiers are athletic enough that they aren't afraid of bending over to fasten their boots into their bindings. The "step-in" kind could, however, be a big plus on long tours with very heavy packs.

A three-pin binding that I am suspicious of is the kind that comes with a flat sheet-metal toe bail instead of a wire bail. These flat metal bails seem to grip the boot's welt *too* well, preventing a small rocking, adjusting movement of the boot's welt, thus accelerating wear and tear and the eventual ripping out of the sole after hard use.

Toe bindings of a slightly different sort are available for boots with the 50-mm soles that I mentioned earlier. The 50-mm plastic sole projects forward in a kind of snout, which is latched directly into a small binding mechanism. Some of these bindings retain the locking pins, others utilize special spring-loaded catches, but almost all offer the advantage of holding the boot toe firmly to the ski without protruding metal sidepieces that can catch and snag on steep, icy slopes. These 50-mm boot–binding systems—the "50/7 mm" Racing Norm or the "50/12 mm" Touring Norm—offer real technical advantages. The problem is that the boots which incorporate them are often unsuitable for backcountry use. I expect to see a lot of development in this area in the future.

A different sort of cross-country binding, in which the boot is held into the toe piece by a cable running around the heel, is seldom seen or used today. It just isn't necessary; toe bindings work as well or better in virtually all circumstances, unless you just want to shuffle around on cross-country skis wearing a pair of old hiking boots. There's nothing wrong with that either, if you just want to walk up a snowy road from here to there. But remember that the whole system—light skis, three-pin bindings, and boots—makes possible a really dynamic, sporty, and sometimes almost effortless style of Nordic movement.

There is, however, one useful extra that you can add to the extreme simplicity of the three-pin binding. Almost all such bindings come with some kind of a heel plate, a small device to help the heel of the boot grip and prevent it from sliding off the ski when you want to weight and twist the rear of the ski, especially in downhill turns. Some of these plates have small, metal teeth that grip the boot's sole; in many of the lighter weight racing-type boot–binding systems, a raised plastic ridge on the heel plate fits into a notch in the boot heel itself. A more complex but more effective version is the "heel locator," a kind of plastic spur that screws onto the rear of the boot sole and slips down between two vertical plastic pieces mounted on the ski just behind the boot. This system allows unimpeded vertical movement at the heel but when the heel is down it gives great lateral stability whenever the foot edges or turns. Heel locators don't cost much, and they permit more downhill control in the sloppy, soft, injection-molded boots I've already warned you against. But it's my own feeling that you don't really need heel locators if you have a pair of really good, leather-soled boots. But a lot of brilliant Nordic skiers swear by them. Heel locators can also create a potential hazard. Nordic bindings have so much flexibility that they don't need a release mechanism to be safe; at most you might sprain your big toe. But in a backwards twisting fall the heel locator can trap your foot on the ski and conceivably cause a broken leg—*caveat emptor*.

Mounting the bindings on your skis, by the way, is usually better done by a ski shop (you would hate to drill through those new skis) but the traditional rule of thumb still works, even with new, space-age skies: Bindings should be mounted so that the front of the toe of the boot is directly over the balance point of the ski.

Poles

Your last item of ski equipment is another good place for a first-timer to save some money. As a beginner, purchase a cheap pair of bamboo poles (they're actually made of "Tonkin," a bamboo-like plant from South China). Don't even think about

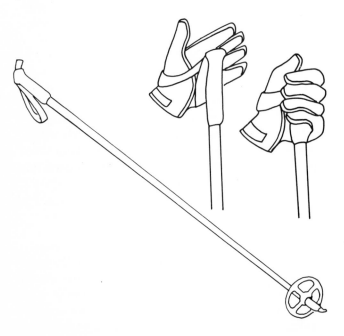

8. *Nordic poles and how to grip them. Note the large basket for backcountry use in deep snow (racing poles have small, non-circular baskets). All poles, Nordic and Alpine alike, are gripped this way.*

quality, just make sure they are the right length, the top of the grip reaching your armpit as you stand on the floor. If you got better poles when you were learning you would probably fall on them and bend them anyway. If your bamboo poles survive the inevitable falls of your early days on skis, they'll make a good spare pair later. Eventually, as you begin touring away from the beaten track, you will want a better, stronger set of poles.

Good poles, for longer backcountry trips (where a broken pole would be more than a slight inconvenience), are made of metal (lightweight aluminum alloy) or fiberglass. Springy fiberglass and carbon fiber poles dominate cross-country racing, but the backcountry skier should stay away from specialized racing poles, easily spotted by their small and often asymmetric baskets, which are useful only in packed tracks. For high-mountain Nordic touring where avalanche danger is real, I strongly recommend a pair of aluminum ski poles which knock down and screw together to form an avalanche probe pole (I also hope you never need to use them in this way, which is covered in detail in Chapter 9). Two very good such double-purpose poles are made in the U.S. by Ramer and Lifelink. Some pole manufacturers also make extra-large baskets for use in deep powder snow, but I confess I've never used, needed, or wanted them.

Wax and Waxing

This final part of our Nordic equipment review deals with alchemy. At least that's the way it's always seemed to me. Cross-country waxes mystified me when I first began Nordic skiing, and even now that I'm rather familiar with them after all these years, I still find them a bit mysterious. What right-thinking person would believe that rubbing one pasty substance on a ski could both make it grip securely going uphill and help it slide faster going downhill? Yet that's the way it is.

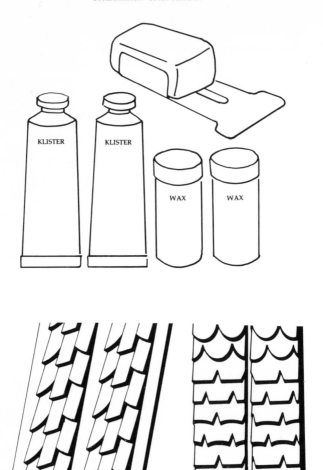

9. Basic waxing paraphernalia plus typical base patterns of several "no-wax" skis—in this case the designs used by Rossignol and Trak.

Actually the ski doesn't grip the snow—it's the other way around. Snow, all snow, is composed of tiny particles, whether new star-shaped snowflakes, metamorphosed shrunken crystals, or just tiny lumps of ice (more on the nature of snow in Chapter 9). By waxing skis correctly, the cross-country skier creates a surface just soft enough for these particles to penetrate and grip—when the ski is not moving forward but is pushed down into the snow—yet still hard enough so that these crystals can't penetrate when the ski is in motion, skimming over the snow's surface. A neat trick.

It all depends on the relative hardness or softness both of the snow crystals and of the wax surface. At cold temperatures, new snow has sharp, pointed crystal arms that are relatively brittle and hard. They're hard and sharp enough to penetrate even a very hard coat of wax. They will also penetrate a softer wax, but will penetrate in so far and so well that they would grab even a moving ski, effectively stopping any forward motion. So it's a fine line. The general principle is: The colder the snow, the harder a wax you must use; the warmer the snow, the softer the wax. Of course, as you might suspect, there's more to it than that, and the way that snow changes with age also influences the wax you'll choose. Fortunately several generations of wax chemists have worked out most of the details for us. If you can read directions, you can at least cope with waxing.

There are plenty of short cuts, secrets, and hot tips, so now that we have a very general idea of how wax works, let's look at the more practical side—how many waxes do you need? We know that any single wax won't be appropriate for every situation: cold new snow demands a hard wax coating while older warmer snow (the crystals are rounded and not as hard) will need a softer wax surface. And—you guessed it—there's a whole spectrum of potential waxes between the two extremes. Luckily for the novice, there are some very simple two-wax systems that ignore the subtle gradations in between, and they work pretty well. However, for maximum performance—the fastest possible glide combined with good grip—experienced Nordic skiers use a more complex array of waxes.

The full spectrum works like this. Snow conditions are divided, albeit crudely, into two categories: new snow and old snow. New snow may be freshly fallen, or it may have been on the ground for days but not yet melted and refrozen. Old snow, for waxing purposes, is snow that has undergone major changes (or metamorphosis, as snow scientists put it)—mostly melting and freezing, sometimes just melting, sometimes other changes. Typically, old snow surfaces are lumpy and icy, or slushy, characterized by granular rather than crystalline snow structure: the crystals have been transformed into grains of ice. New snow conditions require *stick waxes* (also called *hard waxes* despite the fact that they vary considerably in hardness), that come in neat, little cans and can be rubbed directly onto the ski's base. Waxing for old snow usually requires *klister*, a diabolically sticky substance, about the consistency of honey, that's squeezed (like toothpaste) onto the ski base from a tube. I don't believe anyone really enjoys handling such messy stuff (to protect your pack, your other waxes and yourself from total stickiness, carry each tube of klister in a separate plastic bag). In fact, the only excuse for the existence of klister is that it works so well on old snow.

Both stick waxes and klisters are available in a full range of relative hardness and softness, to be used according to the temperature (fanatics will measure snow temperature with a special thermometer, but air temperature will do just fine). The colder the temperature, the harder the wax *or* the klister that must be used. Almost all wax manufacturers use the same color coding on both their wax canisters and klister tubes: green is the hardest (coldest), then blue, purple, red and finally yellow for very warm days—and to be sure, each company throws in a surprise or two, such as a black or silver klister, just to make sure you read their charts. In most ranges, blue is for a cold day and green for a *really* cold day; purple (or violet) will handle conditions around freezing; red is definitely above freezing. A unique yellowish stick wax exists (often called klister-wax, perhaps because it combines the worst qualities of waxes and klisters in a terrible drippy bubble-gum consistency). It's really for folks who are too lazy to start using klister, and is seldom worth it!

But relax—you don't really need so many waxes and klisters. More than anything else they exist to let cross-country racers fine tune their skis for maximum speed. For touring off packed trails, a simpler approach to waxing usually prevails. Adequate grip for climbing is usually more important than maximum speed, and serious tourers are generally less concerned with getting their wax just right. If it works, good! My best advice on waxing for the Nordic beginner is: Keep it simple! Pick a brand of wax that's commonly available. Get that brand's simplified two-wax system (one can will be for cold, dry snow, the other for warm, wet snow, sometimes indicated by plus and minus, for temperatures above or below 0°C.) and use them until you've pretty well figured out how they work. Next, try one additional hard wax, stick with it for awhile, and so on. By the time spring rolls around with its typical klister conditions, you should be ready.

A few words on application. With the more precisely designed camber of modern fiberglass skis, the way we wax (and to some extent the waxes themselves) has changed. The tip and tail sections of the ski base are often called the *glide zone*, the center section underfoot is termed the *kick* or *grip zone*. This center section is where you will apply the waxes we've just described, beginning underfoot and waxing out toward the tip and tail. You may only need a couple of feet of waxed ski base; if the skis don't hold going uphill or don't provide sufficient "kick," then you can extend the wax further toward tip and tail. Technically the waxes we've mentioned are all called *grip waxes*; a separate but compatible category of *glide waxes* or "speed waxes" exists for waxing the tip and tail sections of the ski, solely for increasing speed on downhill stretches or in a track. These glide waxes are important for racing, but most backcountry skiers just don't bother with them (despite the fact that they protect the skis' bases as well as increasing performance). I sometimes rub on some Alpine speed wax for really sticky snow, but I don't believe such waxing refinements are important to most touring skiers. Yet another sort of Nordic wax, *binder* or *base wax*, can be invaluable for granular spring conditions. Applied under other waxes, it keeps the whole wax job from being scraped off in a hurry.

A few more tips for applying this mysterious and magical substance. Clean the skis first, and make sure they're dry. Wax just won't adhere to damp ski bases. If in doubt about the wax of the day, use the harder (colder) of your two options. It is easy to apply a softer wax over a harder one, but not vice versa. For cold, new snow conditions, rub on thin layers of hard wax and cork them smooth (a waxing cork for polishing and a scraper for removing old wax, or a combination cork/scraper are the minimum waxing tools). Multiple thin layers will work better in cold snow than one thick layer. In warmer snow, a thicker, rougher layer will be better. And finally, when using klister, apply it sparingly.

It's not uncommon for the would-be Nordic skier to fall into a state of profound depression after hearing or reading an explanation of cross-country waxing. Cheer up, it's not that bad. The beginner can more or less ignore the complexities of waxing and stick with a simplified system. At the advanced level there is a satisfying, puzzle-like quality to the waxing game; outwitting the snow becomes, believe it or not, a real pleasure. Besides, as a modern cross-country skier you possess a couple of other advantages in the sticky-fingers sweepstakes. First, no more gooey pine tar to seal the hickory bases of wooden laminated skis; modern polyethelene ski bases need very little maintenance and can be waxed just as well as the classic wooden ski. And for those who don't want to bother with even the simplest waxing system, there is yet another modern alternative: the no-wax ski.

No-Wax Skis

Waxless skis, like fiberglass construction, have definitely come of age. When writing *Wilderness Skiing* eight years ago, I was very hesitant to recommend them seriously. No longer. The first significant no-wax ski was the American-made Trak ski, with a fish-scale pattern in its plastic base. The scales, like tiny shingles slanting backwards, resist backward sliding yet let the ski slide forward. A number of other systems have appeared (and some disappeared) over the years but the Trak fish-scale base is still one of the best. There are also skis with parallel mohair strips inset and glued to the base in the center or kick zone of the ski. The hairs of the mohair point backwards and are very effective on hard, crusty, frozen snow. However, if the mohair strips protrude too far from the base of the ski, they tend to interfere with lateral slipping of the ski in turns. Some skis have steps in the base, straight or rounded notches running across the kick zone. And finally, there are skis with tiny backward-slanting mica flakes embedded in the plastic base material itself (ingenious but slow). Actually the most efficient waxless bases seem to be those composed of small repeating all-over patterns. Different ski companies, like Rossignol and Fischer, have developed their own patterns analogous to the Trak fish-scale. This definitely seems to be the wave of the future in waxless skis.

But do waxless skis work as well as classic, well-waxed cross-country skis? Sometimes not, sometimes even better. The waxless ski was originally a gimmick developed to sell Nordic skiing to a public that was put off by the muss and fuss of waxing. In most cases a well-waxed ski will outski any no-wax model, but there is one important exception—changeable conditions around the freezing point (0°C). Newly fallen or falling snow around freezing is a waxing nightmare; nothing seems to work very well. And such snow conditions are often the rule rather than the exception in California's Sierra Nevada and the coastal mountains of the Pacific Northwest, both regions famous for heavy, wet, warm snowfalls. Frankly, during the winters I've spent around Lake Tahoe in the Sierra, I've always preferred waxless skis. Yet in the San Juan Range of Colorado, the other mountain region where I've spent a number of winters, waxless skis just don't make sense, except for beginners on their first day out. Here you can ski for weeks on end in consistent cold temperatures, over squeaky powdery snow, and

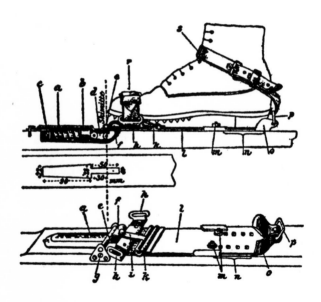

The famous Zdarsky binding was the last word in ski equipment circa 1896.

never use anything but hard blue or occasionally green wax. So if you live in the Rockies or the cold Midwest, don't take waxless skis too seriously. Waxing in these regions tends to be as easy as it is effective. If you live in the wet, warm West, give no-wax skis a second thought. (If you're not used to snow, 32°F/0°C may sound neither warm nor wet—it is freezing, after all—but actually it's bloody soggy.) Ultimately, however, every touring skier has to make his or her own peace with waxing, and it doesn't have to be a pain.

Enough! Enough of this talk about equipment! One could spend a lifetime discussing it and forget to go skiing. One could even write a whole book about Nordic ski equipment, and Michael Brady has done just that. His book, *Cross-Country Ski Gear* (The Mountaineers, Seattle, 1979) is a veritable encyclopedia, and if you want information on the molecular weight of P-Tex ski bases, or anything else about ski gear, consult it. But now I want you to grab a pair of skis, no matter how funky and beat up, and do some skiing.

3

Nothing is free—the child
must pay his dues to walk
as we must too to ski,
we too bruise body and ego
(knee and me) pick ourselves up
(dusting off snow) and return
to the same mindless repetition—
humiliating, liberating exercise.
Again and again we try the same
simple turn on the same
featureless snow and eventually learn
to say yes to our skis instead of no.
Nothing is free—but the skier
is as free as anyone, or freer.

3
Your Basic
Bag of Tricks

Your apprenticeship on Nordic skis may
last a couple of days, but after only a few
hours on skis you'll probably want to take
off into the woods on your first mini-tour. And you
certainly can, if the terrain isn't too rough.
Technically, backcountry skiing is quite open-ended.
You don't need great ski technique to have great
adventures on skis, five minutes, five miles or five
days from the end of the road. But you must be able
to cope. Which brings us to an interesting question:
how much ski technique does a backcountry tourer
really need? And how hard should you work at
acquiring it?

I have a number of friends who are veteran ski
tourers yet who, from my point of view, can hardly
ski. Touring for them is almost synonymous with
walking on skis—nothing wrong with that, it's still
easier and more pleasant than walking on
snowshoes. Downhill runs are approached with a
certain trepidation but mostly avoided. I think such
skiers are laboring under the misapprehension that
ski technique in itself is difficult, and so they never
really "get around" to improving their skiing.

On the contrary, the point of technique is to

make skiing easier. Of course you'll encounter some frustrations and problems along the way, but I'd like to convince you to make a real effort from the very beginning to learn to ski well. Every hour you spend concentrating on technique at first will pay a handsome dividend later—more speed on the flats, less effort uphill, more security downhill. And that's what this chapter is about: the basic stride for skiing on the level; techniques and tactics for climbing hills; and finally, balance and the beginnings of downhill control.

The Basic Stride

The great Nordic cliché (perhaps it originated as a slogan to sell cross-country skiing to a skeptical public) has always been: "If you can walk, you can ski." It would be more accurate to say: If you can run, you can ski! The *basic* or *diagonal* stride, that fundamental, typical, and most effective of all Nordic techniques, is more like a form of graceful slow-motion running than anything else. Yet on a long backcountry tour, skiing under a heavy pack tends to resemble plodding more than running. So I guess there's some truth to the old cliché after all.

First things first. Your first task in learning any kind of skiing is simply to get used to moving around with these long extensions on your feet. Pick a flat area to begin—a nice, open meadow will do fine, or a snow-covered golf course! Put on your skis, grab your poles, and just start moving around. Simply walk a bit, here and there, shuffling or sliding your feet and skis forward over the snow rather than lifting them at every step. Easy, right?

The only problem you may encounter will be turning around in place. If you move too fast, you're certain to cross either the tips or tails of your skis; so move slowly, shifting either the tips or the tails around in a series of small steps. As you walk you'll tend to use your poles as outriggers, helpers, maybe even props to hold you up if you find yourself tripping over your own feet. After about five minutes of walking around on the level, the whole business will seem more reasonable, the skis less awkward, balancing on them easier. You're ready for a little speed.

To put some oomph in your skiing, the easiest thing is to use a track—a pair of parallel ski tracks that will guide both skis while you work on a more dynamic stride. If you're practicing at a touring center or an organized Nordic skiing area there will certainly be some flat tracks around. If not, you can make a nice one in about five minutes. Just head off straight across the meadow, walking in as straight a line as possible; go a hundred yards or so, stop, turn around, and there you have it: a short but useful practice track.

Now you're going to ski back and forth in your track, letting each ski slide along in its packed-out slot, trying, with each pass, to get a little more speed out of your skis. The first time try to walk briskly, much faster than before, stepping out with smart strides like an impatient commuter hurrying to catch a train. As soon as that feels comfortable, I want you to try running—or more precisely, jogging—along your track. At first, trying to run on skis may feel choppy and jerky, but at least it's more dynamic and active than walking. And it will help you identify the basic stride we're after, something in between walking and jogging that works much better than either.

What did you feel? What is the difference between a fast walk and a jogging/running motion? In walking you put your front foot forward *and then* shift your body weight forward onto it. In running, your body is moving forward *even before* the front foot lands to receive your weight. There's nothing new here—walking and running are things we've done all our lives. The point is that effective cross-country striding works more like running: you don't push your ski forward and then step onto it; instead, *you push yourself forward* over the new front ski.

You shove off one ski onto the other, and as your body moves forward, that new ski, bearing all your weight, glides forward in the track. As the gliding ski comes to a stop, you simply follow through with your forward motion and push off that ski in turn. Net result: you find yourself gliding down the track for an extra foot or so each time you stride from one ski to the other.

So the basic stride is actually a rhythmic alternation of two phases: pushing off one ski, and gliding on the other. In English these two phases have always been called the *kick* and the *glide,* although kick is not a very accurate image. It would be far better to say *push-off*. What the skier really does is to thrust himself forward with a rapid extension of his rear leg. This "kick" is directed straight down (and helps the base of the ski grip the snow), but because the skier's body is already tilting—almost falling—forward, the leg's extension looks like a movement to the rear.

However, the kick, or push-off, is only half of the stride. Its whole purpose is to create a strong glide. In order to glide as far as possible, once you've thrust yourself forward onto the new ski, you must *hesitate*. That's right, for an instant you do nothing at all, and just remain balanced on that front ski while it slides forward. One of the commonest problems with the basic stride is a too-rapid rhythm, which never really allows the gliding ski enough time to cover any ground. Of course, by hesitation, I don't mean that you freeze up motionless—the basic stride always involves continual rhythmic motion. But the rhythm is a kind of "one-and-two-and-," where the skier glides forward on the "and" while preparing for another kick. Perhaps the most accurate image for this stride is that of running or loping along in slow motion.

Work on developing this double sensation, push-off and glide, for at least a half-hour before trying anything else. It won't come to you all at once, but it will come. The feeling of the basic stride is something you grow into, bit by bit, as rhythm and timing develop. And a critical part of this rhythm and timing is the correct use of your arms and poles. I haven't mentioned them yet—on purpose. Your first half-hour or so on cross-country skis should be spent trying to get feet, legs, and skis to cooperate.

In the basic stride, arms and poles work together, but the arms are more important. So put your poles aside temporarily and ski up and down the practice track without them. Relax your shoulders and let your arms swing back and forth with each stride—as if you were running or ice skating. Surprisingly, without poles, your natural arm movements are just right: as you stride forward onto the right ski, your left arm swings forward; as you push off that ski in turn, the left arm is swinging back and the right one swings forward. But don't concentrate on your arm movements while you practice; it will only confuse you. Without poles, the movement is totally natural. Simply try to *feel* yourself doing it.

Next (and still without poles), exaggerate the forward swing of your arms—your arm stretches horizontally in front of you at the end of the swing. Why? Because it helps bring your weight forward onto the sliding ski. As your hand drives forward, your whole body tilts forward with it, and you find yourself gliding faster and farther on that forward ski. The swinging, forward motion of your arm adds power to the kick or extension of your rear leg. Another hint—as you glide forward on the front ski,

10. *The diagonal, or basic, stride.*

keep your front knee bent, almost as if you were trying to push the knee forward too. When you push off this leg for the next gliding step, you can develop much more power from straightening a well-bent knee.

Now it's time to take up your poles again and add the final element to your basic stride. With poles, it works like this: when one hand swings forward, it brings the pole with it. (Don't reach ahead with the pole; indeed, as your hand swings all the way forward, the pole will still slant back somewhat.) Then, on the backswing, plant the pole in the snow and give a strong backward shove. In fact, it would be more accurate to say that the pole "plants itself," and that the complete backswing of the arm creates a powerful push. You don't even have to grip the pole hard, as even with a relaxed grip, your hand will push down and back on the pole straps. Finish the movement with a full follow-through to the rear, gripping the pole lightly between thumb and first finger at the end of the push. The full swing of your arms results in effective pole action, whereas if you attempt to stick the pole in the snow and push yourself forward on it, the movement will be inefficient and probably out of synch with the all-important kick and glide. Worse yet is the common beginner's mistake of planting the pole too far forward in an attempt to pull oneself ahead with it. The goal of correct pole action is to add even more power and precision to the basic stride.

Remember, the complete arm/pole action helps in two ways: driving the skier's weight forward on the front swing, and giving an added push with the pole on the backswing. Both are equally important.

It doesn't take long for these different elements to come together, and before you know it you're no longer huffing and puffing down your practice track, but skiing it, smoothly and swiftly. Good work! Just to keep the record straight, let me add that what you've just learned has almost always been called the *diagonal stride* (because of the complementary action of opposite arms and legs), but I prefer to think of it as the *basic stride*, since it is the quintessential Nordic movement for covering ground. The basic stride will be useful both for climbing and descending hills—it is the basis for the Telemark turn. Best of all, in an hour or two almost anyone can learn this most fundamental of Nordic techniques. Of course, it may take you a lifetime to perfect it.

You see, the real difference between an expert and a novice cross-country skier is not in the technique they use—both ski with the same diagonal stride—but in the subtle refinement of the same

11. *The follow-through in the basic stride. Note the full extension of the body, the bent front knee indicating good forward weight transfer, and the relaxed rear hand and trailing pole.*

simple set of movements. Olympic athletes in their grueling 50-kilometer races use exactly the same stride you have just learned, but they execute it with a power, precision and endurance that no beginner is capable of. Actually, that is an oversimplification, as modern racing technique relies heavily on arm strength and "double poling," but the basic comparison is just. The basic stride is the key to cross-country skiing on the level. The rest is just a variation on this theme. The backcountry skier, of course, has to go well beyond this base and acquire a number of other techniques for ups and downs, rough terrain and unusual snow. But it's well worth mastering the basic stride before branching out. So if at all possible, I strongly recommend a couple of days of skiing in tracks, or at least on level terrain, early in your Nordic career.

It will take both time and patience to refine this all-important technique. Worth it? And how! Even when a heavy pack or a steep hill slows you to a crawl, the basic rhythmic movement will stand you in good stead. And an efficient stride can turn the level stretches of a tour from drudgery into play. But backcountry skiing isn't all flat. You've been wondering about that, haven't you?

Hills and How to Ski Up Them

Before we make a big deal out of climbing uphill on skis, I ought to point out that if your skis are well waxed and the hill is not steep, you can just walk straight up. Or if you're feeling energetic, sprint up with the basic stride you've just learned—shortening your steps to a kind of a jogging trot rather than a long kick and glide. The trick to getting the maximum grip from your wax is keeping your weight directly over the center of your foot (and ski), not back on the heels. This means keeping knees and ankles well bent so your hips are pushed forward. If your skis begin to slip a bit, try slapping the ski down in the snow as you stand on it instead of just sliding it forward. This ability to simply ski straight up a hill without slipping back is, of course, one of the unique advantages of Nordic over Alpine skis. And indeed, skiing over gently rolling terrain, you will hardly notice slight uphill sections except perhaps through a change in the rhythm of your stride.

But even the best wax job has its limits, and as the hills grow steeper, you'll eventually start slipping back. What then? If the crest of the hill is only a few steps away, simply push with your poles to keep from slipping. But this is too fatiguing for more than a few feet, so next try the *herringbone*. This is no more than spreading your ski tips out at an angle—your skis will form a kind of "V"—and walking duck-footed up the slope. As you spread your ski tips apart into this V-shape, the skis naturally tilt up onto

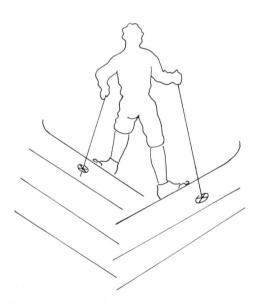

12.   *The herringbone.*

their inside edge and this is what keeps them from slipping down the hill. As you walk uphill in this rather ungainly position, keep both poles behind you, below the skis as additional pushers, and swing each leg up and out enough that the tails of your skis don't cross. And that's it—just stomp your way up the hill. Looking back down at your tracks you can see why this funny technique is called herringboning—more after the famous Harris tweed pattern than after actual fish bones.

Herringboning is a fine but fatiguing technique. The steeper the hill, the wider you must spread your skis in a V—and the harder you work. There must be a better way . . . and there is. Instead of attacking the hill head on, we'll use a little strategy and zig-zag up it. By *traversing*—heading diagonally up across the slope—you effectively reduce the angle of the snow under your skis, and once again the wax will hold. This way you can also take advantage of the different contours of the hill, climbing around small steep sections, utilizing slanting benches, and avoiding dense trees and underbrush. Trial and error tells you how steeply you can traverse before your wax slips, so all you have to learn is how to connect a traverse in one direction with one in the other, linking a zig with a zag. At first you may want to just step your skis around in a V (like the herringbone) until you are facing the other way. But again, there's a better way.

The *kick turn*—a snappy maneuver that turns the skier around 180° in place—is the answer. It's actually easier to do on the side of a hill, but it's usually easier to learn on the flat. And though it looks like a cross between yoga and ballet, be encouraged by the thought that hundreds of thousands of skiers before you have gotten through its pretzel-like complexity and ultimately found it quite easy. Really. Take a moment to study the sequence drawing of a kick turn; it will help you make sense out of what I'm about to say. A kick turn works like this: braced on your poles, swing one leg (say your right leg) back, then vigorously kick it forward and up and place the ski vertically on its tail in the snow. Pick up your right pole and plant it out of the way behind your back on the other side. Now flop your right foot and ski down, letting it pivot on the tail, until the ski is parallel to the left one, only pointing the opposite way. Don't start laughing now or all is lost! Then quickly shift your weight so that you're standing on that right foot, and swing your left ski around beside it. Whew!

Get a friend to demonstrate this if you can, because it's one of the most absurdly contorted maneuvers in all of skiing! So much so that downhill ski schools tend not to teach it any more. But cross-country skiers need and use it all the time, so the sooner the better. A couple of tips: use your poles for support, not decoration. The little backswing is necessary to get your kicking foot high enough. And don't stay in the cross-footed middle position any longer than you must—shift your weight and move! The kick turn is well worth the bother and is really essential for linking traverses up a hill (and down, too, sometimes). Standing horizontally on the side of a slope, it is easiest to kick the lower (downhill) ski with both poles braced on the uphill side. A kick turn with the uphill ski is a faster way to link two ascending traverses but is a good deal trickier for the beginner.

---

13. *The kick turn.*

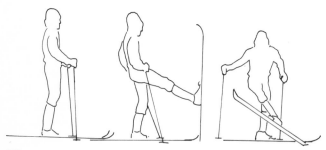

14. *Sidestepping.*

And finally, for those short steep pitches where you don't want to traverse around but where the herringbone obviously would be a killer, try *sidestepping*. The name tells all. You stand sideways across the hill and step up, one foot after another, in a crabwise sideways motion as though climbing a set of stairs in this sideways position rather than head on. By setting each ski down solidly and flat you will create a set of horizontal steps in soft snow. On hard or icy slopes you will want to edge your skis into the

hill, making them grip by simply rolling your knees and ankles into the hill (to tilt the ski at more of an angle). Unlike the herringbone, sidestepping is very easy, but it's also very slow—a good technique for short pitches. For long climbs up serious slopes, the Nordic tourer instinctively prefers to traverse. You can also sidestep while traversing, which is sometimes more effective than either would be alone. But the basic idea is to use your skis, not raw strength, on uphill stretches, making strategy more important than technique. The experienced backcountry skier will spot the easiest way to the top of a given hill (traverse up there to the right, then follow that ascending bench, then take that gentle ridge back to the crest) rather than attacking the hill directly. You get no points on a ski tour for reaching the crest of a slope a few minutes ahead of your companions, but out of breath and too exhausted to enjoy the descent.

It's true: who goes up must come down. One way or another, gracefully or otherwise, but preferably under control, stable and safe. And that's what we're ready to tackle next.

Downhill Basics:
Balance and Control

So far we haven't talked about falling. Like all beginning skiers, you'll have your share of falls (and believe me, experts crash too). Most falls are minor, a few will shake you up, but one of the beauties of cross-country skiing with three-pin bindings is that falls are generally very safe. But there are falls, and there are falls. Learning to ski on the flat, you probably wobbled a bit at first and fell over a few times. I didn't tell you how to get up because people interested in backcountry skiing should be in good enough shape to simply scramble to their feet (the same is not true, alas, at downhill ski resorts). But now, when skiing downhill at higher speed, falls might be more serious. So our very first job is to develop enough balance and stability to stay on your feet when things get exciting. Of course, falling is still part of the game but it will become less and less frequent. Meanwhile, remember this: it's safer and softer to fall on your seat than on any other part of the body, so if you're on the brink of losing your balance on a downhill stretch there's no disgrace in simply sitting down. That is, try to fall back and into the hill, rather than forward, over your skis. It's a bad idea to extend your arm to "break" or cushion your fall; you risk a sprained thumb or wrist. Better to just relax and collapse gently into the snow. And if you do make a spectacular "head plant" or "beater" (short for eggbeater, a rolling, tumbling fall), and I'm sure you will, then get yourself organized, and swing your feet and skis parallel, placing them horizontally across the slope below you, before getting up. Not only will it be easier to get to your feet, but you won't start moving again until you're ready.

Now, with all this grim business about falling out of the way, you're ready to learn how *not* to fall. First, you need a good practice hill. Select a gentle slope, not too long, with a flattish spot on top to push off from and, most important, a long, flat run-out at the bottom, or even a gentle upslope that will bring you to a stop before you learn to stop yourself. This slope can be packed out or not (no deep powder, please), a downhill track with a generous run-out is fine, and the beginner or "bunny" slope at a downhill ski area isn't bad either. At any rate, here you are on top of your practice slope, looking downhill with mixed emotions. What next? In real life, just push off and enjoy the ride, wait for your skis to coast to a stop, then climb back up and do it again. But since we're not actually out on the hill together, I'm going to hazard a couple of explanations.

First some useful ski vocabulary. Looking downhill in the steepest direction, the line a rolling snowball might follow is called the *fall line*. Nothing sinister, it has nothing to do with falling. Skiing

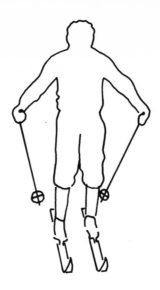

15. *A straight descent, or schuss, becomes a traverse when the skis are aimed across the hill. Note the wide stance and the arms spread for balance.*

straight down the fall line is called *schussing* (a German word we inherited), and it's also the fastest way down the slope. Skiing any other line, diagonally down the slope, is called *traversing* (the same as climbing up). The more across the hill you aim your traverse—the greater an angle you make with the fall line—the slower you'll go. *Voilà*: basic speed control! Your first runs down the practice hill will be schusses (straight down); the point will be to develop balance.

Skiers have to balance in two planes, side-to-side and front-to-back (lateral and longitudinal balance), and the mechanism for each is a little different. Take side-to-side balance. The best thing is to spread your feet and skis in a *wide stance* (skis about hip width apart). Then flex your legs (ankles, knees, and hip joints) and holding your hands widespread in front of you (for even more lateral balance), push off down the hill. This wide stance is your basic position for running down slopes of a uniform steepness—it's not a crouch but a relaxed, flexed, wide-based position. Your weight is equally distributed across the flat of both feet, and you don't lean forward or back. Naturally you're looking where you're going, not down at your skis, and you ought to feel stable and solid on your skis. The wide track is the key; balancing with feet close together is like balancing on a tightrope—it takes time.

Practice this straight descent in a wide stance a few times until you're really comfortable. If you find it exciting and want to go faster, try starting higher up the hill or pushing with both poles. But as soon as you feel comfortable with straight running, you're ready to learn a bit of control: how to slow down and stop, how to turn right and left. Before we get into it, however, there's one more aspect of balance that you may not need to develop right away, but will soon enough. This is fore-and-aft balance, and it's called into question whenever you ski over rolls and dips in the terrain. If you started skiing at a developed touring center with packed tracks, you may already have followed a track that led you over a series of dips and hollows. To preserve maximum balance over such "breaks" or changes in the terrain,

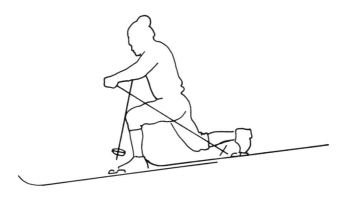

16. *The telemark position.*

drop into what we call the *telemark position*. It's like a slow-motion basic stride, but without the kick: push one foot way ahead of the other, flexing your knees into a low position as you do so. The extended front ski encounters the wall of the dip, for example, bearing only part of your body's weight and glides over. Once it's past the obstacle, the rear ski follows easily. By sliding the front ski ahead, you have, in effect, created one very long ski that has a great deal more fore-and-aft stability than two shorter skis. You won't use this telemark position very much at first, and initially it will even seem tippy to you because you are balanced on a narrow rather than a wide track. But the telemark position will become progressively more useful in dealing with heavy backcountry snow, so don't neglect it.

But back to the task at hand: gaining a little control by learning to slow down, turn, and stop. This is what all downhill technique is about, but as a Nordic beginner you have two choices: step turns and wedges. Since they're both useful, we'll learn them both. Step turns first, however, because they

17.   *A step turn up the hill from a traverse.*

relate more closely to what you've already done, and because they will continue to develop your balance over a moving ski.

Step Turns

Step turns aren't very hard to understand—or to do. It's just a matter of "stepping" your skis around the corner, pointing one where you want to go, then stepping the other one alongside it, and repeating the process until you either come to a stop or are aimed in the right direction. Try a step turn as you finish a short schuss down the practice hill. At the bottom, just as you reach the flat, lift the tip of your right ski

and step it over to the right. Then step smartly onto it and step your left ski parallel. And repeat. Before you run out of momentum you can probably step all the way round until you're pointed somewhat back uphill. Of course, you would stop anyway, but you can use these step turns to slow down as well as stop by aiming yourself progressively more up the hill while actually descending.

Try a step turn again, this time from higher up on the hill. The whole secret is shifting your weight to the new ski as soon as you have stepped it into the direction you want. This weight shift is similar to the forward weight shift in the basic stride, only here it's both forward and to the side. At the same time, you will be improving your balance over a single ski. Not bad.

Step turns are really useful when linking traverses *down* a slope you might otherwise not be able to ski. You traverse the slope crosswise to control your speed as far as you want. Then a step turn *up the hill* brings you to a stop. A kick turn points you in the other direction, and off you go on a new traverse. This is a prudent but time-honored way to descend a slope that seems a little too threatening. A classic example: one of the steepest developed ski mountains in the west is KT22 at Squaw Valley. The name comes from the 22 kick turns that the first skiers had to use to link traverses all the way down.

So now you can ski! Combining traverses, step turns, and kick turns will get you down some pretty serious slopes. (And it's not just a beginner's cop out; experts too use the same strategy in special snow, such as breakable crust, when they can no longer pull off a downhill turn.) Now it's time to stop practicing and start touring. Pick simple, short cross-country tours of a few hours or a few miles at first, and, if possible, ski with experienced friends. Believe it or not, you're ready. If you have ever achieved a minimum of control, if you can zig-zag down a slope the same way you zig-zagged up it, you're already

prepared for your first backcountry skiing
adventures. Go to it! But don't stop learning either.

Wedging

The wedge (or snowplow, or stem) is a real ugly
duckling of a maneuver—a well-done step turn, for
example, is more graceful and more fun—but the
wedge will give you one more mode of downhill
control, and at the same time, open the door to some
more advanced downhill turns—christies and
telemarks.

To get started, we'll need our gentle practice
slope once again. (Be sure it's packed down, not soft
or deep snow.) As before, schuss down toward the
flat in a good wide stance. As the hill eases off,
weight the *heels* of both feet, and twist them apart so
that the tails of your skis (not the tips) spread apart,
forming a "V" pointed forward, down the hill. What
will you feel? As your skis open up into this
"wedge" position, you have the sensation that they're
scraping or brushing across the snow, and you come
to a stop a lot sooner than you would have just
sliding down the hill. Great. Try it again, and as you
push or scrape the tails of your skis out into this
wedge-shaped position, pay attention to the edges of
your skis. Pushing the skis out tilts them up onto
their inner edges; and it's these edges brushing
across the snow that slow you down. If you want to
use your wedge to stop on a dime, do two things:
push the tails of your skis a little farther apart to
create a wider wedge (like a bigger slice of pie), and,
at the same time, try to bear down with a little more
pressure on the inner edges of both skis. *Voilà*: more
friction and you stop.

This maneuver, the wedge, is a real beginner's
standby, but don't despise it for all that! On both
cross-country and Alpine skis it gives better control
at very slow speeds than almost anything else you
can do. (I'll never forget the shock of my ski class at
a resort in California's High Sierra when they saw

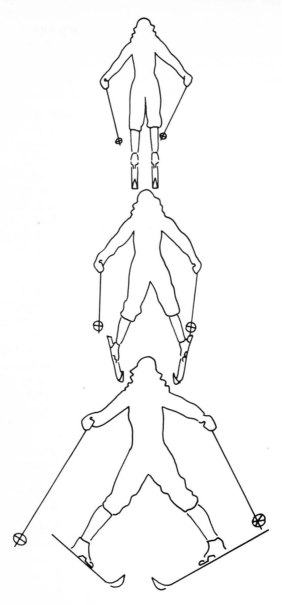

18. *A straight wedge to a stop from a downhill run. The first wedge position, a moderate or gliding wedge, slows the skier somewhat. The final position, a wide-braking wedge, brings her to a full stop.*

triple Olympic gold medal winner Jean-Claude Killy snowplow to a lift line!) On your cross-country skis with moderately flexible boots you will have to make a wider (or fatter) wedge in order to break your speed than an Alpine skier would. But there's no one correct angle for your skis. Experiment while straight-running down your practice slope with wider and thinner wedges to see just how much braking force you can develop.

Here are a few hints to smooth out any problems you may encounter while wedging. As you push the tails of your skis apart, the tips may cross. This won't occur if you remember to start from a wide stance—that way your ski tips have room to move a bit closer without crossing. The same problem may occur if your legs are too stiff: keep your knees bent and loose as you press your heels out. But beware, too, of letting the knees knock in together as you try to put pressure on the edges for a wedge stop: apply pressure more with the edge of the foot than the knee. Finally, remember that you're not just pushing the two skis apart but also *twisting* them at the same time—a rotary outward displacement of the heels of your boots. Why this stress on the heels? First, of course, to control the tails of your skis. But equally important, since your ski bindings only hold down the toe of the boot, you must weight the heel of your foot in order to maintain ski contact and control.

After a few tries you should be able to slow yourself and to stop at will in a wedge. But you can do more. If you exaggerate the wedging action of one foot and ski, you will begin to turn. Like this: as you're wedging straight down the hill, press and turn the right ski out a little harder. That ski becomes dominant, steering you to the left, the direction in which it's pointed. Topsy-turvy but logical. In your V position, the right ski tip points left and vice versa. So pressing and pushing on the right ski will turn you left; pressing and pushing on the left ski will turn you to the right. Let me be more specific: in

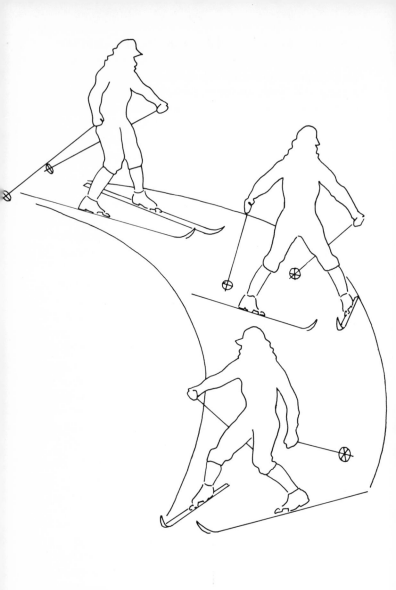

19. *A wedge turn to the right. The skier simply presses, or wedges, her right ski outward to create the turn.*

technical terms, what you do is shift your weight to one side, pressing harder and even leaning over that ski; at the same time, you *steer* the ski around by twisting your foot and knee toward the direction you want to go. More obvious in practice than on the page. But the important point is that this turning action is identical to how you made the wedge in the first place, i.e., pushing on the ski while twisting the heel out (and, hence, the toe in).

To experience your first wedge turns, exaggerate the wedging action first on one side then on the other. You will find yourself making a series of gentle curves down the hill. Now, instead of wedging out wide to stop, try turning to a stop: keep wedging out one ski until it guides you all the way around, into the hill. This takes less effort than a plain wedge stop, so practice it several times and to both sides. That's it. Now you have two means of turning: step turns and wedge turns. Splendid.

These wedge turns, simple though they are, will be enormously important in developing more advanced downhill skills on Nordic skis (what the next chapter is all about). So I want you to concentrate most on the points that carry over into advanced turns. The wedge itself is a stable, triangular platform, and the fact that each ski is already tilted up on edge and pointed in a new direction makes it easy to turn in a wedge even if you do everything wrong. Avoid the most common mistake—trying to turn your body around the corner rather than your skis. Your body is heavy and relatively hard to turn, and twisting your torso around to one side or other only indirectly affects your skis. The skis, on the other hand, are light and designed to turn as well as to go straight. If anything, tilt *away* from the intended direction of your turn; this will put pressure on the ski that's going to do the job for you. The active, turning ski is often called the *outside ski* because it will be on the outer side of the arc of your turn. (This is the right ski if you're turning left, the left ski if you're turning right.)

Sounds like a lot of words, but this is important shorthand in describing ski technique, so we'd better get used to it. If I talk about shifting all your weight to the outside ski in a turn, you'll know what I mean. And by the way, you don't have to shift *all* your weight to the outside ski in a wedge turn, just some of it, pressing on that ski harder until it dominates and steers you around the corner.

Once again, you're not twisting your body into a turn, but rather steering the skis (in this case in a wedge) around the corner while you ride the turning

20. *Linked wedge turns viewed from behind. Alternate weight shift and wedging of the outside ski creates a series of turns. Note that the body leans away from the direction of the turn.*

21. *The traverse revisited. As the slope steepens, the uphill ski is advanced, and progressively more weight is carried on the downhill leg and ski. Arms are always spread wide for balance.*

---

skis. This pattern will hold in every ski turn you ever learn, on Nordic or Alpine skis! Turn with your feet and legs (a bent knee can add a lot of leverage). Keep your upper body, your torso, quiet, almost motionless. And balance with your arms and poles. A universal pattern for good skiing.

Before congratulating yourself on having mastered all the basics of Nordic skiing, I do hope you'll spend a little more time practicing both step turns and wedge turns. (The wedge, by the way, is nothing more than a modern term for the venerable snowplow; and the action of wedging is also often referred to as *stemming*, especially when wedging only one foot at a time. Be sure to practice both kinds of turns from a traverse across the hill. Use step turns to turn uphill and stop at the end of your traverse. Use the wedge turn to link one traverse with another, turning downhill (or through the fall line, as skiers put it) and continuing around till you reach the direction of the new traverse.

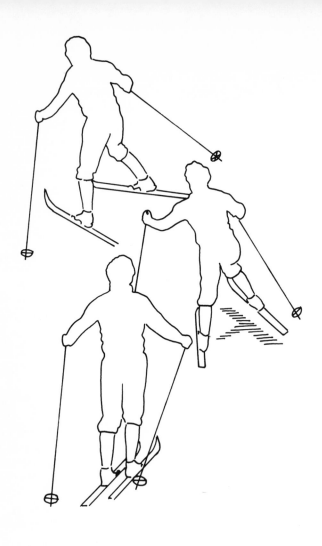

22. *Stemming, or wedging, only one ski from a traverse. The uphill ski can actually be lifted and stepped into position for the coming turn.*

So far, I haven't given you any special tips about traversing. It's just the same as schussing—only you aim across rather than down the hill. When you do get around to traversing steeper slopes, try this: advance your uphill ski a bit (so that the skis can't cross!), and put a bit more weight on the lower, downhill, leg (which will be straighter, therefore stronger). And always keep your arms comfortably spread in front of you for lateral balance. To link two traverses with a wedge turn, try this: shift all your weight on the lower ski and simply step the tail of the uphill ski out into a wide wedge; then progressively shift your weight onto it to come around, just like a regular wedge turn. Stepping one foot out into a wedge will get you into the turn (and into the fall line) a bit faster, especially on slightly steeper slopes.

But you shouldn't be skiing steep slopes yet, especially not on cross-country skis. You *are* a skier now, however, and you should be touring. Armed with the basic stride, uphill skills, and a couple of ways to stop and turn, you could even handle some major wilderness tours by skiing conservatively and prudently. But more important than anything else is mileage. Skiing and touring until everything we've talked about becomes second nature. How long will it take? A few days? A few weeks? A whole season? That depends on you. Five days in a row of skiing will do more for your technique and confidence than several months of weekend skiing. But you *will* get there, and you *do* possess the basics. I know experienced wilderness skiers who possess no skiing skills other than those described in this chapter. Yet they routinely take week-long trips in the backcountry of the Sierra, Yellowstone, and Colorado. A little technique can produce a lot of adventure.

Of course there's more. Instead of just coping with the wilderness in winter, you can become a real virtuoso on skinny skis. That's what the next chapter is about, and it's not as hard as you might think.

4

The reason you turn at all
is that your skis were meant to
and not because you want to.

Nor were you designed to fall
and so your body stands
upright, till mind bends.

Skiing just happens, that's all—
accept the soft white ride
with thanks, not pride.

4
Expanding
Nordic
Horizons

A quiet revolution has taken place in Nordic skiing over the last five years or so—the growing awareness among serious cross-country skiers that their light, narrow boards, pin bindings and flexible boots really are effective tools for thrilling downhill skiing. True, Nordic skis are not designed expressly for downhill runs. More than anything else, our light cross-country skis are designed for easy striding, literally for crossing country, and so in most cases their downhill performance is a compromise. But in the downhill domain, our Nordic horizons have expanded enormously in the last few years. For two reasons: first, the skis themselves (in which the compromise between kick and glide on the one hand, and turning ability on the other has become more evenly balanced). And second, but maybe more important, the efforts of a small number of three-pin fanatics to expand the downhill limits of their sport (which have led directly to the rediscovery and current renaissance of the telemark turn).

The telemark, like the diagonal stride, is a purely Nordic phenomenon, impossible without the free heel-lift supplied by touring bindings. The modern telemark was really rediscovered by American skiers after having been nearly forgotten, or at least relegated to the status of an antique, in the Scandinavian countries of its origin. The telemark is both functional and elegant, all you can ask of an advanced ski turn—but it is not a universally applicable technique. No turn is. To feel completely at ease on a wide variety of terrain and snow, the Nordic virtuoso needs to know and use other downhill turns as well, christies. There is a whole family of christies, characterized by parallel skidding skis. The telemark, too, is not only one turn but a family of related turns characterized by the extended, split-ski position we have already encountered for running over bumps and hollows. Both turns have their places, although I would say that the telemark is both more natural and more important for the backcountry Nordic skier.

In this chapter I'll explain not only how to christy and telemark, but when and where each one is more appropriate, more useful. But first, a couple of thoughts on what it means to become an expert Nordic skier. There's more to it than prowess on the steep and the deep. Downhill technique seems all-important because for years the Nordic tourer felt almost excluded from the challenge of downhill skiing, and because downhill runs are—no two ways about it—the most thrilling moments in skiing. But something else is necessary before you can consider yourself a hot Nordic skier—*a truly efficient basic stride!*

I've already pointed out that both beginner and expert use the identical technique to cover level and rolling ground; one simply does it better. So how do you get there? How do you refine that basic stride? Probably you'll need an instructor, a coach or a very skilled friend; certainly you'll need to spend time in a packed track, skiing without a pack—even if your heart remains in the backcountry surrounded by untracked snow. The packed track frees your attention from controlling the direction of your skis, enabling you to concentrate on the fine points of your stride.

Work on a more powerful, more explosive kick. On a more positive and complete forward weight transfer to your gliding ski. On keeping that forward knee bent as you project your hips (your weight) forward over it. On simplifying and refining your arm/pole movement, swinging them through close to the body with no excess waving, following through

23.   *Double poling to improve the basic stride.*

with a relaxed back hand at the end of the push. While you're thinking about your poles, take the time to learn *double poling* for more speed on slight downhills, or double poling action combined with a kick to keep up momentum on the flat. The technique of double poling (reaching and pushing with both poles at once) seems obvious, but the trick is to let your upper body break at the waist and collapse forward over the poles for maximum power.

All this adds up to a more efficient stride that will eat up the miles with more speed and less effort. Even on a ski expedition, struggling with a giant pack, an efficient stride will save you a lot of energy, although you never get up any speed. So it's worth the effort even if you have no interest in ever entering a cross-country race. One more point: the better your stride, the easier it will be for you to telemark in tough snow! In skiing, as in many other sports, people learn integrated movement patterns, often referred to as the basic motor skills of that sport. Striding is one such basic skill, and we'll find the same movement pattern used for starting telemark turns.

What are the other basic motor patterns needed for advanced Nordic skiing? You've already acquired several of them. *Lateral stepping* is one. Coupled with effective weight shift, it produces a step turn. And if you feel energetic, the same stepping skill will let you actually skate on skis. Wedging and wedge turns have introduced another skill—*steering*: weighting a ski while simultaneously twisting both foot and knee in the direction of a turn. Steering is something you'll use in every turn from here on. You'll also become more conscious of *edging*. You have already noticed that as you wedge your skis they tilt up on edge, but you probably haven't made a special effort to control the edges of your skis. As we steered the outside ski of your wedge, a bit more edging seemed to occur but this was more in the class of a "happening" than something you did on purpose. Now we're going to get serious about edging—or more exactly, *edge control*, both edging and flattening the skis. Edge control (a very generalized sort of skill) is all we need at this point to get into our first advanced turn, the stem christy, and it will do wonders for our telemarks later.

Christies

Logic insists that I tell you what a christy is (you remember the name came from Christiania, which is now Oslo, Norway) before discussing how to learn it. Very well. A christy is any turn that ends with the two skis parallel, sliding or skidding around on the same set of edges. You may start a christy with your skis "stemmed" out into a wedge shape; and then it's called a *stem christy*. Or you can keep them parallel through the whole arc of the turn—typical of Alpine skiing—and then you have a *parallel christy*, or *parallel turn* for short. Christies require more speed than wedge turns, but they're more graceful, take less effort, and have a number of other advantages as well. Sounds good, how do we start?

First, you must learn to skid or sideslip. This involves the edge control I was talking about. Find a short steep slope, only a few meters long, and make sure the snow is moderately hard. If it isn't, sidestep up and down a couple of times until it's packed out. Or better yet, learn sideslipping, and then christies, at a downhill-ski area where the slopes are already packed. Such firm snow will really speed your progress at first; later you'll be able to apply these christies and parallel turns in unpacked, untracked snow. (But if you have nothing but very deep

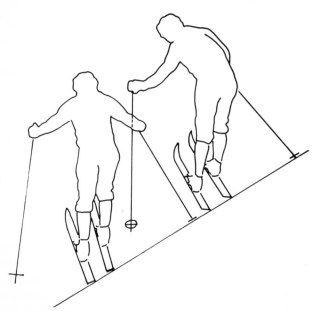

24. *Sideslipping on cross-country skis. The edges are set and released primarily with the ankles, somewhat with the knees.*

powder or deep, heavy snow to ski in, then skip to the next section and learn to telemark first.) Let's assume, however, that we have found a good short steep practice slope; what next?

Stand across the hill, skis horizontal as though you were traversing. Now think about your edges. If you're not slipping down the hill, it's probably because you've already tilted your skis into the hill, making the edges grip the slope with an inward (uphill) push of your ankles and knees. Next, exaggerate the grip of these edges, the uphill edges of your skis. (Bear in mind that we're not necessarily talking about metal edges; any ski edge—plastic, wood or metal—can grip and release, although metal edges are a real plus on very hard snow or ice.) You've pushed your knees further into the hill to grip more; now relax your feet and roll your knees back out. Your skis will flatten out on the slope, and you'll slide laterally, or sideways, down the hill. Your first sideslip. To stop, just re-edge your skis. Practice a little more, increasing and releasing pressure on the edges of your skis. Use your poles for balance. If possible, avoid leaning your body into the hill when you slide. Instead lean *out*, over your sideslipping skis.

A note on vocabulary: skiers refer to sideways bending of the body as *angulation*. You angulate your knees and ankles into the hill to make the edges grip; you relax, or de-angulate, to let them sideslip. Likewise, you angulate your body out, down the hill, in order to stay in balance over your sideslipping skis. All this sounds a bit complicated and I guess it is. But well worth it. The edge control developed through sideslipping—not just setting and releasing the edges of your skis, but also becoming more aware of them—will make advanced ski turns a hundred percent easier. And sideslipping is useful in itself: if you come upon a section too steep for you to ski, sideslip down it! In addition to sideslipping straight down, you can also sideslip diagonally forward by releasing your edges while traversing. Of course, sideslipping on cross-country skis only works well on hard, or icy, or packed snow. If you try to flatten your skis in deep soft snow, nothing will happen.

The Basic Christy

Now, how about those turns. Let's begin by learning a simplified version of the stem christy, which I'll call a *basic christy*. Think of it as a wedge turn that ends in a sideslip, two things you already know. It's just a question of getting the skis from a wedge (or converging) position to a parallel one. Do it like this: Wedge straight down the hill (not too fat a wedge, please), and start turning to the left. As you come around, out of the fall line, you find yourself bearing down mostly on the right ski, your steering ski. So exaggerate this a little and put all your weight on that ski, which completely lightens the inside, left ski, allowing you to easily lift it up a few inches and slide it in parallel to the steering ski. What happens? You're still turning because you haven't stopped steering that outside ski only now the two skis are skidding (sideslipping) parallel through the finish of the turn. You'll probably skid right to a stop the first time you try.

Let's take another look. What did we do? To turn at all (as in a wedge) we must steer the *outside* ski in an arc. But to trigger the christy or parallel phase of the turn, we use the *inside* leg—lightening and lifting that ski, and pivoting the tail inward until the ski is parallel to its mate. Because the outside ski is already turning, brushing over the snow through its steering action, you'll discover that you don't need to "release" the edges in order to skid. Once parallel, your skis will both skid and keep on turning, actually sideslipping in a curve or arc to complete the christy. Two more points will help make it easy. Don't slide that inside ski in right next to the other one; pivot it parallel, but keep a *wide stance*. You'll have better balance during the christy finish. And

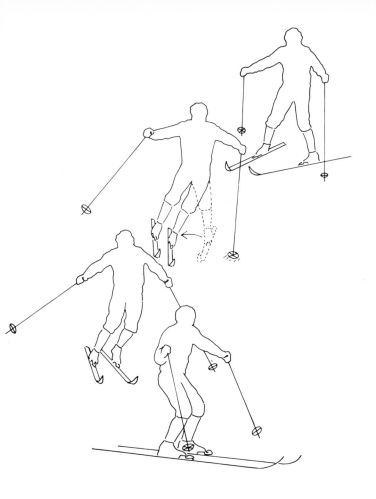

25. The basic christy, from a wedge turn to a skidded parallel finish. Note the transition from one position to the other, which takes place, initially at least, after the wedged skis have been steered into the fall line.

finally, trigger that parallel movement near the *end of the turn*, after you have come around, through the fall line, in your wedge and are already slowing down a bit.

With practice—and that comes next—you'll start to feel more confident and more solidly balanced over your outside ski. As a result you'll be able to bring your inside ski parallel, triggering the christy, sooner and sooner—actually in the fall line, or even earlier. Thus mileage will transform your basic christy into the much spiffier *stem christy*, another version of the same turn.

The Stem Christy

In a stem christy, you no longer steer your wedged-out skis slowly through the fall line before bringing them parallel. Instead, you simply step the uphill ski into a wedge position (we have inherited the German word "stem" for this action), and immediately commit yourself to it—shifting your weight, and pulling the other ski parallel to begin the christy with no further ado.

Why even bother with the initial stemming action? It actually helps a lot. Once you've stemmed the top ski out (you're in a traverse, let's say) you've accomplished several things: that ski is pointed more down the hill, angled in the direction you want to turn. And by placing that ski out at an angle you

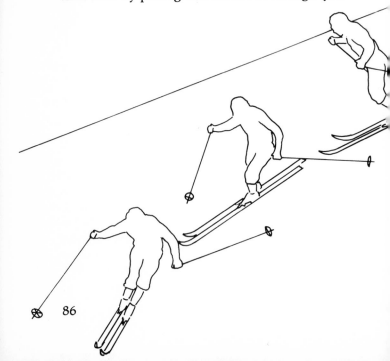

have actually changed its edge, tilting it onto its inside edge in preparation for the coming turn. All this in the guise of getting ready, with no desperate effort or early commitment of weight to the turning ski, which explains why stem christies are easier and certainly more popular among touring skiers than their grown-up cousins, pure parallel turns (christies without a stem opening to start off). On easy snow, firm and smooth, the stem part of your stem christy may become quite small indeed; but unless you are an experienced Alpine skier who has taken up Nordic cross-country after mastering parallel turns, you will find a pure parallel christy on skinny skis extremely difficult for quite a while. The stem christy, on the other hand, is very easy.

Here are a few final tips to make it even easier. Plant your pole! That is, use your inside pole (the

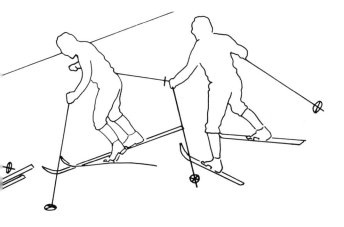

26. *The stem christy, in which the uphill ski is merely "stemmed" into position rather than both skis steered toward the fall line in a wedge.*

pole on the inside of the turn) for support. Simply stick it in the snow at the very moment you lift the inside ski and move it parallel to the other one. Planted at that moment, your inside pole "props you up," just when you're losing the support of your inside ski and foot. Do you want to make tighter, shorter radius christies? Once into the christy phase of the turn, bend both knees a bit more and twist them more vigorously into the turn. The tails of the skis will slide more and the turn will come around faster. (Our Nordic christy, by the way, is a bit different from the Alpine version; on cross-country skis it's easier to lift the inside ski parallel than to slide it, and, with free-heel bindings, we must shorten our turns with more steering rather than forward pressure.) To make a longer, slower christy, simply stand a bit taller and relax your ankles somewhat to let your skis sideslip even more through the arc of the turn.

The essence of christy-style skiing on skinny skis is that the parallel skis skid or sideslip. A skidding ski is far easier to push around—to steer with bent knee and foot—than one that's tracking forward on its edges. Of course, that's true only if the ski can

skid in the first place, but obviously in deep snow, heavy wet snow, and a dozen other tenuous varieties of white stuff, the ski will just sink in and be unable to skid. So there are clearly a lot of situations where christies are maybe not the hot tip. Are they, in fact, very useful to the backcountry skier?

You bet! Christies, and parallel turns too, are definitely useful for off-trail Nordic skiing—although generally not as useful as telemark turns, which we'll learn next. They come into their own for steep slopes, for short-radius turns, and on hard snow. Typically all three of these conditions are found together. On steep slopes speed control is essential; this means making shorter turns, back and forth across the fall line—hence christies. And also, steep slopes don't hold deep new snow well, as it often sloughs off, leaving a harder surface layer—once more, ideal for christies! And finally, you'll find a surprising amount of hard snow in the backcountry: old, settled, consolidated snow, spring corn snow, wind-slab and plain old ice—all perfect for christies.

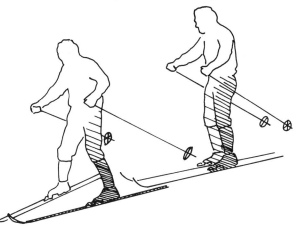

27.   *Triggering the stem christy. Note the all-important weight distribution and weight shift to the outside ski at the start of the christy phase (weight is indicated by shading).*

However useful the christy may be to the backcountry skier, the telemark turn (our next major topic) is even more useful. Don't wait until you perfect your christy—and don't even bother to start learning parallel turns—before learning to telemark. You can, in fact, learn the two turns almost simultaneously. But I've described the christy first, and I hope you'll learn it first, for a very special reason: in my experience, skiers who can do effective christies have an easy time picking up the telemark turn. But telemark-only skiers have a hell of a time learning to christy. It's hard to explain just why, but I believe that the edge control (not the skidding itself) learned through sideslipping and christies carries over to the telemark turn, while there's no comparable transfer of skills in the other direction.

Parallel Turns on Nordic Skis

Eventually, you *will* want to learn parallel turns on your skinny skis. Because the parallel turn is nothing more than an extension or refinement of the christy you've just learned (a stem christy without the stem), my comments about it logically belong in this section—even though I've just suggested that you tackle telemarks first. So file the following advice in your memory bank, and use it later, when and if you need it.

The best way to learn to "parallel" on cross-country skis is to go to a downhill ski area and buy yourself a lift ticket. Stay on beginner to intermediate packed slopes, and simply imitate all the "parallel" skiers you see. Better yet, rent Alpine equipment—plastic boots and shoulder-height skis, and learn to make parallel turns with them (see Chapter 6 on Alpine technique) in ski school or on your own. Then go back to your free-wheeling, free-heeling skinny skis and you'll most likely be able to make parallel turns on them. The reason I propose such a roundabout program is that every Nordic ski tourer I know who can make really effective parallel turns on

28. *A parallel turn on "skinny skis," characterized by bent knees and ankles, and a somewhat wide or open stance.*

---

skinny skis in an honest-to-God backwoods situation learned how first on Alpine skis. I certainly did and my Alpine experience stood me in good stead. Parallel turns look better than stem christies and, yes, they feel better when they work. You can also eliminate any weight shift in a parallel turn and, as a result, make beautiful turns in deep powder, where stem christies would be disastrous.

For those of you who have already had a little experience with parallel turns on Alpine skis, here are a few tips for *adapting* them to cross-country equipment. Stick with a wide stance, no feet-together stuff. Exaggerate both knee *and ankle* bend for greater leverage in turning both skis downhill together. Use more up-motion to unweight your skis at the start of the turn than you would on Alpine skis. If you're on hard or solid snow, use a lateral parallel step to put early turning pressure on the outside ski of the turn—in soft snow, don't shift your weight at all. Since you can't use forward leverage (tip pressure) with your Nordic boots and bindings, revert to the old-fashioned technique of heel thrusting, pushing both feet sideways while weighting the heels, in order to complete hard turns (a good idea for any Nordic christy). And finally, a strongly anticipated upper body and pole plant will really help (again, see Chapter 6 to interpret this mysterious instruction). Basically, parallel skiing on cross-country skis resembles the Alpine ski technique of twenty years or more ago.

Adapting parallel turns to cross-country skis, as I said, is fairly easy; learning them for the first time on skinny skis is devilishly hard. If you're bound and determined to try, a gentle, packed slope will make things easier because you can ski more directly in the fall line without picking up too much speed and thus not have to turn so far at first. Good luck! And in the meantime we'll move on to telemark turns—the most graceful of all Nordic ski turns and, in the right circumstances, the most efficient.

Telemarks

For the Nordic touring skier, telemark turns are definitely the hot tip. What I call the telemark renaissance is the most exciting new development in Nordic cross-country technique in the last decade. The excitement is not in the turn itself—telemarks have been around for a long, long time—but in the discovery that they work amazingly well in a heretofore-unsuspected variety of downhill situations. Also, using the telemark one can become a very competent downhill skier on skinny skis with no Alpine ski experience at all. But before singing its praises any further and talking about different applications and uses for it, I'd better tell you just what a telemark turn is and how it works.

A telemark is a downhill turn in which the outside ski is strongly advanced (remember, that's the right ski if you're turning left and vice versa) and set at an angle to the trailing (inside) ski in order to lead or steer the turn. Put even more simply, it's a turn done in the telemark position, which we've already encountered in Chapter 3 as a stable position for running over dips and hollows. The image I want to give you is that of a partially kneeling skier: kneeling, on the trailing rear leg and knee, while the lowered body is supported on a very bent front leg. Check the accompanying illustrations to make sure you have a clear picture. Front thigh almost horizontal, rear thigh almost vertical. But what on earth, you're wondering, is the real practical advantage of this obviously unnatural position?

It works out like this: Any downhill ski turn is the result of two factors, the muscular twisting, or steering (which the skier must supply) and the shape of the ski itself. You'll remember from our equipment review that skis (except for X-C racing models) have a feature called sidecut—a curved, waisted profile—that helps them turn. This is particularly helpful in the christies we've just learned; the wider tip of the ski creates more friction and lets the tails slide out into the turn. In addition, to a slight extent, the ski simply tends to follow the curved shape of its side or edge, tracking in a slight arc rather than a perfectly straight line. This is what happens in a telemark, only more so. When one ski is pushed ahead by about half a ski length and then turned in front of the other ski, what happens? In

this position, we can think of the two skis as one
long ski with an exaggerated sidecut or arc to one
side. This curved shape, created by both skis, leads
the skier around the arc of a telemark turn. You can
also think of the front ski as similar to the front
wheel of a bicycle, another long, narrow shape—turn
it, and inevitably the rear wheel, or ski, will follow.

So much for theory, how about practice? To
learn to telemark easily and quickly ("telemark
without tears") I want to suggest several different
exercises and approaches, each of which will give
you a better feeling for some aspect of the turn. The
basic skills you need are striding and steering, both
of which you've already learned. As usual you'll
need a practice slope—not necessarily packed this
time, but the snow shouldn't be too deep, too icy, or
too steep.

The Telemark Stride

First, on a very gentle part of the slope, or even
on the flat, you want to become comfortable getting

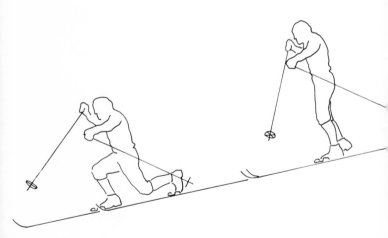

into and out of the telemark position itself. Think of it as a basic stride, with a deep knee bend and a few seconds of hesitation thrown in. Stride forward onto your right ski and let the right knee bend much more than usual as your weight comes onto it, allowing the trailing left leg to bend also until the left knee almost touches the ski. And then hold it for an extra second or so before standing back up on your front, right leg and striding into another deep knee bend, this time on the left ski. That's right: a slowed-down, exaggeratedly flexed basic stride. And, as you stride into and out of this telemark position, don't forget to use your poles just the same way you normally do while cross-country running.

Let's call this curious sequence of deep knee bends a *telemark stride*. And now we're ready to put a little turning into it. Start down a very gentle slope with your newly acquired telemark stride, only this time, as you stride forward onto the new ski, turn it at a *very slight* angle across the other one. That is, point your toe inward in the air as you swing the foot forward. As you might expect, each time you

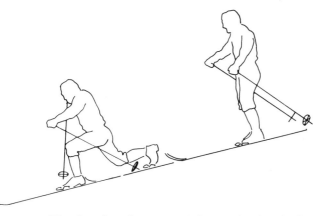

29.   The telemark stride: a series of alternate deep knee bends down an easy slope, gradually turning the front ski slightly across the other to create small changes in direction. Ideal practice for striding rhythmically into the telemark position.

step forward at an angle, you'll start turning in that direction. Not a very big turn to be sure, just the beginning of a slow change of direction, heading the way your front ski is pointed. And then, after that brief pause, stride onto the other ski, angling it in turn, to veer back the way you came. Result: a series of gentle turns, more like slight deviations from the fall line than real turns, which leave a long, stretched-out pattern in the shape of a letter S down the slope. You're accomplishing several things at once. The striding action helps carry your weight forward onto the advanced ski. The most common problem in telemarking is shuffling the outside foot timidly ahead without committing the body's weight to it. At the same time, linking one stride to another prepares you for eventually linking one turn smoothly to another—with no traverses in between. A super exercise! My friend Steve Barnett is the first person I know to describe this exercise. In his book, *Cross-Country Downhill*, which was also the first serious discussion of advanced downhill turns on skinny skis, Steve called this move a "crooked

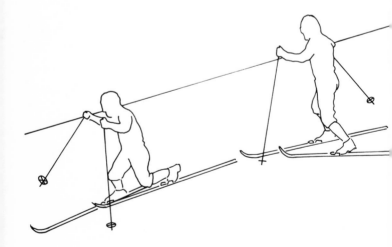

stride," which is pretty descriptive. (I recommend reading Barnett's book, a handsome paperback devoted exclusively to downhill skiing on Nordic gear, for yet another perspective on the same ideas and turns covered in this chapter.)

Repeat these "crooked strides" a few more times down the hill in order to practice what is essentially the beginning of a full telemark turn. But this isn't enough to give you the feeling of a complete telemark, so let's try another preliminary simplified maneuver—the stem telemark.

The Stem Telemark

This one's easy: just start a downhill turn in a wedge; but as you reach the fall line, advance the outside ski about half a ski length while smoothly kneeling forward into that now-familiar telemark position. Surprise! You'll whip right around out of the fall line, completing the turn in classic telemark fashion. The trick for getting the best result from this one is to be sure that you start the turn in a

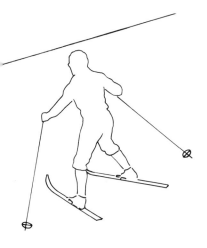

30. The stem telemark: advancing the outside ski into a telemark position from the familiar wedge.

relatively narrow or pointed wedge (what Alpine skiers call a "gliding wedge" as opposed to a wide, fat "braking wedge"). Also, be sure to shift your weight strongly to the front ski as you advance it. The wedge position sets you up with the outside ski angled across the inside one. But it's all relative. If the front ski is angled too much across the inside or rear ski of your telemark, then the two skis seem to work at cross purposes. You have to have some difference in angle or your telemark just won't turn; but the rear ski should follow smoothly along, more parallel than perpendicular, to the lead ski. It should actually slide in even more parallel as the telemark progresses.

But don't worry about the refinements at first. Play around with this stem as a way of making sure that when you drop into the telemark position you'll already be turning. Once again the pattern you experience is something like this: from a traverse, for example, stem the uphill ski out into a small wedge; start to steer this ski down the hill in the familiar wedge turn. Once things are going smoothly, slide that outside, steering ski ahead, moving your weight forward with it and riding smoothly through the finish in a narrow telemark position.

This hybrid turn, the stem telemark, works great, but it's still not the graceful swooping turn that is our goal. (Don't worry, we're almost there.) But seriously, why bother with these two preliminary versions, or exercises, instead of trying the full telemark turn right away? The answer is that these exercises are very simple, and lead to a better, more dynamic telemark turn in the long run. To see why, let's go back to basic skills for a minute.

Balance and Edging in Telemarks

In addition to a modified basic stride—the telemark stride that we've already worked on—and the positive steering action of the leading, ouside ski, which we obtain automatically from the stem

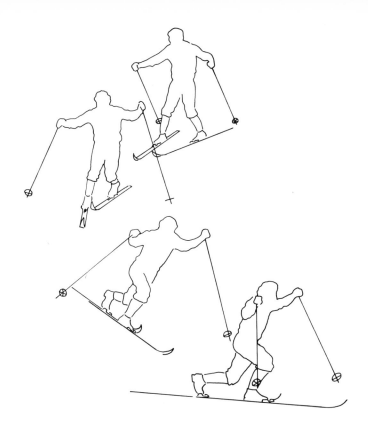

31.   Another view of the stem telemark. Note the inward inclination of the body in the second figure, which provides the needed edging of the front ski.

telemark, we still need two more skills for the perfect telemark: balance and edging. These final two skills are closely related.

Consider balance. We've already learned to distinguish two kinds of balance: lateral, or side-to-side, and longitudinal, or fore-and-aft balance; and we know that long base of the telemark position offers us great fore-and-aft balance. But, by the same token, the telemark position is so "narrow track" that lateral balance is a bit shaky. Don't throw up your hands! Spread them wide while telemarking, a first step toward better side-to-side balance. But basically, my strategy is to have you experience different aspects of the telemark first while you get used to its distinctive balance requirements, without the need for total commitment and perfect balance throughout the turn.

When I watch even pretty fair Nordic skiers trying to teach themselves to telemark, this is what I see: They extend their leading ski and drop into the classic position; then they begin a wrestling match with the front ski, trying to twist it across into the direction of the turn. All the while they wobble from side to side and are constantly forced to use their poles as props and outriggers. What's wrong? For these skiers, getting into the turn is a hesitant, drawn-out process. Their balancing act starts before they ever begin to turn—and the front ski is invariably not edged against the snow! Aha, edging! You remember that, in your simple wedge turn, the outside steering ski was quite strongly edged (because it had been thrust out from your body), and

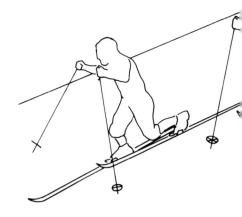

this helped it to turn. The telemark, too, demands an edged steering ski that can "bite in" and lead the turn in the desired direction. This is why the stem telemark works so well: your outside ski is pre-edged in the stem or wedge position and stays edged as you thrust it ahead for the telemark finish. What about the body? Relative to the edged outside ski your body is tilted to the inside of the turn in the stem position and that's just the way it should be in the telemark finish.

The Classic Telemark

Now let's put all these elements together. To make it easy, ski a bit faster. You're heading down a gentle hill in a steep traverse (close to the fall line), let's say down and right, and you want to telemark around to the left. The start is just like our "crooked stride." In one movement, step your right ski forward (and you with it) while starting to turn to the left, turning it a bit in the air as you step. And at the *very*

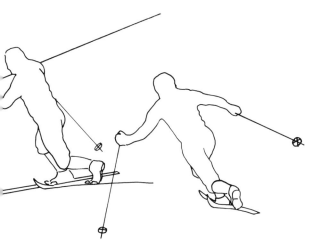

32. *The classic telemark.*

same time let your whole body tilt a bit to the left in the direction you want to turn. That should do the trick—your turn is launched, and it will keep on going. The idea of tilting the body—let's call it banking, the proper term—is one you won't enjoy at first. It feels as though you'll fall right over on your head, but you don't. This initial banking puts your skis on edge, and since the turn starts right away, centrifugal force will support you in the banked position just as it does the bicyclist who leans into each turn. Don't overdo it. With practice you'll learn to commit your body just enough to get the turn started, and that's all. But if you stay bolt upright, all you'll do is wobble as you fight to start the turn. In a sense, speed and commitment are everything in beginning a good telemark. By striding forward, steering the front ski and banking slightly *all at the same time*, you have much less time to lose your balance laterally—and generally you don't!

At this point you're saying to yourself: all very well, but I'm only reading a book; what will it be like on the snow? You're right. It will be strange and awkward at first. But if you follow my advice and spend some time experimenting with our two warm-up exercises—the crooked stride and the stem telemark—then things should go a lot more smoothly when you're ready to commit yourself to a full telemark turn. Look at the illustrations, watch other skiers telemarking, and if possible get an experienced friend to demonstrate repeatedly for you. If necessary, reread the preceding pages. But one way or another, form a mental image of how telemarking works. Then start trying it.

One of the real dilemmas in describing advanced ski turns, Alpine or Nordic, is that the explanations are always more complicated than the turns themselves. But if there weren't a lot to them, then they wouldn't be advanced turns; beginners would learn them after a half-hour on skis—and they don't. So hang in there.

More important than anything else I've said

about the telemark is the fact that it's developed from the basic stride. Stride strongly into your first telemarks, and you'll soon succeed. Try to ease into them, and you might as well not bother trying. This is why the telemark is the Nordic turn *par excellence*; our free-heel equipment permits a graceful, dynamic, efficient stride, and the telemark is the turning version of that stride.

Once you've succeeded with a few telemark turns, the order of the day is mileage, practice, and repetition, just as with christies. And here I have a possibly jarring suggestion: do some of that practicing at a lift-served Alpine ski area. There's no better way to get a lot of downhill mileage in a short time. Your lift-ticket dollars will be handsomely repaid with confidence and competence in the backcountry. Start on the beginner slopes, and gradually venture up to steeper but well-groomed intermediate slopes. However, I want you to avoid the bumps, or moguls, found on the even steeper, advanced runs. Skilled telemark skiers can indeed enjoy a workout amongst the bigger, meaner bumps found on steep runs at downhill ski areas. But they're no place to learn, and, fortunately, these bizarre, bumpy shapes, made by crowds of skiers, aren't found in the backcountry. Don't bother practicing telemarks at a downhill ski area if you know in advance that the snow is extremely hard or icy. You want packed powder *à la* Rocky Mountains, not the black ice of New Hampshire. And while you're practicing, don't neglect deep and untracked snow. Your first telemarks, unlike your first christies, will work just fine in a foot of new snow. And that, after all, has been in the back of your mind all along.

What I want to talk about now is how to improve and refine your telemarks, once you have a turn that works. Clearly, you don't learn everything about this, or any ski turn, all at once. If, on your first attempts to telemark, you tried to think of every single pointer in this section, your brain would be so overloaded with instructions that it would be a wonder you could even stand up. Seriously, don't overload your circuits. To become an expert backcountry skier (or an expert skier period) your best bet is to work on one point at a time, master it, integrate it with what you already know how to do, and then go on to build on that.

Refinements

In this case, the very next thing to work on is your arm and pole action. We've neglected it in this turn so far, except for the suggestion to spread your arms a bit wider for lateral balance. There is also a specific pattern of arm/pole action that will give you a more powerful telemark as well as making it easier to link turns down the slope. Begin by planting your uphill pole (as in the basic stride) just before you turn. Give a strong push with it, which will help you stride that uphill foot forward to start the turn. At the same time, swing (or punch) your inside, downhill hand forward to help complete the forward weight shift onto the front ski. You won't believe the difference! A so-so turn suddenly becomes smooth and dynamic, almost effortless. The push with the outside pole and the complementary forward swing of the inside arm work together to give you a powerful quick weight transfer onto the lead ski; they take all the hesitation out of the turn. Yet the arm action I've just described is identical with that of the familiar, basic stride on the level, here synchronized with the forward stride at the start of the telemark. It's obvious, but a lot of skilled skiers forget it or have never thought of it in this way. It can be baffling at first for experienced Alpine skiers who are just getting into the telemark, since in parallel christies it's always the downhill pole that's planted, not the uphill one.

In the follow-through, or steering phase of the turn, you'll want to stay in more or less the same position: outside hand and pole low and back, inside pole and hand reaching forward and ready to plant

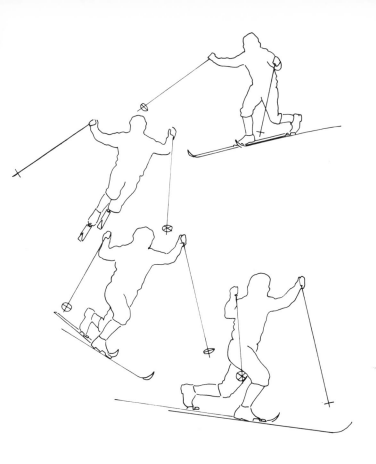

33. *The classic telemark seen from below. Note the bicycle-lean angle.*

at the end of the turn—which, of course, becomes the beginning of the next turn. Planting the advanced, inside pole at the end of the turn is a hot tip because that's the very moment where you may have the greatest problem with balance, say in very heavy snow.

What about the arc of the turn itself? The ideal telemark is more of a "carved" than a "skidded" turn. Rather than skidding sideways as they turn, the two skis (acting like one long ski with an extreme amount of sidecut) tend to track around in a very positive arc. To do so, the edges of both skis have to have a pretty good grip on the snow. We've already talked about the necessary "bicycle lean" angle, the body's slight banking toward the center of the turn, which helps to establish the needed edging. In deep snow, or soft packed powder, or soft corn, you'll find that this slight lean alone gives you plenty of edging. In harder snow conditions you may need more edging. Get it by tightening your ankles in your boots and pushing the knees inward (knee angulation). Your front knee is perhaps a tad more important in this, but both skis should be edged. Don't, however, try to increase the edge hold on hard snow by banking further into the turn with your body; you'll just tunk over in the snow if you do.

There's a limit to how much edging you can achieve in a classic telemark position. In order to angulate more with the knees you can stand a bit taller, skis less extended fore and aft, in what some folks call a "half telemark." But the limit is physiological, because with the outside hip advanced in the classic telemark, the upper body is unable to angulate out over the edged skis to stay in balance past a certain point. The answer is simple. In really hard snow conditions, you must accept a certain amount of skid. At a certain point, you're better off using christies and parallel turns, which are skidded to begin with! It's no accident that the telemark renaissance originated in the Rocky Mountains and then spread to the Pacific Northwest, both regions famous for soft snow conditions where edging in a telemark is never a problem. In very deep snow, new powder for instance, edging is never a problem because the snow holds the banked skis perfectly; however, flotation—or rather its opposite, where the ski tips dive beneath the snow—may well be a problem. Don't put quite as much weight on the front ski, and lift up with the toes while pressing down with the heel to make sure the tip of that front ski floats up in the snow.

Now how about the size of the turn? Long-radius, medium, or short? (These are descriptions which actually have no precise meaning in skiing, and are relative only to each other.) Your first telemarks were probably all the same; how can you make them shorter? or longer? To begin with, the radius of a telemark turn is mostly determined by the angle the leading, outside ski forms with the trailing, inside ski. A slight, shallow angle produces a long-radius turn; the greater the angle, the shorter the turn. So far so good, but if the front ski is angled too far across, an awkward, very skidded and out-of-balance telemark results. So if you really want to shorten up your telemark turn, begin with a moderately angled stride—as though for a medium-radius turn—and then, once the turn is established, steer the front ski extra hard, driving the knee inward to edge and help shorten the turn. At the same time you'll want to be sure your rear ski doesn't get left behind: keep sliding it in to a more parallel position with a more active than normal rear foot. From what I've just said, you've already guessed that it's a lot easier to make medium- and long-radius telemark turns than short ones. You're right. To carve a very long-radius telemark, stride forward with the front ski almost parallel; start the turn more by banking the body than steering the forward, outside, leg; and through the arc of the turn weight the rear ski a trifle more than normal to keep it tracking steadily.

The matter of weight distribution between the two skis is a very subtle one in advanced telemark turns. I have repeatedly advised you to put your weight forward onto the front turning ski. This is because it's so bloody difficult to get enough weight out there. But in reality your weight will still be somewhat on both skis. That's fine. And as you finish the turn, swinging out of the fall line, it's often good to shift a bit more weight back onto the rear acceleration of gravity parallel to the slope—is so the start of a new turn, all your weight will be on the lower ski (the lead ski of the last turn) in order to lighten the uphill ski for striding forward into the turn.

Finally, a few words about telemarking on steep slopes. It's all relative; what's steep for one skier may be flat for another. You'll find your own perception of steepness altering as your skill increases. But whatever your level of technique, when it's steep enough to make you nervous, then it's *steep*! Telemarks are quite tricky on really steep slopes because the force acting on the skier—the

34.   *Telemarking on a steep slope. With one dynamic step the skier swings his top ski forward, across the other ski, and into the fall line.*

ski so it will "hold" and not "wash out." Of course at much greater: more speed as you start into the fall line, and more pressure sideways as you come out of it. On steep slopes, the best bet, if you're anything less than a true telemark wizard, is to use the stem telemark we practiced earlier. The stem will keep your speed down as you steer from a traverse toward the fall line; it's a great safety turn in soft, steep snow. The expert will avoid telemarking through a full 180° arc on the steep, but in a different way. In a far more dramatic move than stemming, he will simply step his upper ski across the tip of the downhill ski, right into the fall line. This starts the turn in a hurry, but the two skis are momentarily almost at right angles, which means trouble. So, as soon as the skier's weight comes onto the front ski (now stepped into the fall line), he must "flick" the rear ski in parallel to the front ski, with a sideways movement of the rear foot and leg. This is a rapid, dynamic, and athletic start to a telemark turn, which must be performed without a trace of hesitation. But it works well on steep slopes. The real telemark portion of the turn occurs only from the middle of the turn on—just as in the stem telemark. And if the end of the turn gets a bit hairy, plant the inside pole for support and step out of it by bringing your inside foot forward early. You may occasionally wind up skidding out of such a steep telemark in a wide-track parallel position, which should tell you something.

So where does that leave us? We've seen a lot of variations and refinements of the basic telemark turn; are there still others? Indeed there are, many and subtle, but they can be discovered only with practice and with backcountry mileage—and that's up to you. The telemark, as Doug Robinson wrote in a ski-touring article for *Outside* magazine, "is a great turn, but a panacea it ain't." This is why I've insisted that the complete Nordic skier master both christies and telemarks. The two complement each other in a marvelous way. Telemarks are more efficient for medium- to long-radius turns; christies (and parallel turns) are more efficient for medium to short turns. Telemarks are generally superior in soft or deep snow—and unbeatable in heavy crud and breakable crust, where skis just won't skid; while christies work better on hard surfaces. On the steep, I prefer christies (and parallel turns) because speed control demands a short turn, and skidding is a good way to kill speed. In open moderate terrain I prefer telemarks for their graceful, floating/flying feeling. But these are only general guidelines. There's an exception for every rule.

And talking technique, questions of personal motivation, attitude, even philosophy come into play. Why are we skiing? Why elect backcountry touring? And why bother to master these various techniques. If you were carrying the mail across the High Sierra, the way Snowshoe Thompson did a century ago, you could get by on long skis and little technique. If, like me, you're looking for freedom, relaxation, mobility, and security on skis in the backcountry, then you'll want to develop a broad spectrum of techniques, and use them as conditions dictate.

If you're trying to prove a point, it may be very satisfying to use telemarks exclusively, and in situations where others don't dare to; or even to use Nordic equipment everywhere, no matter what (to make the first three-pin descent of this, or traverse of that). But there is a critical point here. Is backcountry skiing the pursuit of difficulty or delight? The answer is purely personal, but you should know when you're making the choice. Becoming too ardent a champion of one particular style of skis, skiing, or turning may well put you in the camp of hard-core fanatics who invest a certain technique with moral virtue just because it *is* difficult, and they *have* done it. Of course, seeking out and mastering difficulty is enormously gratifying, be it a mountain, a steep slope of challenging snow, or a new technique. One of the reasons for the current telemark renaissance is the fact that a number of expert Alpine skiers in the Rockies turned to three-pin bindings and skinny skis in search of new challenges, new difficulties to overcome, new limits to push. Skiing the backcountry offers all of us personal limits to overcome; but they should be your own, not someone else's.

Some friends of mine recently completed a major ski traverse in Alaska on the lightest of equipment, 47-mm light touring skis, the works. The expedition was a big success—and a first! But one of them confided to me that in such steep and glaciated terrain they would have had a much easier time of it on Alpine ski mountaineering equipment. In short, they were skiing to prove a point. For me there is another point altogether, adapting myself to the winter landscape as completely as possible, feeling at home in a surrealistic, snow-covered world. This means adapting both equipment and technique to the conditions at hand. For me there is no single right way!

For this reason I've tried to present as wide a spectrum as possible of Nordic techniques, and for this reason too, I want to introduce you to Alpine skiing in the backcountry. Nordic boards are the touring skis of choice—for their incredible lightness, for the freedom of movement they afford—but they have real limits, primarily of steepness, and beyond those limits it's time to switch to a new style.

5

*Skiing in the third person: the skis
themselves know where & how to go,
turn, traverse or fly, & all the skier
needs to add is why—but gently,
from a distance, without believing
himself, or in himself, too much.*

5

Stuff for the Steep

When the going gets heavy, so does the gear—relatively speaking, that is. The limits of Nordic cross-country skiing all have to do with downhill control, and all are directly related to equipment. When you want to ski steeper, icier, narrower or otherwise more desperate slopes than you can handle, or dare to try, on cross-country skis, then it's time for a new set of equipment and the particular style of skiing that this equipment makes possible: Alpine touring gear and advanced Alpine turns.

The main functional difference between Alpine and Nordic turns is the way that edging and steering forces are transmitted from foot to ski. Why? The steeper the slope, and the harder the snow, the greater are the forces that the skier must exert to maintain control. To create edging, turning, and pressure-control forces we have the physical strength of our whole body, but in the end, all these forces must be transmitted to our skis through our feet! And beyond a certain point the foot just isn't strong enough to do the job. There are 26 more-or-less wobbly bones in each foot, and when the time comes to really crank those skis, the feet need help.

Indeed, one of the practical limits of Nordic skiing on steep slopes is the extreme muscular tension the foot must maintain to hold an edge, and the resulting fatigue. In Alpine skiing, a stiffer boot provides far more foot and ankle support, and a relatively rigid binding system transmits strong edging and twisting forces quickly and efficiently to the ski. And of course, Alpine skis are quite different too, a good deal wider and with more pronounced sidecut for easier downhill turning.

Turning is the crux. Alpine ski equipment, and the technique that goes with it, are totally oriented toward efficient downhill turns. At downhill ski areas, you only ski downhill—lifts handle everything else. As a result, the Alpine ski equipment used at ski areas is hopelessly inappropriate for any backcountry skiing, anywhere. Downhill boots bruise you if you try to walk in them; the bindings totally inhibit your movement for walking and climbing; and the skis work great downhill, but since weight is no factor they're a real pain to hump up a mountain. But the technology is there—plastics, fiberglass, strong and light metal alloys—and those of us addicted to Alpine touring on steep terrain have always known that it was only a matter of time before really good Alpine equipment for the backcountry would be available. I can honestly say that the time is at hand. When *Wilderness Skiing* appeared in 1972, almost all the Alpine touring equipment we wrote about was makeshift adaptations of regular downhill gear. No more.

Compared to the millions of downhill skiers in this country, the number of touring skiers is small indeed; and that minority of touring skiers that actually seeks out steep, demanding Alpine terrain seems minuscule indeed—by commercial standards. So we're lucky that things are different in Europe. It's the history of skiing all over again. The Alps are simply bloody steep mountains, generally steeper than ours (it's hard for someone who hasn't skied or climbed in Europe to really accept that there's such a difference between the Alps and, say, the Colorado Rockies, but there is). That's why, for reasons of security and downhill control, off-*piste* skiers in the Alpine regions of Europe have typically favored heavier equipment. Most, but not all, Alpine touring equipment is imported; and it's only because this branch of the sport has become so popular in Europe that we can, at last, get high-quality boots and skis for Alpine touring and ski mountaineering.

All touring equipment we've looked at so far has been a compromise, and Alpine gear is no exception.

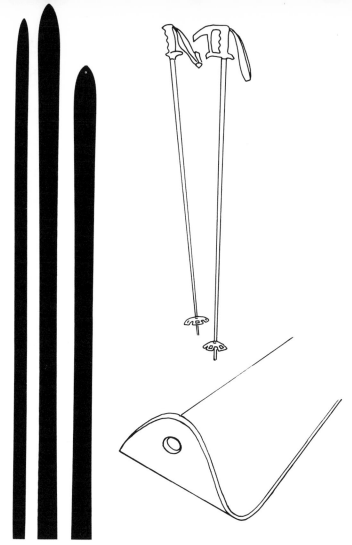

35. *Alpine touring gear. Boots are modeled after downhill ski boots, but are more flexible and have lug soles. Plate-type bindings hinge at the toe and lock down for the descent. Normal Alpine ski poles, sometimes fitted with special self-arrest grips. And mountaineering skis: the silhouettes above show the different dimensions of a cross-country ski, a normal downhill ski, and a shorter, wider Alpine touring ski. Most have broad, rounded tips with a pre-drilled hole for constructing emergency sleds.*

But the compromise works in a different direction. For Nordic touring we saw ultralight skis and boots, primarily designed for covering ground but beefed up a bit (sidecut, edges, etc.) to offer more downhill control. In Alpine touring gear, we see skis and boots that are designed primarily for downhill control but which have been lightened and softened for level walking and uphill climbing. Both compromises work well, but now we're ready for a closer look.

Boots

I'm starting with boots because they have changed more in recent years than any other item of Alpine ski touring equipment. Plastic touring boots—a cross between the typical plastic downhill ski boot and high-altitude mountaineering boots—are here to stay. And they're great! Downhill skiers gave up leather boots over ten years ago. Plastic, buckled boots provide more support, a better fit (since they can be heated and molded to allow for strange-shaped feet), and, if well designed, can be both warmer and lighter than equivalent leather boots. Moreover, since plastic boot materials don't break in, or break down, plastic Alpine boots can be made softer from the start, since they won't lose whatever stiffness they have. But typical Alpine boots are still too heavy and inflexible for the uphill half of the touring experience. Or were until the first synthetic Alpine touring boots appeared a few years ago.

For the 1981 ski season, only four such boots were imported to the U.S., the San Marco and Dolomite models from Italy, and the Kastinger and Koflach from Austria. Many more such boots are available in Europe, and who knows what the future will bring? But as of this writing, that's your choice. All these boots are good. They differ from each other in small design details and you should choose one on the basis of availability and subtlety of fit for your particular feet. Small sizes for women are hard to obtain, since it's falsely assumed (by the importers, that is) that women aren't attracted to strenuous backcountry adventures. It's to be hoped this mistaken policy will change.

All these Alpine touring boots, at first glance, look like typical Alpine downhill boots—made of colored plastic, fastened with from two to four buckles or cable/buckle systems. Look closer. They have a thinner sole than downhill boots do, with a thin-profile lug sole attached to it (this is a potential weak spot: be sure the toe of the lug sole is held to the boot sole with small screws, or add a couple yourself). Several models have a short gaiter-like snow cuff attached to the top of the boot to keep snow out. They have removable, insulated inner boots (just like double mountaineering boots). Perhaps most important, they are not very stiff. Of course, that's relative; these ski mountaineering boots are about as stiff as beginners' plastic boots that you might rent at a downhill ski area. In other words, much softer than experts' or racing boots, yet at the same time a good deal stiffer than any leather mountaineering boots. They have been designed to be quite stiff laterally—on the sides—for edging support, while the hinged uppers flex forward for adequate ankle bend. Even so, for walking uphill, Alpine touring skiers will tend to undo or loosen the top one or two buckles on these boots.

In the last analysis these are as much ski-mountaineering as ski-touring boots. They work as well for ice climbing as they do for Alpine skiing. And ever since Reinhold Messner began storming up 8000-meter peaks in the Himalaya wearing his plastic Kastinger ski boots, they have become quite respectable. The most important reason for buying a pair of these boots, however, is that while they're adequate for scrambling, for snow and ice climbing, and for hiking uphill, on skis or off, they will also let you ski downhill at the very upper limit of your technique. No compromise here: these are marvelous ski boots.

If you can't find a pair of these plastic Alpine

touring boots, or are unwilling to spring for them (they are not cheap, about as much as a medium-priced downhill boot), then there are still a couple of alternatives. You can dig up an old pair of leather, lace-up ski boots at an auction or ski swap, and maybe even have them resoled with lug-pattern soles. Or, if a good deal of winter mountaineering is to be part of the game, you can probably use heavy leather mountaineering boots, especially double ones. But to tell the truth, I'm not too keen on this last option; such mountaineering boots often give you the worst of both worlds—too stiff for the free-heel kick-and-glide of Nordic skiing, too soft for real support in difficult Alpine skiing. They're advisable only if you're simply using skis to get up to the base of a climb.

You might as well go for it—and get the best boots. Since the whole point of Alpine touring is thrilling, yet secure, downhill runs in a backcountry setting, the plastic touring boot is well worth the expense. Even more important than your skis, they ought to open up new dimensions of control and comfort.

Bindings

Alpine ski bindings are an engineer's nightmare, or delight. And Alpine touring bindings are even more so. Unlike the Nordic boot/binding system, so flexible that it's almost impossible to hurt yourself in a fall, the Alpine binding is a potential leg breaker. In its downhill mode, the binding must hold the boot rigidly to the ski, which, in a tumbling fall, acts very much like a six-foot lever trying to do evil things to your leg. Hence the development of release bindings which free the boot from the ski under a steady but excessive torque (momentary impacts have little chance of injuring you). This is nothing new; release bindings have existed for some twenty years and the current generation of downhill bindings are about as sophisticated and foolproof as you could wish.

But touring bindings are another story. An Alpine touring binding must function in two modes: in the uphill mode it allows free upward heel swing for walking and climbing; and in the downhill mode it clamps the boot firmly to the ski for downhill turns. In addition, it should be as light as possible, yet strong and trouble-free in the backcountry. And, since no mechanical device is perfect, it should be easy to repair in the field. All this plus an effective release mechanism that will release *only* under dangerous stress, keeping the skis solidly attached the rest of the time. In other words, a binding's retention is as important as its release. An unwarranted "pre-release" can cause not only an unpleasant fall but an injury or worse. A broken leg ten, twenty or fifty miles from the end of the road and the nearest ski patrol can be just as serious as falling over a cliff, and an accidental ski release on a steep slope could cause either. (Although I don't relish talking about potential hazards, we must admit their existence before we can avoid them.) Bindings, along with good judgment, technique and physical condition, are among the principal defenses against a backcountry ski accident. If you've chosen Alpine touring gear in the first place, you're likely to be on steeper slopes, where any accident could be that much more serious. You need the best bindings you can find.

Once again, the Alpine backcountry skier is in luck. Touring bindings exist that do everything I've just described, and then some. But not all "touring" bindings do the job. Old fashioned cable bindings, like the classic Silvretta, are no longer worth considering: they break too easily and have totally inadequate release systems. Likewise, heel-and-toe systems such as the old Su-matic and the Marker Rotomat TR should be ruled out because they allow only a few inches of heel lift in the touring mode— not nearly enough. The modern solution is a plate-type binding. In such bindings the ski boot is

121

clamped to a rigid or semi-rigid plate that pivots up and down at the toe. This allows free heel lift in the touring mode, and, for downhill, the whole plate clamps down at the rear. The release function varies from model to model; in some cases the entire plate releases.

A number of these modern Alpine touring bindings are sold in the U.S., although none in great numbers. I have a favorite, however—at least as this book goes to press. This is the Ramer binding, a real masterpiece of functional design. The Ramer binding is the brainchild of Paul Ramer, an ex-aerospace engineer who first decided he liked skiing better than anything else and then decided to fill a big gap in the equipment picture with an Alpine touring binding that actually worked. I used my first set of Ramers more than five years ago, fell in love with these cunning devices, and promptly broke them. Not only have the weak links been redesigned, but Paul has completely reworked the binding over the years, making it stronger, lighter and more nearly idiot-proof. On top of everything else, it is approximately half the price of any comparable Alpine touring bindings—such as the Iser, the Vinersa, the new Silvretta plate model and a couple of others—all imported and all costing around $200 (1981 prices). So you see why I can recommend it without hesitation—Alpine touring gear is expensive enough already!

The newest Ramer models are made of thin steel alloy instead of the original thick aluminum. The plate is thinner, bringing the foot closer to the ski for better edge control; the hardware is more robust and easier to adjust, and, best of all, the release system has been greatly improved. Release is controlled by two spring bars at the front of the plate that pinch the toe pivot points; the tighter the spring bars are clamped, the greater the release force required. In the new models, the spring-bar pivot sockets have been redesigned, and there is a wider range of adjustment, including very low release-force settings. (Unlike sealed downhill bindings, incidentally, Ramer pivot points should be lubricated every day before skiing.) These changes have pretty well banished my only doubts about this binding, namely that the release forces were formerly a little on the high side. If you ski with these bindings, you can now start out with the lowest of five settings. If you experience any premature release, tighten them one position at a time. This way you'll arrive at the lowest practical setting, which is also the safest.

One thing hasn't changed in the new Ramers, and that is the unique climbing system. The rear clamp that holds the plate down for the descent also swivels around to place a plastic plug under the boot plate. This elevates the footbed for climbing directly up steep slopes without straining the Achilles tendon. Super! For the very steepest slopes, an extension for the climbing plug lifts the heel of your boot even farther off the ski, letting you walk comfortably straight up the hill at angles that would be impossible with other systems. (Most of the other bindings I mentioned have also incorporated some kind of add-on climbing plug under the heel, but the Ramer still outclimbs them all.)

If I sound enthusiastic about this binding, I am. It's a fine achievement: sophisticated, practical, rugged, and affordable. And from reports I've gotten, it's now outselling the European Alpine touring bindings in Europe! Paul Ramer is a dyed-in-the-wool equipment freak, in the best sense of the word, who has made a number of major contributions to backcountry skiing (his personal avalanche beacon, another sophisticated yet affordable device, is discussed in Chapter 10). He publishes an annual newsletter/review of Alpine touring gear (write to Alpine Research Inc., 765 Indian Peak Road, Golden, CO 80401); it's one of the best ways to keep up with new developments in this fast-changing, high-tech area. Keep up the good work, Paul!

And now—what are we going to screw these bindings into?

Skis

Here we return to a wider range of choices. You can mount touring bindings on almost any Alpine skis and use them to ski up and down a peak. However, there are enough different sorts of skiing that fall under Alpine touring that no one type of ski will be ideal for all of them. A ski expedition to a major Andean or Himalayan peak may need one kind of ski; the powder hound who wants to tour away from a ski area to find untracked snow in the back bowls may need another; the extreme skier looking to descend steep, narrow couloirs and chutes on frozen summer snow may want still another. They will, at any rate, all be Alpine skis, and all will have certain points in common.

Alpine skis are a good deal wider than any of the Nordic skis we've talked about so far, and they also have a good deal more sidecut (widest at the tip, narrow at the waist and wide again at the tail, with a very approximate ratio of about 9:7:8 cm from tip to tail). They have bottom camber too, but typically less than cross-country skis since the camber is not designed to affect gripping and gliding, but only to distribute the skier's weight more evenly on the snow. And Alpine skis nowadays—for touring or for straight downhill—are very sophisticated in their construction: fiberglass or aluminum alloy, or both, are what give an Alpine ski its strength, resilience, and a host of other qualities, but these structural materials surround a space-filling core of wood, or, more commonly today, foam. And that's just the beginning. Alpine ski design is so complex that one actually can't say, "a metal ski is better for such-and-such a purpose," or "a fiberglass ski is better for powder, or ice." What *can* we say?

The parameters that affect ski performance off the packed slope are: flex and flex distribution, torsional stiffness, weight and length. *Flex* describes the relative stiffness or softness of the ski bending under your weight. A soft-flexing ski will be much easier to ski in deep powder than a stiff ski: the tip especially will bend back and float up to the surface, making it easier to turn. But the tip can be relatively soft while the tail section is stiffer or the ski can be even-flexed throughout. Soft tips, at any rate, are a must for deeper snow, whereas stiffer tails could be a help on harder snow or when skiing with large packs on shorter skis (not so much tail to stand on). *Torsional stiffness* is the resistance to bending around the long axis of the ski and guarantees that as you edge the ski with your boot, at the waist section, the tip and tail sections will edge just as strongly. Torsional stiffness is next to impossible to judge for oneself, in a ski shop for example, but it is the quality most responsible for the "hold," or bite, of the ski's edges on hard snow or on ice. Here you must rely on the ski's reputation for holding on hard snow, or your own feel for it if you try out a demo ski. And if you're thinking more of powder than hard conditions, it may not matter. *Weight* is self-explanatory, the lighter the better, all else being equal. And finally, the *length* of Alpine touring skis—a controversial subject.

Ideas on the length of downhill skis have changed radically in the last decade—sometimes faddishly, first getting shorter then longer again as manufacturers rode every hint of a trend to sell a few more pairs. But a reasonable pattern has emerged. Beginners should stick with what I call a "learning-length" ski, about chest to shoulder height. But don't consider a ski this short for serious touring. It's a good idea to rent such skis as you first begin to puzzle out Alpine ski technique at a downhill ski area. You'll soon graduate to a second length category, the "compact" or mid-length ski. Compact skis run roughly from shoulder to head height or a few inches higher; this is a very good length to consider for Alpine touring. A good compact ski will perform like a full-length ski in almost every way except for stability at higher speeds—and frankly, after spending hours climbing to the top of a peak, high speeds are the last thing on my mind. I want to savor the hard-earned descent and, if possible, stretch it out. The so-called full-length ski is any ski significantly longer than head height. Typically, a full-length ski for most men would be around 200 to 205 cm and for many women from 185 to 195 cm.

Now let's see if I can be a bit more specific. How are you going to choose the right length ski for your own touring ambitions? Unless you're already an expert skier with a preference for long boards, stick with compact skis. They have a host of advantages. Their slightly shorter length not only makes them lighter (to carry or to climb on) but gives them a lower "swing weight"—this is the inertial resistance that you must overcome in order to pivot your skis into a new direction. Think of the front and back of your skis sticking out from your boot like levers. If there's any excessive resistance out there at the tip and tail—for example in deep, heavy, wet snow—the longer those levers are, the harder it will be to turn the ski. In other words, a compact ski won't fight you as much in difficult snow; it will turn faster and more easily. If a "full-length" ski is simply shortened to produce a compact model, as many companies have done, you would gain this ease of turning at the expense of performance. Take flotation in deep powder, for instance: a traditional full-length ski has more bottom surface area, and as a result, will float you higher in the deep stuff. To compensate for a shorter length, a compact ski for powder or for all-around touring should be comparatively wider. This not only makes up for lost flotation but makes it immensely easier to ski in heavy "junk" snow, breakable crust, and similar horrors (wide skis are less likely to catch outside edges in such glop). This extra width is a small matter, just a wee bit wider, but it works, and virtually all the compact skis designed for high mountain skiing have it.

A final performance factor is the relative stiffness of compact skis. With less ski to support you, you'll need a slightly stiffer ski than in a full-length model.

But even so, the tip area should be as soft as possible to bend upward in deep and difficult snow (turns will be easier, and the ski won't dive and bury itself).

If you're already an extremely good Alpine skier with a marked preference for long skis, then you'll have no problem using such skis in the backcountry. Look for a light, soft model that nonetheless holds on hard snow. In this category I ought to mention the American-made Hexcel ski. It has a unique aluminum honeycomb core that makes it one of the lightest conventional skis ever produced. Ski mountaineers with a bent for long skis discovered this when the Hexcel first appeared, and it's still a favorite. Not all the models that this (or any) ski company produces are suitable for backcountry skiing and, worse yet, the model names of those that are change from year to year. But in this full-length category, look for so-called "de-tuned" (softened) recreational version of a slalom ski (designed for quick, easy turning). A final advantage of the full-length option is that you have more edge to use on icy slopes, but this advantage is at least partially cancelled out by the nearly effortless turning of the shorter compact ski.

The better a skier you are, the easier it will be for you to make a logical choice. I arrived at my own choice after several years of experimenting with compact skis in the backcountry. For steep, rugged touring situations I prefer a 190-cm ski (180 will do), even though I normally ski downhill on 205s. Linda Waidhofer, my companion on any number of backcountry ski adventures, is a slender, light-boned woman and a brilliant skier, who normally skis on 190-cm skis but prefers 170-cm in any situation where she either has to carry them to the top of a peak or might encounter desperate snow on the way down. Neither of us care much about setting downhill speed records in the backcountry, but both of us have a *toute neige, tout terrain* ("any snow, any terrain") philosophy of backcountry touring. Good compact skis make it easier to ski in challenging conditions, and when you're skiing bad snow with a heavy pack you need all the help you can get. The only thing you can't do on these somewhat shorter skis is go really fast, say at recreational racing speeds—they tend to wobble and vibrate too much. You *can* ski moderately fast on them, provided you have well-developed fore-and-aft balance and a quiet, stable upper body (we'll talk about this more in the next chapter).

To complete the picture, I should mention that there are a limited number of skis available in this country especially designed for Alpine touring and mountaineering. They all fall into the compact category, although there are a number of important design and production differences among them. Such skis are Kästle's *Tour Randonnée* model, the *Alpes 3000* from Rossignol, the Fischer *Tour Extreme*, the Head *Alpinist*, and a new ski, the *Duret*, from France. The Fischer ski is my favorite. It's surprisingly stiff for a mountain touring ski, but it performs well even in rotten, soft snow and holds remarkably on frozen snow and ice (perhaps because of its unique slightly wavy, or serrated, edge profile). Rossignol's Alpine touring ski is very soft and even-flexing, a good soft-snow ski, while the Kästle *Tour Randonnée* seems to be a good all-around compromise design. I haven't skied the Head or the Duret models yet (but reports on this last ski are very positive). Don't expect to find them all in the same shop. You'll be lucky to find a ski shop that stocks one of these specialized skis, but keep looking—they're worth it!

Poles

No big deal here. Just about any old Alpine ski poles will do. Alpine poles in general are considerably shorter than Nordic poles; your forearm should be horizontal when holding the pole with the basket in the snow (in a store, turn the pole upside-down and grasp it under the basket to judge its height). Lightness, strength, and good balance in the hand are all desirable.

Two special models designed exclusively for backcountry skiers and ski patrol personnel are the Life-Link and the Ramer poles. Both convert into avalanche probes (handles and baskets pop off, and the shafts fit together)—something you hope you'll never need but which could easily save a life. The Ramer poles are adjustable in height, a nice feature which you pay for with more weight and an slightly awkward "feel"; they're also made of a somewhat heavy but malleable aluminum alloy that can be bent back straight if you fall on it and bend it. The Life-Link is my favorite since it is light and perfectly balanced, but it's made of 7001 aluminum, a light, strong alloy that will probably break rather than bend if you crash on it with a big pack. Take your pick. If you ski with brute force, a heavier pair of poles will last a lot longer. If you rely on technique rather than strength, you will doubtless appreciate—and not destroy—a lighter, better-balanced pair of ski poles.

Climbers

Since one of the main reasons for using Alpine gear in the backcountry is to tackle and enjoy steep descents, it follows that you will often have to deal with steep ascents too. This is where climbers come in. Alpine skis, we've learned, are designed strictly for downhill control, but that doesn't mean you can't also ski uphill on them, exactly as you do with cross-country skis. The same maneuvers—herringbone, sidestepping, and ascending traverses—are used, and the same touring waxes: hard stick waxes or soft, gooey klister. It all works. But climbing uphill on your edges (herringbone or sidestepping) is desperately fatiguing after a few dozen meters, and it certainly won't get you to the top of a big peak. Nordic waxes, too, have their limits. They are designed, you remember, for both kick *and* glide, that is, gripping *and* sliding, a compromise. So, not surprisingly, there is a limit to the steepness of a slope on which you can reasonably expect to grip with any wax, no matter how soft and sticky. Nordic waxes, then, which adhere perfectly well to the bases of Alpine skis, should be used only for moderate climbing and, above all, for flat-to-rolling terrain where you can take advantage of their up *and* down capacity. For long, steep, direct ascents (crossing a high pass or climbing a peak on skis) you'll want to use *climbers* or, as they are often called, skins.

Climbing skins were first made of sealskin, long strips of it with the hairs pointing backward so the ski could slide forward yet would not slip back. They were fastened to the skis' bottoms with various complex arrangements of straps and buckles. Animal lovers relax! The sealskin climber is history, although we skiers still talk about "skins." Modern climbers are all made from "mohair," a kind of synthetic fur, thin strips of which are also embedded in the bases of some waxless cross-country skis. For Alpine touring, the best climbers are stick-on "mohair" skins, backed with a renewable glue-like adhesive. These do away with buckles or metal clips that wrap around the skis' edges (and are constantly being cut, while at the same time they prevent effective edging). One squeegeed application of the glue that comes with these modern skins should last for ten to fifteen uses. No snow or water gets under these skins. When you strip them off at the top of the climb, just fold them in half, sticky sides together, and you won't get any glue on the inside of your pack.

Coupled with an efficient Alpine touring binding, such as the Ramer (which raises and holds the heels of one's boots a few inches off the skis, its steep climbing mode), a pair of skins can halve the time of many ski ascents. Typically, at least on harder snow surfaces, you will wind up walking straight up the fall line with skins on your skis, rather than traversing. And you will be astonished, even frightened, at the degree of steepness you can

130

manage. As I've said, skins are for steep direct ascents, waxes for alternating ups and downs.

There's yet another mode of climbing—the fastest of all if you're dealing with frozen spring snow—just walking uphill with your skis on your pack (this is when you'll appreciate the lesser weight of compact skis). Carrying skis on your pack, with crampons (mountaineers' spiked, metal frames) on your boots, and using your ski poles for support, much like a mountaineer's ice axe (or even actually using an ice axe), you can ascend frozen, spring-snow slopes far steeper than anyone in their right mind would try to climb on skis. One touring buddy of mine calls this strategy the "stair chair," a short-cut up passes and peaks on shadowy spring mornings, that can open up unlimited horizons of steep adventure skiing.

But reaching the top with your skis is only a prelude; the promised run down had better be worth it! For one thing, all this Alpine equipment we've just looked at will cost you double, or more, what a good Nordic touring outfit would. Believe me, it is indeed worth it. If total freedom of the high snowy hills is your goal, then this Alpine touring gear and the technique that goes with it will open up the last, best defended, most exciting slopes, ice and crust, the steep and the deep. You'll need more than a stem christy to pull it off, however; and you'll find that even a parallel turn is only the beginning.

6

With aluminum poles and steel edges
we impale ourselves against the steep white
snow of this couloir, as butterflies
might
on pale cotton, ignoring the _whys_
that have led us here, struggling instead
with the _how_, our blind dread
of falling, smashing on far-off ledges . . . .

Up here there is no safe turn,
no perfect ski-school form to avoid
this void
beneath the downhill ski.
Salvation here is something we earn
through deeds not prayer,
We leap in the air,
turn our skis while fall-
ing, land on a moving wall
of snow, feel dizzy, almost free.

There's an image here we'll keep
intact forever: a red
butterfly moving slowly downward
between somber granite walls,
frightened, happy, weightless,
a skier falls and falls . . . .

6

Parallel
Plus

he parallel turn is what Alpine ski
technique is all about. Graceful, fluid,
efficient, it opens up terrain that can't be
skied any other way. Parallel turns are also natural
extensions of the family of christy-style turns we've
already learned to do on Nordic skis. You can think
of a parallel turn as a stem christy without the stem,
that is, a purely parallel christy from beginning to
end.

For many skiers—particularly intermediate skiers
at downhill ski areas—just learning to turn "parallel"
is the major goal. Kicking their dependence on the
stem is the desired end result of all the technique
they struggle to acquire in ski-school classes. But the
backcountry skier with sights set on the steep and
the deep, on out-of-bounds chutes and far-off faces,
who wants to ski the back of the beyond
comfortably and securely—this skier will have to go
beyond a simple parallel turn.

The basic parallel turn, then, is only the
beginning of advanced Alpine ski technique. It's an
ambitious program, but in this chapter I hope to

explain (and even simplify) not only the mechanics of modern parallel skiing, but the variations on this theme that you'll need to handle challenging snow.

We're going to jump right into things, skipping over the beginner, novice, and lower intermediate levels of Alpine skiing. These first steps and basic techniques are virtually identical (except for the diagonal stride) to what I've already described for Nordic skiing: climbing uphill, schussing down, wedging, the wedge stop and turn, sideslipping, basic and stem christies. All are nearly the same on Alpine skis. If you're not already a Nordic skier and you want to start from scratch at a downhill area, no problem. In terms of downhill control, you'll make faster progress initially, and you can always pick up Nordic skiing later. The transfer of skiing skills works in both directions. Sign up for ski school, pay your dues, and you'll be an intermediate, or christy-level, skier before you know it.

Once you've gotten into parallel skiing, you'll find there are a number of directions advanced parallel technique can take. Two of them, exciting in their own right, are of no concern to the backcountry skier; one is ski racing, which depends on faster, more carved turns, and the other is mogul skiing (moguls are the bizarrely shaped bumps formed by crowds of skiers on popular runs, but conspicuously absent in the backcountry). But two other directions are ready-made for the wilderness skier; and they constitute an "open sesame" to all-snow, all-terrain freedom in high mountains. The first is deep-snow technique, for conditions ranging from powder to "Sierra cement." The second is radical short swing, a technique for handling extreme steepness. Both involve major modifications of an advanced parallel turn.

So that's our strategy: first develop a basic parallel turn, then transform it into an advanced turn through anticipation and unweighting —two new terms you'll hear about soon—then adapt it to deep snow, and finally to extreme steepness.

Basic Parallel Turns

By hook or by crook you've become an intermediate Alpine skier. Christies are old hat. You skid through most of the arc of your turn in a comfortable parallel position and in what we might call a medium stance, skis neither spread nor squeezed together. You've been skiing mostly on packed slopes at a lift-served downhill area, and I want you to continue to do so for a while longer. Untracked snow will wait, and you'll be glad of more developed skills when you're ready for it.

You have also modified your christy style a bit, compared to the way it's done on skinny skis. The stem or wedge phase of the turn is smaller, narrower. You shift your weight to the outside ski as soon as possible, and then instead of lifting the inside ski in parallel to the other one, you brush it in over the snow—a smooth easy gesture we'll call *inside leg steering*. All of this works because Alpine boots give you more precise control of your skis' movement on the snow.

At the same time, you can now ski a variety of terrain. When the slope is shallow, the stem part of your turn almost disappears; you barely need anything to get that christy started. On steeper slopes you probably exaggerate the stemming action to get the outside ski into the turn as fast as possible. Now, how about that first parallel turn?

There are several possibilities. Try a *hockey stop* first. This is a sudden, almost violent parallel stop from a wide-track schuss. Crouch lower than normal and spread your skis slightly wider in your straight run, then suddenly and decisively twist both bent knees and feet sideways. You skid to a parallel stop. It will work, too, because anatomically the wide-track, bent-legged position gives you a lot of extra twisting strength. The hockey stop is too rough a movement to be directly useful in starting turns, but it does merely give you the feeling of turning both skis at the same time. So try to apply this parallel

pivoting of both bent legs to your downhill turns—
while reducing the amount of "oomph" you put into
the twisting start. The only problem with this
approach to parallel is that it tends to develop a
rough, almost brutal turn. So after a little practice
with hockey stops, try another approach—*early weight
shift.*

Here I want you to think about stepping onto the
uphill ski before you stem it out to start the turn. By
shifting your weight to the uphill (soon-to-be-
outside) ski before pushing it out in that familiar
stem, you accomplish a couple of things at once. The
outside ski seems pinned to the snow by your
weight, so, in effect, you're unable to stem it to the
side. But at the same time, the usual twisting action
that accompanies a stem start will cause that ski to
turn beneath you. *Voilà*, a parallel start! Let me say it
again: instead of turning your outside foot
(stemming) and *then* shifting your weight, shift your
weight *first*, then turn your foot. This will keep you
from stemming, and you'll turn parallel. At least you
should—but it will feel awkward.

Why is it that stem christies feel secure, while
parallel turns feel awkward (at least at first)? To
create any turn at all (stem, telemark, or parallel) the
skier has to twist at least one ski into the turn, and
change its edge. You do this in a stem christy by simply
stemming out the tail of your uphill ski—and all the
while, you're securely balanced on your other,
downhill foot. There's no commitment until
everything is ready, set up for the christy phase of
the turn. Not so in parallel skiing. The commitment
is total because you must twist both skis and change
both edges at once, at the very start. You've already
practised twisting both feet in the hockey stop and
also shifting weight early in order to keep your
upper ski from stemming out of sheer force of habit.
But what about those edges?

Steering both knees in the direction of the turn
tends to tilt the skis onto their new, inside edges, but
to really do the job with dispatch you have to bank

your whole body slightly to the inside of the turn. And there's the rub; it feels as though you're just going to fall over. Of course, you don't. Centrifugal force is there to prop you up at what we call the "bicycle-lean angle"—that same inward tilt which was so important in mastering telemark turns, and which the kid on a bicycle discovers for himself. What counts for the skier, however, is not physics, but feeling. And at first it feels terribly insecure to commit your upper body into the new turn at the same instant that you shift weight and steer both skis. A bit like sticking your head into the lion's jaws. But do it anyway! Your early parallel turns will be a hundred percent better for it—and, no, you won't fall over. But be careful, at the same time, not to overdo this inward tilt at the start of the turn. You don't want to get your weight onto that inside ski; but you do want to move into the turn enough to help establish your skis on their new edges. As usual, a happy compromise!

By this point you're skiing in a crude sort of parallel turn, probably pretty wide-track (for balance and strength) with a rather hasty and often over-pivoted start. Since you're practicing at a downhill ski area, it hasn't escaped you that expert parallel skiers seem to float into their turns effortlessly, nearly motionless, the skis responding to some invisible signals. It's a trick. They're using one additional missing technical element, anticipation, which is going to totally transform your fledgling parallel turn.

But first things first. Before you worry about a truly sophisticated parallel turn, it's important to log at least a few days of downhill skiing with this basic wide-track version of the parallel turn. Mileage will make everything that follows that much simpler. The critical thing at this stage is developing a sense of both skis pivoting together, however crudely, into the turn. Also, at this basic parallel level, stay on gentler slopes where you'll have the confidence to ski a bit faster than usual. The extra speed will help smooth out your turns, which should be medium- to long-radius, not short arcs. This will allow the skis to do more of the work for you. And whenever possible, use small bumps or convex rolls in the terrain to start your turns. Mark the spot with your inside (downhill) pole and pivot both feet just as you pass the crest of the hump—the skis will seem lighter and easier to pivot as they drop down the other side.

All these tips, plus a few days of practice, should add up to a rough-and-ready parallel turn. Not bad when conditions are easy—but still far from bombproof. To achieve a turn that works everywhere, easily, we need a couple of new elements.

Advanced Parallel Turns

The real key to modern parallel technique is *anticipation*. It lets you initiate turns in a smooth, relaxed way rather than forcing the skis violently into the new direction. How does it work? The simplest explanation is that the skier's upper body (torso, arms, head) is turned downhill before the legs and skis. You "anticipate" with your upper body the coming action of your lower body and skis. Why? For one thing, the upper body contains about two-thirds of the skier's weight; if it's already pre-turned, (anticipated) then there's a lot less physical work required to turn the rest of the skier. But there's more to it than that.

You've already noticed that really good skiers tend to make continuous, linked turns down the hill, rather than individual turns, separated and linked by traverses. They're not just showing off. Anticipation makes it easier to link turns down the fall line than to do isolated turns; it offers a way of using the end of one turn to launch the next. This is a subtler but more accurate way of looking at anticipation. Think of it as a total pattern of skiing in which the legs and skis work actively against the heavy and relatively stable upper body, building up a kind of tension at the end of one turn that can be "released" into the start of a new turn. This is the single most important idea (or technique) in advanced Alpine skiing. But it's far from obvious. To make it less obscure (I can't promise it will be simple), I'm going to go over anticipation in detail, twice: first, to describe the way it works when linking advanced turns; second, to describe a series of steps you can use to master it. So hang on.

Imagine that you're finishing a turn. Coming out of the fall line you steer your feet and drive both knees forward and inward, in the direction of the turn; the skis respond, coming around in a nice parallel arc. All the while, your upper body does nothing at all; it's passive and relaxed, neither needed nor involved in finishing the turn. The legs do it all! But your torso is so much heavier than your legs that it has almost twice as much inertia. This means your upper body will turn more slowly than the legs and skis, seeming almost to lag behind them. Thus as your skis come around *across* the hill, your body is still facing more or less *down* the hill. Aha! you say, there's that anticipated position again, only instead of the trunk turning down the hill, this time the legs and skis turned up the hill beneath the torso! Same result, only better, because the active lower-body steering has set up a kind of tension between torso and legs. You feel "wound up," legs and skis twisted one way, upper body the other. And just when this tension is greatest, you start the next turn.

It's easy. You're looking downhill, torso turned downhill, reaching downhill with your downhill pole. Simply plant that pole and support yourself on it as you rise up and forward—that is, down the hill. What happens? As your body moves out and down the hill—in the direction of the coming turn—your skis flatten (de-edge) under you, and both legs and skis "unwind." They pivot back beneath the body, realigning themselves in a more natural position, which also happens to be the direction your body is heading, into the new turn.

Great! Only don't try it yet. That's what's supposed to happen, but that's not the way to learn it. I merely wanted to build up a mental picture of how anticipation works to link turns, before giving you a specific learning sequence. The image of the *pre-turned body leading the skis into the turn,* drawing them after it, is the one I want you to hang onto. The timing and mechanics of the turn are secondary at this point.

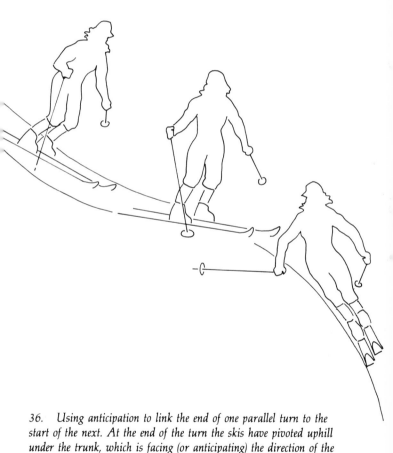

36. *Using anticipation to link the end of one parallel turn to the start of the next. At the end of the turn the skis have pivoted uphill under the trunk, which is facing (or anticipating) the direction of the coming turn.*

Even so, to complete our understanding of the anticipated parallel turn, there are a couple of points I should stress. The *pole plant* at the end of one turn (which is, of course, the beginning of the next) is not an accident, and it's not optional. By planting the pole down the hill (rather than up front by the ski tips) the skier in effect "anchors" his body facing the fall line, so that the inevitable unwinding from this position occurs only at the level of the skis! This guarantees the maximum turning power (unwinding) from your anticipation.

Unweighting is also a part of the anticipated turn. Unweighting is anything you do to take pressure momentarily off the skis in order to turn them more easily. A change in terrain can produce unweighting (those small bumps I mentioned), and so can vertical movements of the skier (flexion or extension). Since you're strongly flexed at the end of a turn (knees and ankles bent from steering) it seems natural to use a re-extension of the legs, or strong "up-motion," to unweight the skis. This is the "up and forward" motion I described as the body moves down the hill into the new turn. And since it lightens the skis, they have an easier time pivoting back beneath the body. They appear to turn *by themselves*. The anticipated body moves up and forward, down the hill, and the skis just follow. Bravo!

What I've just described is too complex for you to do all at once. Luckily there is a simple sequence of steps that will teach you this almost sinfully effortless turn (effortless, that is, once you've got it). You'll notice that I described how the end of one turn leads to the start of another—two curves, linked in an S down the slope. To develop a feeling for the anticipation that makes this possible, we're going to take that first turn out of context and practice it in the form of an *uphill christy*. At the end of a full turn, after all, the skis are steered out of the fall line and *up the hill*.

Start across the hill in a traverse. Sink and relax your ankles so that the skis sideslip a little, and immediately steer them both up the hill, an uphill christy. At the same time, though, concentrate on keeping your upper body facing the original direction of the traverse. Pick a distant object, like a tree, and keep your torso aimed at it while you turn. In other words, legs and skis turn uphill; the rest of you doesn't. This is easier to achieve if you relax the muscles in your lower back and keep both arms rather widespread in front of you. Now we'll add one more element: tilt your downhill wrist forward so that the pole is aimed ahead of you. Now as you continue to practice this special uphill christy, you'll come to a stop and plant this pole below you, supporting your anticipated upper body solidly on it. Let's call this whole sequence—an uphill christy with anticipation and a pole plant—a *pre-turn*. Think of it as a preparatory uphill turn before a complete downhill turn, or as the tail end of a preceding turn that will be linked to the following one. The whole

37. *Practicing the pre-turn to a stop across the hill. The mass of the upper body is motionless, facing down and ahead, while the skis turn uphill beneath the trunk.*

point of the pre-turn is to "wind you up" in an anticipated position, ready to launch the new turn.

So far, you've skied the pre-turn completely up the hill to a standstill; this means you have no momentum left to launch the new turn. So this time, traverse a bit faster and start your pre-turn, but before you have lost too much speed by turning uphill, plant your downhill pole, and supporting yourself momentarily on it, rise up and forward. What happens? The skis, seemingly by themselves, start to pivot back down the hill, easily returning to the line of the original traverse. That's good enough for now. I'd like you to practice this quite a few times—to both sides of course—feeling the reaction, or unwinding, from your anticipated position in the pre-turn as your skis pivot back down to the traverse.

You're only a short step away from the full turn at this point. To achieve it, I want you to repeat the same maneuver with a little more speed, and this time, as you plant your pole and rise up, shift your weight onto that upper ski and commit your body to more of a downhill lean. Your skis will pivot even farther down the hill than before, and you'll be balanced right over the outside ski, ready to steer the turn around like any other christy. You've got it!

To ensure success on your first efforts, you can steer the pre-turn right up to the crest of a large roll for a little terrain unweighting at the critical moment when you commit your body into the new turn. You'll know when you've got it because it feels as if the skis turn downhill absolutely on their own! You're only a mildly astonished passenger, riding them around a preordained arc. Now you know why expert skiers make it look so effortless. It is—and it's a great feeling.

But don't stop now. Keep working with the pre-turn until the anticipated start to the parallel turn becomes second nature. Initially it helps to make a definite pre-turn before every downhill turn. And since the pre-turn (uphill) slows you down, you'll want to build up a bit more speed, or make a steeper traverse than normal so that you'll have enough momentum to carry you around the intended downhill turn. But remember that the pre-turn represents the tail-end of a preceding turn taken out of context. So as you get the hang of it, you'll want to start linking one turn to the next, the end of each turn serving as the pre-turn to launch the following one.

As the pattern grows familiar, you'll probably start to wonder just how much anticipation is needed for a given turn. Do you want your torso oriented completely facing down the fall line (maximum anticipation) or would it be just as effective to turn the body only a little down the hill? It depends on the radius of the turn you want to make, on how fast you want your skis to pivot down the hill. The "unwinding" effect produced by anticipation starts the skis pivoting into the turn and lasts until skis and

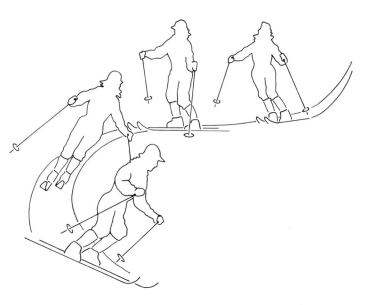

38. *The advanced parallel turn. The skier uses just enough anticipation at the end of one turn to start the next one.*

legs have realigned themselves under the torso. So a lot of anticipation means a lot of initial pivoting—and a short, quick turn results. If the body is turned only a bit toward the fall line, say just a few degrees from the axis of the skis, then the skis will tend to pivot only that amount, not much at all; a slower, longer-radius turn will result.

Fortunately you don't have to think all this out in detail for every turn. A good rule of thumb is to steer the same size pre-turn as the downhill turn you want. A long, rounded pre-turn will give you just enough anticipation to produce a long, rounded downhill turn. A short, sharp pre-turn will put you in a much more anticipated position, suitable for triggering an equally short, sharp turn down the hill. Not bad. This also explains why skiers tend to link the same size turns down the hill—it's the easiest, most natural thing to do once you've begun to ski with anticipation.

And there you have it—the secret of easy efficient parallel skiing. But make sure you go beyond merely understanding the anticipated turn, or practicing it only once or twice. You need literally hundreds of repetitions before this turn becomes a habit. Nothing less will do. If you have to think about anticipation when you're turning, you still haven't got it. So back to that *sine qua non* of ski learning, practice and more practice, mileage and more mileage. But at this advanced level, practicing turns should be more fun than ever.

I've assumed throughout this chapter that you've been practicing parallel skiing at a lift-served downhill ski area, by far the best strategy because the lifts give you far more time for practicing downhill technique. But when do you get to use these parallel skiing skills in the backcountry? As soon as possible. You're more than ready. Especially for spring touring, which means corn snow on high peaks. Spring snow conditions are the closest the backcountry can offer to the packed slopes you've been practicing on; with the anticipated parallel turn, you can already handle quite a range of terrain. But not everything. A few inches of light new snow won't cause problems; the same turns will work in the same way. But *deep* powder, or heavy wet snow may stop you cold. And on the steepest slopes you may still be a bit too nervous actually to use your advanced parallel turn. So let's continue, adapting our new turn to the sorts of challenging circumstances you're sure to encounter in high Alpine touring.

Deep-Snow Technique

Skiing Powder

Ask veteran skiers about their most magical moments on skis, and nine out of ten will talk about powder: that certain morning, sparkling light, untracked slopes, feathery powder billowing up *over your head!* Floating, dancing, in the most surreal of all ski environments. And afterwards, a perfect set of tracks is all that's left—that and the memory of that breathless, weightless state of grace known as powder skiing. Well and good, but who would believe that learning to ski powder could be so frustrating! Curiously, expert skiers swear that it's easier to ski in powder than on a packed slope. Yes, it's true, but, for most people, *learning* to ski in deep snow is much harder than learning to ski on the pack.

More than anything else, the problem is that of being out of your element. In deep snow you're no longer standing on firm (albeit snow-covered) earth. You find yourself *in*, not on, the snow, with a constantly changing, shifting, almost insubstantial base of support. So before you can ski powder, you need to get comfortable in it. In this context, I'm thinking of powder snow as at least a foot of new light stuff. If there are only a few inches of new snow on an old base, you'll wind up skiing on the hard surface beneath, and you won't need to modify your balance or technique an iota—a delightful sensation to be sure. But we're going for the real stuff—powder, the deeper the better—and this time it doesn't matter if you're standing at the top of a lift, or on the summit of a peak or pass you've just climbed on skins. Powder is where you find it.

Try for balance and stability first—if you feel you're about to fall nothing will work. So the first thing to do is a lot of straight running. Start off traversing, not too steeply, and simply try to get the feel of the soft, compressible snow underfoot (or should I say, underski). As you traverse, bounce up and down a bit to feel how much give and how much resistance the new snow really has. And above all, *keep your weight evenly distributed on both skis.* This is the major difference between hard-snow and soft-snow technique. On a packed or settled snow surface, you've long since learned to support most of your weight on the downhill ski; and likewise in turns, the outside leg and ski carry most of the body's weight. Not so in deep snow (powder or otherwise). *Even weight* is the watchword. The reason is obvious: if you load one ski more than the other, it will tend to "dive" while the other ski floats up toward the surface. For the skier, the effect is like trying to ride with one foot on each of two strong-minded horses going opposite ways. A head plant in the white stuff is the usual result.

So traversing, just cruising along with weight equally balanced, is the first step. Stop with an uphill christy, but, since the deep snow will keep your skis from sideslipping, do it like this: sink to a low position, then while twisting feet and knees up the hill to turn, actually press the tails of your skis away from you and down, into the snow. The sensation is somewhat like "grinding" the heels out into a turn, with a twisting extension of the legs. If you've skied for more than ten years, you'll probably recognize this movement as a version of the old Austrian "heel thrust." No longer in vogue, or even needed on hard

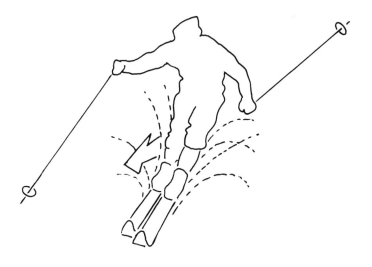

39.   *Finishing a turn in powder. The skier uses a twisting-extension of the legs, pushing the tails of the skis down and outward to slow down and complete the turn.*

snow, this movement—a twisting extension of the legs that presses the tails out sideways, out into the turn—is still incredibly useful in deep and difficult snow. Try it, you'll like it.

Well then, things are going well. You've done quite a few traverses and straight schusses, too. You're starting to feel more at home, comfortable and better balanced in this new and fluid medium. And sure enough, you can make some kind of an uphill christy at the end of your traverse. Let's develop this uphill turn by making a series of traverses and uphill "pull-outs," starting each traverse at a steeper angle than the last, until finally you're starting straight down the hill—a moderately steep hill because the powder will slow you down considerably. Now the uphill christy represents the second half of a full turn through the fall line. You

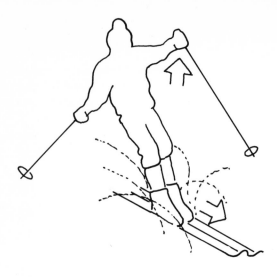

40. *Initiating a parallel turn in deep snow. Note the lift, aided by the outside arm, and the forward thrusting of both feet toward the fall line.*

can see the method in my madness: by practicing the second half of the turn first, you'll build your confidence so that when you finally do turn downhill into the fall line, you'll have been there before, you'll know how to finish that turn! Through this sequence of ever steepening traverses and uphill turns, you'll get used to plunging downhill in deep snow, and also grow accustomed to the surprisingly long time it takes to complete a turn.

Deep-snow skiing, you see, is a bit like skiing in slow motion; there's so much extra resistance from the deep snow that even strong movements take a lot longer to produce an effect. The skis come around all right, but slowly.

This is why, before trying to link turns directly down the slope, you need a short adjustment period: turning in to the new conditions, adjusting your stance—and your expectations. If you still feel a bit wobbly as you head downhill at a steeper and steeper angle, adopt a slightly lower stance; spread your arms and poles extra wide for increased lateral balance, and try to stand not merely even-weighted but *flat-footed* as well—certainly not leaning forward (the tips will dive) but not sitting back either. The old myth about sitting back in powder dies hard, but it *is* a myth. In very heavy and very deep snow, you may want to weight your heels a bit more, and in extremely heavy glop you can actively pull your toes (and ski tips) up toward the surface; but that's the exception, not the rule. A generation ago, by the way, sitting back in deep powder was all the rage. The sign of a skier who had mastered the esoteric "Alta technique" for the deep fluff was his "invisible chair" posture—thighs horizontal, as if seated. Such exaggerated positions are a real strain and with today's softer skis, mercifully unnecessary.

But now that you can pull out of the fall line in deep snow, how about actual turns down the hill? Start with what I call a *light christy*—"light" because of exaggerated unweighting (but a much more modern maneuver than the old French ski turn of the same name). Like this: from a steep traverse, near the fall line, sink, anticipate with your torso, and get your downhill pole ahead ready to plant. Now, all at the same time, plant that pole (there's just enough resistance in the soft snow to offer a little support), and lift the other (outside) hand and pole straight up as you yourself rise up and *push your feet ahead of you and down the hill.* Hey presto! the turn starts, you find yourself dropping into the fall line, and you sink once more, pressing the skis on around as you did in your repeated uphill christies.

Only the beginning of this powder turn is new, and it contains two complementary movement patterns that will become your most effective tricks in deep snow. One is the outside arm movement, a snappy vertical lifting gesture at the start of the turn. This does a lot: It adds to your up-unweighting; it takes pressure off the fronts of your skis, making it easier to pivot them into the turn; and it banks your body to the inside of the intended turn, insuring that the skis are tilted up against the powder—much like water skis. Not bad! For beginning powder skiers, lifting the outside arm can make the difference between turning and going straight.

41. *Linking short-radius turns in deep powder. In this exaggerated view we see one turn finished by extending the legs down into the snow; the next turn immediately begins with a relaxation/folding of the legs so that the skis float up and are easily turned.*

The other key move is the forward thrust of the feet in the direction of the turn. This lightens the tips for easier pivoting, and at the same time the active motion of *both* feet guarantees the proper equal weight distribution over both skis. Altogether it's a great turn, powerful and effective and, as we'll see, capable of many variations. (For readers of an analytical bent, I must confess that this "light" initiation does put your weight momentarily back on your skis. Not to worry, this is a far cry from the "sitting back" position I was railing against. As the skis encounter resistance from the deep snow, they will slow down enough for your body to "catch up" in a perfectly balanced position later in the turn.)

So much for your first downhill turns in deep powder. You will be surprised that you can turn at all—but you can. Sometimes it seems that nine-tenths of the problem in deep powder is pure disbelief. And there's no way to get beyond this except to pull off a couple of turns without falling, and then keep on doing it! Your second run will be easier than the first, and so on with each successive powder descent. In no time you'll be hooked and, like me, you'll probably never get quite enough powder skiing.

The very newness of deep powder skiing will prevent you, at first, from linking easy turns straight down the fall line. Instead, you'll probably make one turn, traverse a bit to catch your breath, literally or figuratively, and then make another. These first powder turns will also be rather large—it's hard to be dynamic in a new medium. As you continue to practice powder skiing, I want you to work on shortening the radius of your turns and linking them more smoothly and continuously. This means more active leg action, more anticipation, and reaching constantly down the hill with your outside pole, ready to trigger the next turn. Short, linked turns in powder will eventually be easier than isolated long-radius turns, because each new turn serves as a dynamic recovery from any possible loss of balance in the last turn. Even so, separate long-radius turns are easier to learn at first—another skiing paradox.

As you ski the fall line with more and more
confidence, the strong up-movement (extension) at
the start of each turn will diminish; eventually, you'll
simply relax your thighs at the end of one turn and
allow the snow to push your skis upwards again, at
which point you pivot the tips once more into the
new direction. Many sophisticated powder skiers
have compared the sensation of finishing one turn
with downward pressure and starting a new one
with relaxation, to the feeling of skiing bumps. You
create an invisible "pressure bump" beneath your
skis with your heel thrusting action at the end of the
turn; then perceive the resistance of the snow as an
upward push that helps launch the next turn. Press,
relax, slow down, pivot again. A beautiful self-
sustaining rhythm; when you've·found it, deep
powder will be your natural element.

Skiing "Junk"

Deep snow doesn't always mean powder. What
do you do about two feet of heavy wet "Sierra
cement," big wind drifts, or varying degrees of crust
over unconsolidated snow? This isn't a catalogue of
horrors, but a suggestion of the variety of
challenging deep-snow conditions you may
encounter in the backcountry. These tougher snow
conditions fall into two main categories: heavier
snow (wetter, warmer, occasionally melting, saturated
and rotten) and crusted snow. They don't require a
new technique. For both types, a slightly modified
powder turn, executed with a little more strength
and determination, will usually do the trick.

The basic problem with heavy snow is its greater
resistance: the skis get bloody well stuck in the stuff,
and they don't want to turn. Skiers have traditionally
resorted to "hanging back" in their boots in a
sometimes vain effort to liberate the ski tips, or to
"leap-and-land" skiing—total unweighting coupled
with desperate pivots and awkward landings. These

two approaches work more or less but are totally fatiguing. Or the skiers try to ski much faster in order to somehow "punch through" the heavy wet snow. This last option is to be avoided in the backcountry (and with a pack); it makes a technically difficult snow condition into a dangerous one. And of course, descending traverses linked with kick turns work fine but lack elegance, to say the least.

Best of all is an exaggerated powder turn that I like to call the "Austrian power turn" because it overdoes the heel-thrusting extension that's always been a part of Austrian skiing (but don't expect to learn this nifty turn in the ski school at *Lech am Arlberg*, Austria; it's not an "official" Austrian turn). This extreme bad snow turn works like this: from a traverse, sink so low that you're almost sitting on the tails of your skis, and, at the same time, anticipate totally (torso twisted all the way to the fall line). Plant your downhill pole and start your turn with a strong extension; but instead of raising your trunk, extend your feet away from you—push the toes out and into the turn—while you progressively press the tails of the skis laterally away from you, right into the heavy glop you're trying to ski. A lifting, forward-punching action of the outside arm will help, as will a very narrow track (the two skis move as one); and your body (left back and to the inside of the turn) will be strongly banked, giving you the needed edge angle to pull this one off. It's like a miracle: you'll come sailing around in snow that will utterly defeat any other turn. Let me say it again: from an extreme low position, the whole turn is made by extending the legs forward and down the hill, while thrusting the tails sideways out through the snow.

The Austrian power turn is an extreme exaggeration of your first parallel turn in powder, that's all. And if it sounds grotesque, wait till you try it. The only excuse for such exaggerated movements and positions is that in the heaviest, rottenest snow, they work better than anything else (in light powder, by contrast, one skis upright and relaxed, with gentle quiet movements). Using this turn I've repeatedly been able to turn easily in snow so heavy that other instructors were driven to leaping out of the snow and swiveling their skis 180 degrees. On a backcountry tour, this turn can save you! One disadvantage is that in order to link two of these turns, the skier must again drop down into an extremely low position prior to the forward extension—but that's a small price to pay.

Crusty snow—windslab, suncrust, and combinations thereof—is skied in much the same way as powder. If the crust is really hard, no problem—it's just like skiing packed slopes. If the crust tends to break, you can often stay on top by distributing your weight absolutely evenly over the two skis; shift your weight and you break through.

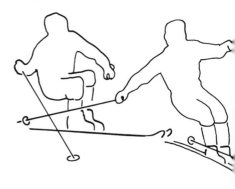

42. *The "Austrian power turn," an awkward but incredibly strong turn for all kinds of difficult and heavy snow. Low start with anticipation, strong forward thrust of both feet to initiate the turn, heel-thrusting extension to finish.*

Be gentle at the initiation of the turn, like skiing on eggs, and try to get both skis to skim lightly over the crust before too much pressure builds up in the second half of the turn. In true breakable crust, ski very slowly, as your skis may become trapped beneath the crust in a bad fall with disastrous results. This means you should ski in the fall line with a lot of turns, and avoid long fast traverses and shaky pull-outs. Fatiguing but safe! And once again, our heavy-duty Austrian power turn will come to the rescue, but only in breakable crust; slam the tails down through the crust while you press them out to the side. Ski it like an ice-breaker navigating frozen waters. If you haven't yet mastered this interesting turn, about your only chance is to "leap and land."

I love skiing deep, junky snow, but only because I've paid my dues, fallen a lot, and learned enough

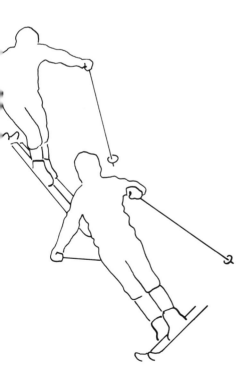

technique to make the stuff ski almost like powder. That, after all, is the purpose of advanced ski technique, Alpine or Nordic: to tame wild snow. Believe me, it's worth the effort. Skiing a 2,000-foot bowl of breakable crust giving way to mashed-potato mush, and *enjoying it*, makes you feel as though you really belong in the backcountry on skis, that you aren't merely a temporary visitor sneaking in and out under special dispensation. If you tour into big mountains expecting perfect conditions you'll be rudely surprised; if you have enough technique to handle any conditions, you'll be perpetually delighted! And there's one last condition we'll deal with right now.

The Steep and the Super-Steep

Control on steep slopes is an art, but not a mystery. The classic elements of advanced parallel skiing, combined into a rhythmic pattern of linked short turns known as "short swing," do the trick. But before getting into the details of such turns, let's consider the question: How steep is steep?

To the skier steepness is as much psychological as geometric. If you look down a new slope, suck in your breath in awe, and wonder how you are ever going to make the first turn, then it's plenty steep! The strange thing is that virtually all skiers—even those who are already skilled alpinists and ought to know better—tend to overestimate the actual steepness of slopes that impress them. Of course, any slope viewed from above, snow-covered or not, will appear steeper than its actual measurement in degrees, and the view from above is the one the skier sees first and remembers. Consider: an easy beginner's slope is anything up to about 10 degrees; slopes from 10 to 20 degrees would be average intermediate ski runs; while slopes ranging from 20 to 30 degrees are definitely the province of advanced skiers only, quite respectably steep. Slopes from 30 to 40 degrees are really steep—frightening to most skiers, even good ones, and only skied by true experts. It's hard to believe, I know. Every skier who comes off a steep slope is prepared to swear it was at least 45 degrees, but it's just not so. As an example, the steepest lift-served slope in California is probably the infamous "Chute 75" at Squaw Valley, so called because the top of this impressive gully attains a steepness of 75 *percent* (not degrees); in this method of measurement 100 percent equals only 45 degrees, and thus the steepest part of this infamous run measures only 37 degrees.

In the backcountry, one can find, and ski, snow slopes and chutes far steeper than those at any ski area. Up to a certain point it's exhilarating; beyond that, for most skiers, terrifying. But it is a great adventure, one that has given birth to an almost separate branch of our sport—extreme skiing! A unique form of competition has developed in Alpine circles to make the "first descent" on skis of faces and couloirs that were hitherto viewed exclusively as ice climbs. In this world of extreme steepness, backcountry skiing blends with mountaineering, and climbing skills are as important as skiing skills in pulling off some of these feats. For me, anything above 45 degrees, or even 40 degrees, is super-steep—a place where you don't want to be unless the conditions are just right, and your technique is unshakable. Slopes steeper than 50 degrees have been skied by masters of extreme skiing, and I suspect that ski descents of 60 degrees have, on rare occasions, been realized, but this upper end of the spectrum is far beyond our scope. Let's get back to basics, mastering the plain old garden variety of steep and scary slopes. Just what's the problem anyway?

Aside from butterflies in your stomach, the main problem of steep skiing is the sudden and dramatic acceleration you experience every time you point your skis downhill, and the consequent time pressure to complete the turn and bring things back under control. This demands a rapid start for each turn, pivoting both skis quickly into the fall line, and an equally rapid and powerful finish, bringing the skis back to the horizontal before they pick up too much speed. We're talking about turns because, as we've already learned, linked turns are the quickest way of losing altitude *and* still staying in control. Furthermore, a lot of steep skiing is found in rather narrow chutes, gullies, and couloirs, bounded by rocks and other unpleasantness, which rule out any possibility of long descending traverses. So the steep demands not only strong quick turns, but short turns continuously linked down the fall line: *short swing*.

Short Swing

To develop short swing, we'll use several different approaches. First, on hard snow (either packed snow, settled winter snow, or spring corn) simply try to shorten the radius of your linked parallel turns. Stress anticipation, keeping hips and torso constantly aimed down the fall line. Ski in a lower stance than usual with legs more bent, and drive your knees more vigorously to finish each turn. A harder, more dynamic finish should produce a sensation of reaction, or rebound, as you release the steering pressure at the end of one turn, letting your skis unwind beneath you into the next one. Finally, to shorten and tighten the radius of your linked parallel turns, tighten up your arm and pole action. Use rhythmic pole plants to mark the timing of your turns, much as a metronome marks time in music. By the time your skis have reached the fall line, long before the current turn has ended, the new outside hand and pole should be well ahead, extended downslope, ready to trigger a new turn.

But in addition to this progressive evolution toward shorter linked turns, you will need one new skill—a strong edge set. This is a technical term for a sudden increase in edging at the very end of the turn. Setting your edges into the snow surface not only brings the skis to a nearly complete momentary halt, but it also creates enough sudden tension in both legs and skis to exaggerate the rebound tendency you've already felt between turns. The skis (and to some extent the skier) tend to pop up off the snow, creating an explosive and total unweighting which greatly facilitates the rapid pivoting at the start of a turn.

This simple sequence should help you develop a strong edge set. First, stand in a traverse position across the slope, flex both knees and slam them quickly toward the hill. Naturally this edges your skis, but the important point is the speed with which the knees are pushed in. The strength of your edge set and the amount of rebound it produces are a

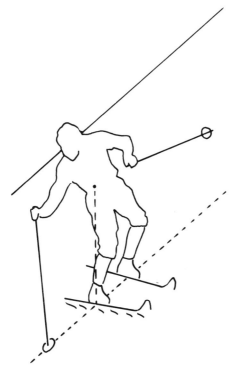

43. *The anticipated edge set on a steep slope.*

direct result of the speed, not the power, with which you edge your skis! Now sideslip vertically a few feet and stop the slide by that same sudden knee-edging movement. Practice this a few more times, on a fairly steep pitch of hard snow, and as you make the sudden stop, synchronize your knee push with a solid downhill pole plant to support your anticipated upper body. So far, so good. Now instead of just sideslipping, make a short sharp pre-turn (your old friend), set your edges at the end and *rebound* back to the original traverse. Typically you won't experience much real rebound at first, so simply give an active hop and feel your skis pivot back to the traverse line. With a bit of practice and a progressively sharper, snappier edge set, this little jump will seem to happen by itself—and you'll find out what I mean by rebound.

Now, of course, it's time to integrate the edge set into your short turns. Again, the first efforts will be so-so. Keep at it. The idea is to replace both speed and an active muscular up-motion with this popping-up reaction off the snow, as a result of that sudden edge set. One afternoon's practice on a short steep pitch of moderately hard snow should give you a pretty good feeling for what I'm talking about.

And then it's a question of finding steep slopes to ski: situations where practice skiing merges into skiing "for real"; perfection through crisis! But please, don't go off armed only with these few pages of hot tips and attack the steepest snow-covered cliff you can find. Work your way up to it, skiing ever steeper slopes as you expand your comfort range and sharpen your short swing.

I've talked about skiing on a hard surface, but don't overdo it. On ice you won't be able to set your edges sufficiently to stop the sideways sliding at the end of a turn, so look for spring snow that's softened after a few hours in the sun, or smooth, steep slopes of wind-blown powder. (Past a certain angle, powder either won't stick or will avalanche away under your skis, leaving you the hard subsurface to ski on.) If in doubt about whether or not you can get your edges in, simply sideslip to an edge set before you commit yourself to the slope. Eventually, as your confidence (and competence) on the steep grows, you may feel yourself ready to tackle those ultra-steep slopes and steep and narrow chutes that I think of as the "super steep." And for this sort of extreme skiing, you'll probably need a few more subtle adjustments, or refinements, of your basic short swing.

Extreme Short Swing

Think of skiing the super-steep as a series of linked 180-degree pivots (skis pivoting rapidly from one horizontal position to another facing the opposite way). Each turn results in a short skid or vertical sideslip, cut short by an edge set that provides the rebound or impetus for the next pivot. There is almost no forward speed, and the skier's downward speed is controlled both by sideslipping and by the strong edge set which almost brings him, momentarily, to a stop.

The whole pattern, including the all-important first turn, unrolls like this. Instead of the classic pre-turn (which you've used so often to launch the first turn in a series) simply sideslip to your first turn. Lock yourself into a position of "hyper-anticipation," body oriented absolutely down the fall line, leaning out over your downhill ski, downhill pole extended well below your downhill boot; then sideslip vertically a few feet to a strong edge set. (Because of the steepness, your uphill leg will be bent much more than the downhill leg, which carries most of the weight and thus supplies most of the force of your edge set.) Immediately, to utilize whatever rebound you have developed, leap straight up, supporting yourself on a solidly planted downhill pole; then pivot both skis rapidly *in the air* as far past the fall line as you can (often almost 180 degrees). To pull this off, you must keep your legs bent as you spring up, tucking the heels of your boots up

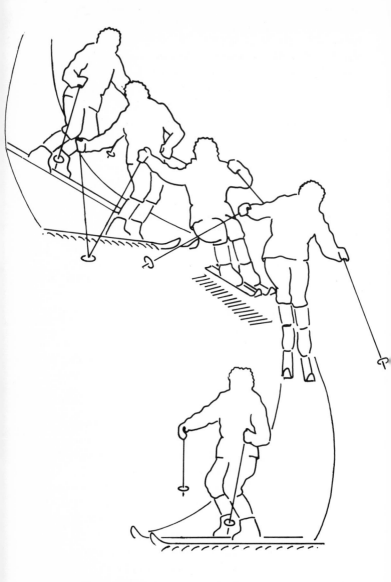

44.   *Short swing on a steep slope. During the airborne rebound that follows the strong edge set, the skier pivots his skis rapidly to the fall line (or beyond) and finishes the turn with a rounded sideslip to a new edge set. Emphatic anticipation throughout.*

beneath you, so that the tails of the skis are raised parallel to the slope and, as a result, won't catch. In effect, you remain in a semi-seated position while you concentrate on pivoting the tips of your skis around beneath you. The next phase of this turn, of course, is the landing, which should be supple and relaxed, most of your weight supported on the new downhill ski as you slide immediately into a new sideslip. At this point in the turn, you will weight the heels of your boots (the tails of your skis) to keep them moving vertically downward—any forward pressure on the balls of the feet would initiate a forward carving action that could not only give you unwanted speed but might result in a closer-than-desirable acquaintance with the rocky sides of a narrow couloir. And so the turn finishes as it began: you complete the steering phase while the skis slip, bringing both skis quickly around to the horizontal, and, as soon as you can, you stop this skidded follow-through with another strong edge set. During the whole turn—indeed, during the whole descent— you never lose your fully anticipated position of the upper body, which guarantees maximum twisting power and leaves the minimum mass (only legs and skis) to turn from side to side.

What I've just described is a more-or-less desperate turn for slopes of more-or-less desperate steepness—the maximum you think you can possibly ski. The middle phase of the turn has been done away with and the strong initial pivoting is done quickly in the air. Such turns have been called "windshield-wiper turns" because of the quick back-and-forth of the skis from one horizontal position to another.

An extraordinarily powerful variation of the windshield-wiper turn has been developed in recent years by such extreme skiers as Jean Marc Boivin and Patrick Vallençant for turning on slopes over 50 degrees (no more-or-less about it, such slopes are really desperate). On these slopes the skier's uphill and downhill legs are spread so far apart that it is almost impossible to get any useful rebound off the lower ski, so the turn is essentially a jump turn made from the uphill ski. Only the start is different. In a full anticipated position, the skier shifts all his weight to the top ski and pulls the lower ski up as high as possible before actually hopping straight up off the uphill ski and executing a lightning-fast 180-degree pivot in the air. The point of lifting the downhill ski up out of the way, before hopping and pivoting, is twofold: the uphill or outside ski can pivot around with no danger of hitting its mate, and the total up-motion is longer and more powerful giving the skier a fraction more time and space to complete his pivot. Skiers using this turn have a strange, one-legged, stork-like appearance at the start of each turn. It is strenuous, almost exhausting, but it works—all one can ask. In Europe one hears this technique referred to as a "pedaled jump turn," but actually it is less a separate technique than a variation of extreme short swing with each turn launched from the uphill ski.

But you don't have to resort to such extremes on all steep slopes. If the angle is a bit less, or if you feel a bit more secure, then reduce the amplitude of your rebound-cum-jump, pivot your skis only to the fall line, keep them on the snow through more of the turn, and drive them around with the leverage of your bent knees. In short, smooth things out a bit. When skiing the steep turn, pivoting both skis quickly into the fall line, and an equally rapid and powerful finish, bringing the skis back to the hori-zontal before they pick up too much speed. We're talking about turns because, as we've already learned, linked turns are the quickest way of losing altitude *and* still staying in control. Furthermore, a lot of steep skiing is found in rather narrow chutes, gullies, and couloirs, bounded by rocks and other unpleasantness, which rule out any possibility of long descending traverses. So the steep demands not only strong quick turns, but short turns continuously linked down the fall line: *short swing*.

A few caveats may make your moments on the

steep and the super-steep both easier and safer. It goes without saying that on slopes of extreme steepness you don't want to fall. Most falls in such situations are caused by sitting back and leaning in toward the slope, rather than out toward the void, over your skis. A natural nervous reaction perhaps, but one you can counter easily by really stressing your anticipation and reaching as far downslope as possible with that downhill pole.

The next most common cause of falling on the steep is losing a ski. Extreme short swing is a violent technique and puts far more strain on the binding/ release system than normal skiing. So if you're skiing slopes where you can't afford to fall, take a moment first to tighten your bindings' release system to the maximum, or block it completely. Should you fall with both skis still on your feet, you have a chance of hitting the edges and popping back up. With one ski off, you'll slide all the way down.

Another problem you don't need (and which could easily cause a fall) is missing a pole plant. Skiing the steep you rely more on your poles than in any other circumstance, but unfortunately many modern Alpine ski-pole baskets seem designed to glance off steep, hard snow. (These are the rigid plastic snowflake baskets.) Make sure the baskets of your poles are soft and flexible enough to twist easily to the angle of the slope. The flexible rubber centers of old Scott-type baskets are probably the best for really steep slopes although they are less effective in powder.

Part of the attraction of skiing the steep is that it brings you very close to your limits. In some cases, with rocks or cliffs below you, the price of an error, or a fall, may be unthinkable. But think about it anyway! Good judgment is as much a part of extreme skiing as good technique. If you've gotten yourself into a situation where all your instincts are screaming: no! don't do it!, you had better listen to them. It's always hard to make the first turn on a steep wall of snow, but if you're so afraid of that first turn that you're sure you'll fall—then you probably will. You have a choice to make, but remember, no halfway measures. Ski it positively or not at all. If rebounding into your first parallel pivot seems improbable, don't chicken out and attempt a giant uphill stem. Stem christies on extremely steep slopes keep you in the fall line too long and often give you too much forward speed to handle. Likewise, if you're facing what seems to be the wrong direction on a slope that's so steep you don't feel like turning, don't try a kick turn! It's a guaranteed disaster. If you're lucky enough to get one ski around without falling, you'll find yourself stuck, spread-eagled and paralyzed, in a situation from which the only exit is a bad fall or help from your companions.

So what do you do if you have to get down a slope that's just too steep for you? Sideslip it! But

45.   *A skier's glissade for slopes that are too steep to turn on with confidence. Often more useful for Nordic than for Alpine tourers.*

even that can be awkward, so try this special version—the skier's *glissade*. Hold both ski poles together, horizontally across your body, and drag the points on the slope uphill from your skis. You can get some support from the poles as well as keeping yourself from leaning too far in toward the slope— much as a climber uses an ice axe in traversing steep slopes. This special form of sideslipping, by the way, is particularly useful for Nordic skiers. On Nordic skis one reaches the upper limits of steepness much earlier than on Alpine skis.

And finally, a remedy of sorts for the most extreme case: falling on a hard-snow slope where you just won't stop, the fall you couldn't afford to take but did anyway. Once more, the backcountry skier borrows a technique from the mountaineers, a *self-arrest*. Self-arresting is usually done with the pick

46. *A skier's self-arrest. It is sometimes easier to drop one pole and self-arrest with the other.*

of the climber's ice axe but the skier can perform a very respectable self-arrest with a ski pole. It won't work, however, with ski-pole straps on your wrists, so I always slip mine off before tackling a slope where a fall could be unpleasant. If you do fall, drop one pole altogether, and slide both hands down to the basket of the other one. Then roll over onto your stomach, lever the point of that pole *slowly* into the snow, holding it about shoulder height, elbows bent, and use the full weight of your body to help scrape or dig it into the hard snow (if the snow were soft, you wouldn't need to self-arrest). An awkward technique but it definitely works. Even on sheet ice, it can slowly bring you to a stop.

Even better than this improvised skier's self-arrest is an arrest using a special claw-like grip on the ski pole handle. Paul Ramer has developed such a self-arrest pole grip, and although I find it a bit awkward for normal skiing, I recommend that you investigate such devices if you plan to spend a lot of time skiing the steep, at or near your own technical limits. One good friend of mine probably saved his life with one of these grips in the course of some extreme summer skiing on Mount Humphries in the Sierra Nevada.

I suppose that's the final word on backcountry ski technique: if it works, it's good. It's nice to look graceful—and better yet to *feel* graceful—while skiing. But it isn't always possible and almost never really necessary. In the backcountry, skiing well means skiing effectively, efficiently and, of course, safely. A highly developed ski technique is often described as "effortless"—it very nearly is—and this may provide a last degree of motivation for polishing your short swing, your powder technique, or your skiing in general.

But don't lose sight of the forest for the trees. The reason we got involved with all this technical refinement was clear from the beginning. Freedom of movement, exhilarating movement, in the backcountry. Freedom of terrain, all terrain and all snow, in an unlimited, *undeveloped* winter playground. My reason for introducing Alpine skiing at all in this book is simply that it opens the door to terrain that's just too difficult for our mostly magical Nordic boards. And we've gone into it in such detail because although these techniques *do* work, they're neither easy nor obvious. But all the technique we've learned so far is academic if you don't take it touring. Keep your sights on snowy, distant summits, your heart in the backcountry, and your skis pointed toward untracked snow, and you'll find that ski technique falls into its proper perspective.

Like the rules of grammar when learning a foreign language, technique on skis is something to master and then forget. The complete backcountry skier doesn't ski in a certain style, but chooses, uses and combines techniques into his or her own style to fit the snowy project at hand. And that's what the next chapter (the last devoted to ski technique) is all about.

7

The path, initially at least,
seems clear, the skier at first

skis dotted lines—turns,
traverses, schusses—& finally learns

something called technique: only then
can we discover snow & begin

to carve out real runs from this white
& yielding medium: there isn't any right

or wrong in such descents
& for a while skiing makes sense.

But with enough time, with no
more fear & a calm mind, the snow

itself begins to change: more & more
ice resembles powder. As before

we return to abstractions & find
the mountain has its own lines,

planes, shapes & curves: go back
to skiing dotted lines—a black

on white pattern of movement & form,
pure form—a new world is born.

But we're still not there, behind
even this intersection of mountain & mind

we sense something always simpler: skiing
not as metaphor but synonym of being.

7

The Best of Both Worlds

E*arly light.* Snowfields flashing mauve, pale pink,
briefly yellow before fading back to frosty morning
blue-gray. Summits high above catch the first
dazzling white. Two skiers appear on a long, rolling ridge,
moving easily, an effortless kick and glide through a dusting
of new powder, thin tracks stretching rapidly across a high
basin. At the foot of a steep slope beneath the pass, they stop,
slap on skins, move on, slower now, antlike, climbing straight
up to the sunlight. The pass, then a long ridge, two hours
later the peak: private pleasures, snowy sights. The air is
warming, the pair moves. Edges holding on wind-blown crust,
they dance down the ridge to stand above a shadowy frozen
chute. Hesitation, check the bindings, an edge set or two to
check the snow, one starts down. Slowly, cautiously, steady
short swing down rock-hard snow, explosions of snow
punctuate each edge set. It goes! The second skier follows.
Lower, as the couloir opens onto a broad snow face, the tight
turning rhythm loosens, snow softens, the skiers figure-eight
each other's tracks all the way down to the lower slopes. Here
the wind has left them powder, and lower, in the shelter of
the first trees, the snow is even deeper. Another quick binding
adjustment and they're off again, flowing to a different music,
linking long, graceful telemarks down rounded ridges,
disappearing at last into forests below, striding in agile curves
around stark white aspen trunks.

Call it a backcountry fantasy. The type of tour, the type of skiing I've just described doesn't quite exist, yet. The backcountry skier, it seems, constantly faces a choice or a compromise: between freedom on the flat and security on the steep, between flotation in powder and light weight on the trail, between light, flexible boots for maximum extention and kick and stiffer boots for edging on ice. It's a pain. But is it really necessary?

For the moment it still is, which is why I've discussed Nordic and Alpine ski techniques separately. But in recent years we've made a lot of progress in resolving some of the contradictions that limit the touring skiers' options. All of us have moved in this direction. Skiers have become more flexible in their thinking, more versatile in using a greater range of techniques; and equipment manufacturers have come up with ever lighter gear, suitable for a wider spectrum of conditions. And the best is yet to come—at least I hope it is. I'd like to see the distinction between Nordic and Alpine skiing in the backcountry disappear altogether. I suspect that one of these days it will, but at the very least, it will require a whole new generation of touring tools, skis, boots, and bindings.

Still we've come a long way. And the answer, for now, is to use an eclectic mix of skiing styles and touring gear that will be slightly different for each touring skier—the best of both worlds! Here are a few examples:

The Uphill Equation

I think it was Pogo who said, "From here on up, it's downhill all the way." That's the story when it comes to mixing and combining uphill touring techniques. Things are looking good indeed. When *Wilderness Skiing* first appeared, Doug Robinson, a superb touring skier, took me to task for implying that the only way to go uphill on Alpine skis was to use climbing skins. He was quite right. Nordic waxes adhere well to the P-Tex bases of Alpine skis, and work just as well, or sometimes better, than they do on Nordic skis because of the increased surface area of the Alpine version. But, strange to say, they haven't replaced skins, which are just as popular as ever. Why? Because each has something to offer. Waxes, of course, permit forward gliding, as well as gripping on hills, and so are ideal in rolling terrain or alternating hills and flats—situations where an alternation of speed and grip is desirable. But skins will grip on far steeper slopes than any waxes, and such steep and direct ascents are invariably slow plodding affairs. So for steady and sustained climbs skins have a valuable place.

But with the introduction of skins for cross-country skis we have come full circle. The Nordic tourer is dipping into the Alpine bag of tricks, just as the Alpine ski mountaineer has done with Nordic waxes. A number of different models of mohair climbing skins, specially made for skinny skis, have appeared in the last few years. Some are short versions, attaching only to the kick zone. But the first ones I ever saw remain my favorites—Skinny Skins, made by Early Winters in Seattle. These are full-length, ultra-narrow (19 mm) mohair skins. They have a renewable adhesive backing and work just like the now familiar stick-on Alpine skins. (Other manufacturers, like Coll-Tex of Switzerland, are now making this sort of narrow Nordic climbing skin.) Believe me, these Skinny Skins are far more than gimmicks! They turn long direct ascents into child's play. They work marvelously in transitional conditions around the freezing point, where waxing (or trying to wax) can lead to a near nervous breakdown, and they hold like gangbusters on frozen spring crust. On top of everything, they weigh almost nothing and don't cost much either. Bravo! The appearance of such Nordic climbing skins fits in perfectly with the telemark renaissance. As Nordic skiers have pushed the limits of their downhill technique, they have naturally sought out higher peaks, passes and slopes to ski from. This has in turn meant steeper ascents, which led to thin Nordic skins.

In the uphill dimension, then, the equation is balanced. We see a real mutual adaptation from each style of skiing to the other. The downhill picture is not as clear-cut, but the savvy backcountry skier can still pick, choose, and borrow with great effect. I have chiefly in mind two important departures from tradition: the use of advanced modern parallel turns on skinny skis, and the use of telemark turns with heavier Alpine gear.

Nordic Parallel, Alpine Telemark

Parallel turns have long seemed a bugaboo on cross-country skis, and frustrated skiers have tended to blame the free-hinging heel movement of their pin-binding set up for an alarming lack of control. I don't believe it for a minute because experienced Alpine skiers seem able to adapt their parallel turns to pin bindings with little or no trouble. The main problem is lack of familiarity with the whole parallel mode of turning, and such familiarity can best be gained with downhill, not cross-country, equipment. So swallow your pride, rent some Alpine gear, spring for a few lift tickets, and get into parallel skiing much as I described in the last chapter.

When the time comes to transfer your parallel skills to the free-heel Nordic situation, perhaps the most important advice I can give you is that old cliché: Bend zee knees! Ankles too! For the leverage of extremely bent knees and ankles can almost make up for the missing power derived from tall, stiff Alpine boots. The ankle joint (two joints really) is a curious and complex bag of bones which allows for a number of compound overlapping motions. But when bent strongly forward (dorsiflexion) the ankle itself is stabilized and begins to behave somewhat as a hinge or sleeve joint, locking the foot in the same plane as the knee. Forgive the technical explanation,

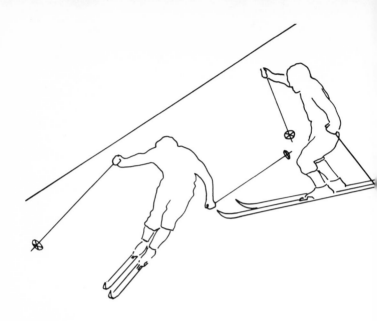

but it's crucial because, in this position, any strong steering action of the bent knee is transmitted right through the foot to the ski. *Voilà!* Strong parallel steering, without the support of rigid boots, and without the forward pressure that is impossible on a free heel binding. Just stand flat-footed, weighting the heels and balls of your feet equally, and you'll find this deep knee and ankle bend gives you plenty of force for starting and steering parallel turns. The rest, as always, is practice and mileage.

But classic parallel turns on skinny skis, even good ones, are far from bombproof in all situations. As soon as the snow gets a bit weird, they have a way of not working. Of course, the logical move in heavy or crusty snow is just to ski with telemark turns, unless the terrain is very steep and you find yourself picking up too much speed in the fall line. Here, a rapid and unshakable parallel turn would be a real advantage. And indeed, there is such a turn—not a normal parallel turn at all but the rather strange one which I call the Austrian power turn and which I described in detail in the last chapter. This

47. *An elegant parallel turn on cross-country boards. The secret is the exaggerated knee and ankle bend.*

48. *The "Austrian power turn" on skinny skis. Forward push of the feet to start, sideways extension to finish.*

turn, which starts in a low, almost crouched, but fully anticipated position, is a kind of living contradiction to everything I've just said about skiing with bent knees and ankles (the exception that proves the rule!). The turn is produced by *pushing both feet downhill ahead of the body*, and by *extending the legs out into the turn*. It works almost as well on cross-country skis as on Alpine boards, because only the heels are weighted and because the straightening of the legs makes them progressively stronger through the turn. It looks strange, but stranger yet is the fact that it works, no matter how rough and rotten the snow. With this turn in your repertoire, as well as the all-important telemark, there aren't a lot of snow conditions you can't handle on Nordic skis. The real limits still are those of extreme steepness.

Lest you think that parallel turns on pin bindings and skinny skis are just a technical exercise, let me share a recent experience with you. Around the beginning of June 1980, my work on this book was interrupted for a week or so by the annual festival of mountain films in Telluride, Colorado, where I live. During Mountainfilm I had the pleasure of taking a group of visiting skiers on one of our classic late spring tours, a 4,000-foot descent on corn snow. In this group were some fine Nordic skiers (from Crested Butte, Colorado, one of the hotbeds of the telemark renaissance, and from Red Lodge, Montana), but the telemark turn seemed to be the only string to their bow. On fairly steep but wide-open slopes of frozen snow at around 13,000 feet, some of these skiers had balance and speed-control problems but most handled it pretty well on cross-country skis with metal edges. In the open bowls of the next 1,500 feet, their skiing was poetry in motion! But in the steep and narrow chutes, lower down the canyon, they took fall after fall and a few desperate slides that made me not a little nervous. Yet these chutes weren't really *that* steep (it's all relative) and would have been easy to ski on Nordic skis using stem christies, easier yet with parallel turns. But only the very best skier of the group could handle them with telemarks. And as if to underline the relativity of such steepness, one last couloir (the longest and by far the steepest) obliged this chap, a real Nordic genius if I've ever seen one, to sideslip down in a skier's glissade. Yet those of the group on Alpine skis encountered no problem with this last obstacle, although they had paid the price of heavier packs on the three-hour climb up.

And so my dream of a universal backcountry ski system remains elusive. No equipment, no technique is universal or universally applicable—at least not yet. But it is clear that the more different techniques you've mastered, the more you can do with whatever skis you happen to be on, whatever snow or terrain you encounter. This is true not only for Nordic tourers who have taken the trouble to master parallel turns; it is equally so for a skier on Alpine gear who is familiar with the telemark. The rigid sole plate of a Ramer or similar binding, in the free-hinging touring position, gives one incredible leverage in steering telemark turns—so why not? The ideal place to use telemarks, if you're on Alpine touring skis, is in deep, wet, rotten snow, so typical and so maddening late in the afternoon of a warm spring day. Such "Alpine" telemarks will work in snow so bad, so soggy and rotten, that no skier in his right mind (or wearing a heavy pack) would dare to try a parallel turn. Try some, you'll like them!

New Frontiers in Gear

The complete backcountry skier, then, is one who knows, enjoys, and uses the whole spectrum of skiing styles, maneuvers, and possibilities. The most serious limitations that such a skier encounters (and none of us is really quite that good) are those of his equipment. This needn't be discouraging. For one thing, all ski equipment is constantly, even rapidly, changing and evolving. I expect that the equipment chapters of this book will be the first to go out of date and need revising. So our ideal, hypothetical all-snow, all-technique ski may well appear, if not next season, then sometime soon.

More likely we will continue to see ever more "hybrid" gear—equipment that cuts across traditional lines and attempts to combine hitherto opposing qualities. One such item is a very interesting ski, the *Expedition* model from Fischer. This ski combines the flex and width of a traditional Alpine powder ski with the extreme lightness of a cross-country ski (aluminum rather than steel edges help in this regard). It can be skied either as a Nordic-style, three-pin ski or as an Alpine ski, and in soft snow works rather well both ways. A fascinating step in the right direction.

An even more fascinating development is Paul Ramer's new "two-pin" system, which should become available to skiers at just about the time this book goes to press. The system features a lightweight plastic boot, modeled after a plastic hockey shoe, which is at once far lighter and more flexible than any purely Alpine boot yet far stiffer in torsion than any cross-country boot. This hybrid boot snaps into a Ramer toe pivot by means of two metal spring bars built into its sole. The result is a free-heel skiing system that offers unparalleled control and safety on downhills (the release system works like the Ramer plate binding) while preserving much of the Nordic skier's freedom of movement on level, rolling, and uphill stretches. The two-pin boot can be used on a cross-country ski, an Alpine ski, or something in between, permitting a wide range of skiing styles. Two-pin telemarks are incredibly powerful (experienced telemarkers will tend to overturn), and parallel turns are remarkably easy up to rather steep slopes. But the real delight of two-pinning is the ease and fluidity with which one slips from one style to the other. This is certainly the best compromise boot/binding system I have seen, or skied, to date; I didn't expect to find one like it for years to come. The future, it seems, is always closer than you think!

As exciting as it is, the two-pin system is not a kind of final answer, the total fusion of Alpine and Nordic possibilities (for example, it's nowhere near as light as traditional low-cut X-C shoes and bindings). With use, we will surely discover its limitations as well as its strong points. But there is a positive side to the so-called limitations of our equipment. Why should one piece of gear have to do everything? The totally broad-spectrum ski, boot, or binding might well be frustrating—doing everything, yes, but nothing well—while specialized equipment always means higher performance.

The trick, as I see it, is not to get locked into thinking of backcountry skiing in terms of only one type of ski, or one style of skiing. You may wind up, as I have, owning quite a variety of touring equipment. But what a pleasure to go on a ski tour with the right stuff, without once getting mad at your skis! I tend to make an initial choice—light or heavy gear—conditioned more than anything else by the steepness I expect to encounter. And then I rely on a broad range of skiing skills to experience the best of both worlds.

Let me repeat something I've said quite a few times already: In backcountry skiing there are no rules; this is surely part of its attraction. There are no judges or stopwatches either. Ski at your own pace, in your own style. You are creating your own definition of backcountry skiing just as you create your own tracks in undisturbed snow. And if you're able to ski where you want to, without crashing head-first into each and every snowbank, then you certainly won't hear an argument about ski technique from me. Nor, I hope, from anyone else.

Part Two

DOING IT: THE BACK-COUNTRY EXPERIENCE

8

The corridors of our labyrinth are all
concentric spirals, white on white.
We inscribe the same patterns in light
powder or hard blue ice. Under tall
pines we glide, weightless and dumb, small
almost imaginary beings. No rest at night:
we dream this same white dream. Who can fight
the snow? Who chooses where to fall?
To repeat oneself forever, up and down,
is purgatory, but to love it, to accept
this white puzzle of snow and tilted space—
In such a maze who can accept or reject?
It's all the same: mountain, plain, country, town.
We would be no freer in any other place.

8

Hot Tips for Cold Trails

Y*ou can ski like the wind.*
Now what else do you need to know about
backcountry skiing? Or more exactly, since
most of what you really need to learn will be learned
on skis in the backcountry itself, what else can I tell
you? My hope in the second part of this book is to
introduce a variety of background information to
make your backcountry ski experiences less hassle-
prone and safer, as well as more varied and exciting.
Since these are reference chapters more than
instructional ones, we may wind up jumping around
from topic to topic a bit more than we have so far;
but you may be able to discern just as much method
in my madness as madness in my method.

This chapter focuses chiefly on day touring,
although most of the information applies to longer
tours too. The next deals with snow itself: the
varieties of snowy terrain, snow structures and
stability, and the whole problem of avalanches, the
most insidious danger in backcountry skiing. Next, a
chapter that summarizes most other ski touring
dangers, causes and prevention, first aid and
evacuation. And finally a chapter on long ski trips,
living in the winter wilderness as well as skiing it,

plus an open-ended view of where your skis may carry you.

An ambitious program, to be sure, but remember that these chapters are only windows on the winter experience; the real thing is out there, waiting.

Day Tours

For a lot of dyed-in-the-wool enthusiasts, this is the real thing: backcountry skiing for the sake of skiing more than for the sake of the backcountry. Skiing as sport, as movement, as freedom and release. Because of course, the deeper you ski into the backcountry, the longer your tour and the farther you get from civilization, the less likely you are to experience wonderful skiing. Your pack will be heavier and more awkward, and an almost inevitable conservatism will tend to limit the exuberance of your skiing in the most remote situations. Not so on one-day tours. You'll be lightly laden, and even if you get into trouble, some form of outside help may be possible, if not easy. You can also choose your snow conditions for a one-day tour in a way that's impossible on a long tour. If you're a week out and rising temperatures turn the snow to mush, then on mush you'll ski. But for short day tours, the choice is often yours. Go the day after a storm if you want powder; or wait a week until the snow has corned-up perfectly. For all these reasons, the finest backcountry *skiing* you ever do will probably be on day tours.

And the range of options for short tours may be greater than you imagine. Here are some possible variations on this theme.

The *all-level tour* is a great idea for beginners who haven't yet mastered the skill for the hills. I certainly hope no one waits to become an expert before actually venturing off the beaten path. Real tours are a possibility and a delight from the beginning. Even in the midst of rugged and mountainous terrain you can usually create an all-level tour by skiing all the way around the shores of a lake.

Touring on roads—snowed-over roads, of course—is another attractive option for inexperienced skiers since it solves two problems at once, steepness and route finding. Small snowed-in mountain roads make ideal touring routes because they contour around hills and zig-zag up and down steep terrain. Even the steepest of these roads can be handled by wedging on the descent. This makes skiing down roads rather boring for advanced tourers but very attractive to beginners. It's also just about impossible to get lost when following a snowy road. Even if the snow has drifted onto a road-cut to the same angle as the surrounding terrain, a thirty-foot-wide band with no trees is hard to miss. The only potential problem about touring on roads, especially remote logging and mining roads in steeper country, is the false sense of security they give you *vis à vis* avalanche danger. Such roads often cut directly across or below obvious avalanche paths. Keep your eyes open.

Day tours can also be classified as *out-and-back tours*, which follow the same route going and coming (again a beginner's favorite, since it's hard to get lost following one's own tracks back to the starting point), and more interesting *loop tours* and *point-to-point tours*. A changing panorama is certainly more stimulating than seeing the same country twice, but presupposes more developed routefinding skills (which we will cover in the next chapter). Popular touring areas sometimes have loop trails that are marked with tree blazes or other signs, but are not actively packed or maintained. Like skiing on snow-covered roads, this sort of tour falls midway between the track and trail skiing of a Nordic resort complex and a pure wilderness ski experience. If you have a choice, plan a loop tour so that some obvious terrain feature, like a ridge or stream, leads you back to your car or starting point. Tired skiers plodding through featureless forest tend to be rather poor at the precise dead reckoning that brings you back to square one.

Point-to-point tours may involve the sort of car shuttling often necessary on river trips, but they're usually worth it. Two good strategies are cutting perpendicularly between two parallel roads, and leaving a road in the snow country to tour parallel to it. The latter idea of touring above, or near, a single road and cutting back down to the road a number of miles later can lead to a tour that's mostly downhill—a real pleasure. This is certainly true along roads that drop dramatically from the high country toward lower elevations.

This brings us to the one-day ski tour whose main purpose is to find and enjoy a wonderful downhill run in a wild setting. Ten years ago this was definitely *not* what the Nordic touring skier had in mind. Today, armed with softer skis and tougher telemarks, more Nordic than Alpine skiers are out in the backcountry looking for untracked powder runs—and finding them! All I need do here is point out that there's more than one way to skin this cat. Touring skiers looking for great downhill runs will generally ascend by a different route than the one they plan to ski down. Sometimes this is for esthetics, to avoid tracking up the slopes they're going to ski. More often it is to balance a gradual zig-zag ascent, perhaps by a circuitous ridge route, against a steeper, more direct descent.

Sometimes ski areas can be pressed into service, and several thousand feet of elevation gained "free" by starting the tour from the top of a high chairlift or tram. Unfortunately this involves what's known as "out-of-bounds skiing"—leaving the marked, patrolled runs of the ski area. Enlightened ski patrols at many downhill areas have a policy of letting touring skiers use their facilities if they sign out, asking only that the skiers telephone back once the tour is safely over. Touring away from the lifts is discouraged or forbidden in periods of high avalanche hazard—a good rule to respect. Unfortunately an equal number of ski areas blindly forbid all out-of-bounds touring from their lifts. This usually results in a state of guerilla conflict between backcountry buffs and the ski patrol, and eventually unnecessary accidents due to lack of communication. The issue is important, because the use of lift facilities to gain initial altitude often permits extraordinary backcountry runs that one could never reach and ski in a single day otherwise.

Some roads that are open in winter, like the one over Loveland Pass in Colorado, can also serve as jumping-off points for incredible downhill-only tours. Starting the tour as high as possible and skiing down as low as possible may be thought of as the recipe for cheap thrills in one-day ski touring—cheap, that is, in terms of the amount of uphill energy expended. In the San Juan Range near my home in Telluride, Colorado, we often organize our spring tours from one valley or watershed to another, climbing up the southern exposure and skiing down to the north where the good snow may extend several thousand feet lower. Another springtime variation for such adventures is that of walking rather than skiing uphill over frozen spring snow, especially with mountaineering crampons on your boots; this is both faster and less tiring than skiing uphill. This is true in general for early morning spring ascents, not just on extra-steep Alpine-type terrain; and surprisingly, flexible crampons work very well with the sturdier Nordic boots.

This is only an indication of the variety to be found in day tours—the excitement I leave to your imagination. There are no *a priori* limits. A day tour may, for example, combine ski touring and climbing. Climb and descend a peak on skis: ski as high as you can, then scramble on to a summit. Or carry technical climbing gear in your pack to enjoy a few pitches of roped climbing in the middle of an all-downhill tour (as in Rock Creek Canyon near Jackson Hole, Wyoming). Or try full-moon touring—indescribably beautiful across open meadows, uncanny in deep forests. Night skiing with a headlamp is usually more frustrating than fun, but I did a lot of it on skinny skis during the years I lived in a snowbound cabin at Bear Valley, below Ebbetts Pass in the Sierra, and I can report that it's good for one's balance.

And finally, one-day epics. As a challenge, a kind of self-testing, and of course an adventure, very experienced backcountry skiers sometimes set themselves to ski in one day a touring route that usually takes several. This takes good conditions, good physical shape, and a lot of drive. And sometimes it hardly seems worth it because the contemplative, looking-around-in-awe side of touring gets lost in the shuffle (or kick and glide as the case may be). Sometimes it's just a case of being in form. A beautiful ridgeline tour from Mount Rose to Squaw Valley in the Tahoe Sierra is an easy day for experienced skiers, but most parties still do it in two with an overnight stop at the Benson Hut. Take your choice!

Choices aplenty, in places to tour and types of touring. I wanted to dispel any notion that you need to mount a mini-expedition to taste the full flavor of backcountry skiing. If you're just getting started, day tours are the easiest way to build skills and develop backcountry judgment, to say nothing of having a good time. When you've been skiing for well over a decade, as I have, you'll look back and realize that you've had a lot more great skiing on day tours than on multi-day trips.

Obviously you don't need convincing if you've read this far, so let's go on to some other basics for short tours.

Dressing The Part

A backcountry skier is someone who goes skiing in the backcountry, not someone who looks or dresses like some preconceived image of a touring skier. The same is not always true for downhill skiing, where fashion seems to play an inordinate

49. *The well-dressed backcountry skier from the inside out:*
A. polypropylene underwear; B. zip turtleneck of fine wool;
C. wool sweater; D. knickers; E. wool knee socks; F. gaiters for
deep or new snow; G. light cross-country gloves and/or
H. Dachstein wool mitts; I. sun glasses; J. wool hat; K. the
ubiquitous pack, which probably contains stormproof outer
garments, extra-warm clothes like a down vest, and a host of
other odds and ends.

role in the perception of who is and who isn't a *real* skier.

It's not just that clothes for ski touring should be functional; they usually have several functions at once (keeping you warm, dry, and cool for example), and they have to work! Your comfort, your skiing efficiency, your reserves of energy, and in some cases, even your survival may depend on what you wear. You need warmth and protection from the elements, yet in active skiing—and fast Nordic skiing especially—your body produces so much heat that adequate ventilation and cooling is the problem. This means a lot of adjustment, which in turn means a lot of layers to add and subtract as needed, rather than wearing heavy, thick clothes.

The Inside Story

Let's start from the inside out. The first thing to get rid of is the classic cotton turtleneck which is sold in ski shops by the millions and sometimes seems like a skier's uniform. When cotton next to the skin gets wet, either from sweat, wet snow falling on the back of your neck or wicking down your back, or any other minor mishap, it simply robs your body of an enormous amount of heat. Remember, snow is only frozen water; on a tour some part of you is always in the process of getting wet and drying out. Most of the time this drying process works from the skin out (springtime sunshine contributes too) so you want to choose undergarments that keep you warm when wet and can dry quickly. Since only a tantric Buddhist lama of the esoteric heat-producing yoga discipline could ever dry out a wet cotton turtleneck, the rest of us had better look elsewhere.

For years my own preference has been for light, extra-fine gauge wool knits, an all-wool, zipper-front turtleneck on top, and wool-blend long johns below. The kind of wool knit I'm talking about is so fine that it's not at all scratchy when worn next to the skin. The zip turtle permits quick ventilation in the middle of the day or when skiing fast, and still warms your whole throat when zipped up. This sort of wool knit was once rare; fortunately it is now widely available. But a new material, polypropylene knit, is probably even better, at least next to the skin. This wonderful stuff has been universally adopted by cross-country ski racers of every country in the last couple of years, because it facilitates the transport of insensible perspiration—super-fine sweat that's always present—away from the body. Result: dry skin, which makes an incredible difference both in comfort and warmth. Formerly all polypropylene underwear was imported from Scandinavia, but it's now made in this country and readily available. For the next layer, however, I've stuck with my fine-knit wool turtleneck with a zipper.

A word here on different philosophies, or systems of insulation for backcountry travel. The biggest problem, whether for ski tourers, backpackers or mountaineers, is always moisture. Some moisture comes from outside (rain, wet snow, etc.), some from your body in the form of insensible perspiration, and some is produced by the warm, moist air in your insulating layers condensing against an outer layer of cloth cooled by cold air or wind. Moisture trapped next to the skin (as by the infamous cotton turtleneck) makes you feel clammy and awful as well as directly cooling you. But moisture in any insulating layer reduces its efficiency. What to do? The commonsense approach is to facilitate water transport away from the body and clothes, increase ventilation as needed, and try to reduce or eliminate condensation.

This strategy has been made infinitely easier, and more effective, by the introduction of Gore-Tex™ outer garments. Gore-Tex is a new type of fabric that is permeable to water vapor but not to water in liquid or drop form—in other words, it's waterproof but it "breathes." Some folks refer to this whole approach to warmth and comfort as a "breathable system."

Perversely, you can do the exact opposite, and get away with it. This is the "vapor barrier" approach, and it consists simply of wearing a waterproof layer next to the skin to keep perspiration moisture *in*. Sure you feel a wee bit clammy, but enthusiasts of this system point out that you don't sweat profusely inside waterproof inner garments because the body adjusts its moisture output in response to the already damp skin. A subtle and ingenious concept, exemplified by nylon wind shirts worn next to the skin, plastic baggies worn inside your socks, and waterproof sleeping bag liners. But there's no getting around it: vapor barriers feel clammy. Some people adjust and no longer notice it. I can't. And since it's hard to recommend something you don't use yourself, I'm going to bypass this approach to wilderness clothing. If you're intrigued, check out vapor barriers in summer before using them in more extreme winter conditions. And remember that vapor barriers only indirectly help reduce condensation, and do nothing for outside moisture. Enough said!

Since I'm approaching the whole subject of clothing from the point of view of my personal preferences (or prejudices), I might as well share one more on innerwear: socks. I find most knee-length socks sold in ski and mountain shops to be unwearable. This is because they invariably have some kind of rib pattern which extends from the leg to the foot, and which imprints itself deeply into your skin after a few miles on the trail. Beware! The very best ski touring socks are made of a wool blend and have lots of tiny, terry-like loops on the inside, which effectively cushion your feet at every step while still letting air circulate. This type of sock is usually made in an ankle-high version for Alpine skiing and is quite hard to find in a knicker sock. Whenever I spot them I snap up a few pairs. Maybe I'm a tenderfoot, but as I was at great pains to point out in the earlier technique chapters, you ski with your feet more than anything else. Treat them kindly.

Over and Above: Outerwear

Tourers have traditionally favored knickers and gaiters over long pants. Gaiters seem a necessity to keep snow from filtering down into your boots, while knickers have a couple of advantages. When your lower legs get wet (as they often do in deep snow despite the very best gaiters) you can change socks instead of pants. Then, too, you can leave the knicker fastenings open at the knees for extra ventilation when needed. Smooth, tightly woven material is preferable for ski pants, rather than fuzzy, textured cloth which only snags snow no matter how organic and woodsy it looks. For over ten years European alpinists and ski tourers have been using high-waisted, bib-style knickers which effectively warm and protect the small of the back and the whole waist area, even when top garments ride up as you move (or when you crash into a snowbank)—but I'm sorry to say, these are hard to find in the U.S. A lot of ski shops sell very light synthetic tricot knickers and some bib-style touring suits that are really great for pure Nordic skiing. Don't be put off by the lightness of the X-C garments. The commonest problem in Nordic dress is certainly overdressing!

Gaiters require a few comments. They can be simple and inexpensive, or devilishly complex, expensive, and overdesigned. Here, as in all wilderness dressing, the trick is to pick what you really need and not reach blindly for the top of the line. Big, easy-to-thread zippers protected by flaps are important. I wouldn't rely on a pure velcro closure, which can become clogged with snow. And Gore-Tex fabric solves the problem of whether or not the waterproof part of the gaiter should reach up to the knee. Short boot-top gaiters are a pain, as you'll always plunge in unexpectedly over their tops. Knee-high gaiters, if well made, can be rolled down for coolness on hot spring days. And finally, if you suffer from cold feet—as a surprising number of women ski tourers do—help is at hand in the form of a gaiter/bootie combination that envelops the ski boot as well as the lower leg and can be both waterproof and insulated. Both Lowe Alpine Systems and Early Winters make such insulated overbooties, specially cut and insulated to be used with Nordic boots and pin bindings.

Above the waist is where you pile on the insulation when you get cold. As one doctor friend of mine observes about the torso, "That's where you live." For warmth, the choices are wool, synthetic pile, fiberfill and down, and their various combinations and permutations. The pros and cons of each are familiar to most outdoorspeople. Down is light, useless when wet, and most down garments are simply too warm to wear while actually skiing. Fiberfill is an equivalent filling for jackets and vests, somewhat heavier and bulkier, but can keep you warm when wet and dries incredibly fast. A relatively new development in the fiberfill/synthetic insulation field is called Thinsulate™; it has only half the bulk of other fiberfill materials but is claimed to be equal in warmth. Synthetic pile is a fuzzy jacket fabric that has had a great vogue in climbing circles, but it's usually very bulky and doesn't allow you to move well for free skiing. Very few pile garments are thin and soft enough to feel good while skiing. Wool sweaters of all weights round out the picture.

The trick is to wear layers, thin layers, preferably with ventilation adjustments like zip or button fronts, so that you can constantly adjust your insulation, not only to the temperature and weather but to your own speed of movement. The biggest mistake is to carry a single warm, heavy garment, like a pile or down jacket, which might be great around camp in the evening but which is too warm to wear during the day. You're either sweating or shivering, never quite right, and it's a real drag.

I can't tell you exactly what to wear (and to carry) because different folks have different thermal needs, but I try to err on the light side for each individual garment, yet always have something extra to put on during rest stops. Insulated vests rather than jackets, coupled with sweaters, light to medium weight, usually provide more than adequate warmth on the trail. They do, that is, in conjunction with a wind- and waterproof outer layer.

The backcountry skier, like the tortoise, asks a lot of his shell. And I'm going to go out on a limb here and say that Gore-Tex outer garments are just what the touring skier needs. Gore-Tex is the latest in a line of highly touted miracle fabrics; the rest promised a lot and didn't deliver. (Who nowadays remembers Reevair?) I resisted Gore-Tex as too gimmicky for a couple of years. But when the ski school I was working for got Gore-Tex uniforms, I found that I could teach skiing in the pouring rain for seven hours and stay perfectly dry. Shock and delight! The damn stuff works! It's not exactly a fabric but a membrane laminated between layers of different fabrics, so the Gore-Tex garments offer a choice of weights, finishes, and colors. It's doubtless not the last word; other manufacturers are scrambling to bring out similar and improved fabrics. When this book is a few years old, you may have to substitute another brand name on your shopping list. But for now this is it.

For the protective layer, I favor a two-piece Gore-Tex combination of overpants and pullover parka, rather than a one-piece suit or an extra-long parka or cagoule. This lets me wear very light wool gabardine pants underneath and still stay warm even in violent windstorms.

Naturally, all these cunning layers won't do a bit of good if they sit in the rucksack while you shiver along, trying to cross that pass. The essence of a layered system of clothes is that you cannot be lazy about adjusting the layers. The effort is well worth it.

Odds and Ends

And how about the little things? Hats, glasses,

gloves, and so on? I almost always tour with two hats: a light, baseball-type hat with a big bill for sun protection, and a wool knit hat for the cold. When you remember that about 40 percent of the body's heat loss is from the head, with its abundance of blood vessels near the surface, it becomes clear that a good hat is more than just an accessory. The so-called balaclava helmet (consult your history of the British Empire for the derivation) is a perennial favorite among mountaineers and backcountry skiers. It covers the whole head and neck and most of the face, and can be rolled up out of the way like a classic ski hat. Personally I favor a normal ski hat that I can pull down over my ears, plus a soft wool neck gaiter (a heavy turtleneck without the sweater) that covers my neck and chin when the weather is fierce. This combination seems to permit freer head movement and hence, for me, better balance, than a balaclava.

Eye protection too comes in storm and non-storm varieties. For general ski touring, wear a lightweight pair of dark glasses. Most so-called "glacier glasses" are overkill, as the leather side pieces cut off air circulation and cause a lot of sweating on warm, sunny days. The best lenses by far are the yellow-brown ones of the Vuarnet type ski glasses. These not only block out harsh, direct sunlight but also accentuate any shadows or possible relief in the snow surface under trying flat-light conditions—a real lifesaver on gray, overcast afternoons! And for stormy weather, high winds, or deep powder, you'll need a pair of goggles. Not just any goggles. The majority of ski goggles are worse than useless; they let you down by fogging up when you need them the most. The only goggles that never fog up are the large, Smith-type double lens models. (They were invented by a dentist named Smith who wanted to see his powder, and have been copied by a number of other manufacturers.) This type of goggle revolutionized powder skiing at ski resorts, and there's no reason backcountry skiers shouldn't take advantage of it. They are quite expensive, as such items go, but should last for years. I consider my Smith goggles to be probably the best-performing single piece of equipment I've ever bought!

And last on the list, hands. The gloves and mitts you choose will vary with the season (multi-layered in January, bare-handed in June), with your circulation (some skiers *always* have cold hands), and with the job you are trying to do (binding repair and photography are almost impossible in big mitts). Silk and metallic-synthetic glove liners are good for extra insulation and for delicate tasks in the cold. Mittens are far warmer than gloves—the fingers heat each other—and you can save a good deal of money by buying raw-wool Dachstein mitts at a climbing store rather than down mitts at a ski shop. Dachsteins don't get very wet (wring them out if they do) and snow sticking to the outside only produces another insulating layer. If that seems too messy, waterproof nylon overmitts can go over the heavy woolen ones. Some skiers, however, are used to skiing in gloves, and even feel they have better control of the pole action on steep downhills. On short day tours, for example, I usually use my leather ski gloves; on long trips or for bitter-cold powder days I prefer my Dachsteins. And in spring, when staying cool and avoiding sunburn are the real problems, there's nothing better than a pair of super-light cross-country racing gloves.

Obviously there are no rules. When I can't find my ski clothes I go skiing in jeans. You can always fake it. But until you've done quite a bit of Nordic skiing, you won't believe how warm you stay as long as you're moving. The more level and rolling terrain you expect to encounter, the lighter you should dress. You'll ski much better. The steeper, the slower, the higher you go, the more extra clothes you should take. Simple, right?

A Few More Things To Carry

All the time we've been talking about extra layers of clothes, some of you have been thinking: that means a pack to carry them in. And with that, the vision of the light, fast-moving day tour goes up in smoke.

Not really. It soon becomes second nature to ski with a pack on your back, and if you're crafty, it need not be either heavy or uncomfortable. Unless you're just dashing off for a couple of hours of skiing, you'll wind up carrying a pack on virtually all your tours. And it will usually contain more than just extra clothes. You will probably carry some food, if only a light snack and some quick-energy sweets. Above all, you need a water bottle (lemonade for the demanding palate) because the snowy environment is every bit as dehydrating as a sandy desert or beach. While sucking snow won't hurt you, as some folks think, it's not very satisfying and, in fact, you can't obtain much water that way. (The little you do obtain should be allowed to warm up in your mouth before you swallow to avoid chilling the stomach.) So the pack contains food and drink, as well as spare clothes, maybe a map or maps and a camera, and who knows what other little personal odds and ends you can't live without, and yes, a few more essentials as well.

Three more items—a wax kit, a first-aid kit, and what, for want of a better term we may loosely call a repair and emergency kit—complete the minimum touring panoply. But assuming that you're skiing in a group, they can be shared out to different people's packs. I might point out, too, that under the right circumstances not every one in the group needs to ski with a pack. A simple day pack will usually hold plenty of food, drink, and extra clothing for a couple of skiers. (Keep reminding yourself that you are skiers, not beasts of burden, and hold things to a reasonable minimum!)

The wax kit should contain fewer waxes and

more wide-spectrum waxes than you would use for running in a track. Keep every tube of klister in a separate plastic baggie to avoid hopeless goop all over the inside of your pack. A small nylon stuff sack should hold all your waxes as well as cork and scraper, the only waxing tools you really need. And skins, if you're using them, can just be doubled over, sticky sides touching each other and thus hidden, and tossed into the pack.

First-aid kits vary in size and scope from a veritable field hospital (too much) to a roll of adhesive tape (too little), depending on one's level of paranoia and/or medical sophistication. But you ought to have something in this department and finding a happy medium is a subject we'll cover in Chapter 10. First-aid supplies, however, almost merge into what I've called the repair and emergency kit— not really a kit in the sense of a number of objects neatly packed together but just a few key items to keep you going when the best laid plans go awry. A roll of tape is the ultimate patcher-upper and can do double duty for sprained ankles or broken ski poles. Either standard two-inch adhesive tape or the ubiquitous gray duct tape, which ski patrolmen call "avalanche tape," will do. From this starting point you should assemble whatever else you need to repair your ski equipment, deal with avalanche hazard if you expect it, and cope with an unplanned night out. Of course, you'll have the same concerns on an extended ski tour as on a one-day trip, and, being more isolated, you'll want a more extensive repair and emergency kit. But for now here are a few suggestions:

In the repair department, I include a fat Swiss Army knife, a tiny pair of vise-grip pliers, a wound-up piece of fairly heavy wire, and a spare plastic ski tip for Nordic skis. With these few items, plus the tape, I reckon I can patch together just about any broken ski equipment, at least well enough to finish the tour. The spare ski tip is not as important now as it was when most of us were touring on wooden skis, but these nifty plastic devices weigh next to nothing and are quite reassuring. (Hitting a buried stump in powder can break the tip off even a fiberglass ski!)

Avalanche safety equipment—radio beacons, avalanche cords, and the like—is quite specialized and will be covered in detail in the avalanche section of the next chapter. Fortunately for everyone, most good Nordic touring, as well as high-mountain spring touring, does *not* take place on avalanche-prone terrain, so you don't often need the full kit.

I do, however, carry one avalanche rescue item on almost every tour, big or little, because it does double duty as an all-around winter survival tool: the trusty snow shovel! A snow shovel is essential to dig avalanche survivors *out* but it's just as useful (and more often used) to dig skiers *in*. I'm talking about excavating some kind of snowy shelter if miscalculation or mishap forces you to spend an unplanned night out. A lot of skiers have survived cold nights out in the middle of winter without a shovel; but if you are able to dig yourself a good snow bivouac such miserable experiences can become almost comfortable. In some cases, a shovel *can* mean survival.

Mountaineering shops have always carried snow shovels, most of them absurd, imported aluminum toys, scarcely strong enough for making sand castles at the beach, whose blades always crumpled when you needed them most. Climbers and skiers alike have sometimes sought out bizarre alternatives: heavy-duty (and heavyweight) grain scoops, steel military entrenching tools, the works. Today, however, there is a snow shovel that does everything you want and more. It is manufactured by Life-Link out of high-impact Lexan plastic; it's light, efficiently shaped, and the blade can even be sharpened with a file if it dulls after much digging in icy crust. I carry this shovel hooked to the outside of my pack with a bungie cord. And whenever I feel a bit irritated at the extra weight or bulk, I just remind myself how much lighter it is than a sleeping bag and tent! At the moment no other snow shovel even comes close to the Life-Link. I wouldn't be without it.

I also include waterproof matches under survival gear. If you're not above timberline, there's always something dry you can burn. And you might consider adding a couple of chunks of fire starter or a small candle to simplify the job of making a fire. The final touch is a small, light tarp, or a climber's bivouac sack, something I generally leave out of my pack if I'm touring in timbered country, but almost always take in the high country. You can improvise great roofs and doors for snow shelters with a small tarp, and it has a dozen other uses if you're really stuck out somewhere. When I lived in the Alps I kept a two-person bivvy sack in the bottom of my rucksack all the time. In more hospitable mountains one slacks off a bit.

There are at least some kinds of equipment the modern tourer need not carry.

Well that's enough, don't you think? Maybe it already seems like too much for a day tour, but you'll be surprised at how little it all weighs (although if you carry a bulky jacket your pack may look a bit full).

And speaking of packs ... I haven't, because for day tours almost any old day pack will do. If your rucksack doesn't have a waist strap, you should sew one on to keep it from bouncing and swaying. Other than that, there are a hundred choices and I'd be hard pressed to say which day pack is best. My own favorite day-touring pack has a padded back (which allows me to be sloppy when packing it); it's a bit on the large size (since I feel that a big pack partially filled is more comfortable than a small one stuffed to bursting); and it has no outside side pockets, which could interfere with the arm swing of the diagonal stride.

The only way to figure out what kind of pack you prefer to ski with, naturally, is by skiing. And that isn't all you figure out by skiing, as we're about to see.

9

Bad snow, most experts agree,
is a phenomenon of transition: snow
whose crystals have not yet
assumed their final form
as hard spring ice or perfect corn.

Skiing bad snow, you get another view:
from time to time a few
turns simply happen, perfect turns
where snow and skis, radius and arc,
are one!

It takes you by surprise.
Afterwards with closed eyes you wonder
about the descent, the snow, and what it meant.

Perhaps we are phenomena of transition?
'Bad snow' only fear and superstition?
When we have learned enough, skied
and fallen enough, we will know
that snow is only snow, that words
like 'bad' and 'good' are just as absurd
as those others, 'ought' and 'should.'

9

Snowy Secrets

f skiing is an art, then snow is the artist's
medium in which to create ephemeral patterns,
experiences, memories. Art or not, snow and the
snow-covered landscape provide more than just
background scenery for our sport. To the
backcountry skier, snow is everything—source of
pleasure and frustration, delight and danger. For
most folks, snow is something that alters the
environment, but to the backcountry skier, snow *is*
the environment. To most folks, snow is boringly
uniform, the same blank surface, the same
featureless depth, white on white; to the backcountry
skier, snow seems almost infinite in its variety, its
shapes and structures, its stability and skiability.

This whole chapter is devoted to snow and its
secrets, but it's only a beginning. It takes years of
skiing and touring to develop a real sense of snow, a
near instinct that tells you when to adapt your ski
technique, redistribute your weight, avoid certain
slopes, or beat a hasty retreat in the face of growing
instability. Snow scientists and professional avalanche
control personnel are the first to admit that, in the
field, they rely on hunches and instinct as much as
on measurable data to decide when snow slopes are

safe. Most of us aren't snow scientists (hydrologists, glaciologists, etc.) and as backcountry skiers, our concerns are essentially practical: where to look for what kind of skiing, and what kind of snow to expect on certain exposures. Finding our way around, "there and back again," without getting lost or confused. And finally, learning enough about avalanches to avoid getting eaten by one.

All this is pretty straightforward except for one thing: in order to understand avalanches at all, you need a fair amount of information about small-scale, even microscopic, processes within the snowpack. So you'll encounter what seems like inordinate detail in the discussion of snow structure and stability. Hang in there! It's important information and, indirectly, it might even save your life. But first things first. We'll start with large-scale snow features through which the ski tourer travels. Then we'll tackle the story of snow itself, next the mechanism of avalanches; and, last, practical measures to cope with avalanche hazard.

A Skier's Landscape

In winter both trails and trail signs are buried and familiar landmarks are often transformed. How do you find your way around? It's not so hard, and I'll try not to make a big deal out of it. Terms like orientation and navigation sound intimidating; _routefinding_ is more like it, and puts the subject on a commonsense level.

Your basic tool is a topographic ("topo") map, usually one of the USGS quadrangles, which in one size or another cover most of the country. Best are maps in the 7.5-minute series, but these beautifully detailed topos do not cover all regions. Topo maps are generally stocked by mountain shops for all the nearby areas, and are far more important to the winter traveler than to the summer backpacker. Using (or reading) topo maps is a basic wilderness skill which is explained at length in just about every

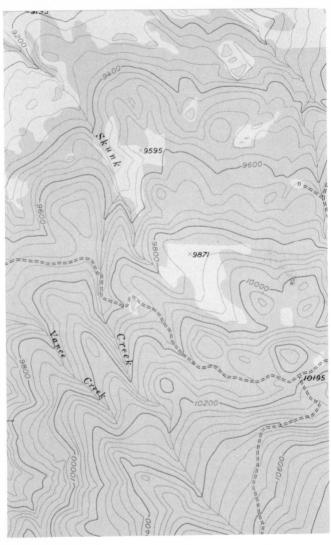

50. *Ideal Nordic touring terrain shown on a 7.5-minute topo map: rolling ridges, hills, creekbeds, small meadow-like flats, and a few small, doubtless frozen, lakes. To visualize this terrain, look first at the marked creeks to get a quick sense of up- and downhill.*

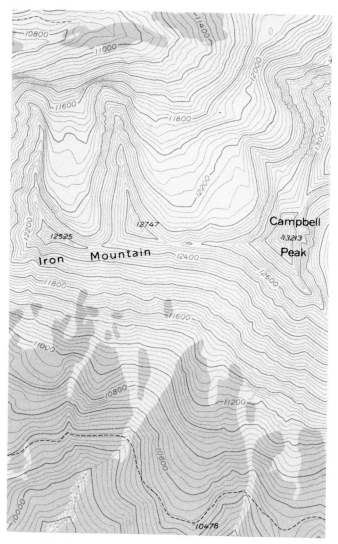

Iron Mountain
12525 · 12747 · 12400 · 11800 · 11600 · 11000 · 10800 · 11200 · 10600 · 10000 · 10478

Campbell Peak
13213
12600

51.   Ideal Alpine touring terrain, also on a 7.5-minute quadrangle. Steep, open slopes descend from both peaks to the south (they will "corn up" rapidly in spring). Open bowls north of the main ridge of peaks are more gently angled and would be more comfortable for Nordic skiers, though they too steepen lower down. To visualize this terrain, look first at the characteristic line of peaks and passes, and imagine the terrain dropping on both sides.

backpacking and hiking handbook I've ever seen. And you should probaby be familiar with such maps from summer hiking if you hope to use them effectively in winter.

Summer or winter, the most important map-reading skill is *visualization*. When you look at the mass of contour lines, don't get bogged down in little details; go for the big features, major shapes and relief. You should recognize peaks (concentric, closed, loop-like lines) and passes (back-to-back sets of U-shaped lines); ridges (nests of U-shaped lines with the rounded end of the U pointing downhill) and gullies (often nests of V-shaped lines with the points of the Vs uphill); as well as steep terrain (contour lines squashed together) and flat terrain (contour lines spread far apart).

With a little practice you can build up an effective three-dimensional picture of the landscape from just these features. You begin with the ins and outs, separating peaks and ridgelines from hollow valleys. Always visualize the general shape of the terrain before looking at small-scale features or altitude markings, or you'll get hopelessly confused.

Two other features of standard topo maps are of special interest to ski tourers. One is the indication of rivers and lakes, printed in blue with river lines crossing contour lines at a bend where they double back on themselves—an easy way to spot a valley. The other is the timberline indications, where green lines give way to brown. This last distinction gives you a lot of information about the skiing. Treeless gullies cutting steeply down through forested slopes (tongues of brown contour lines cutting perpendicularly down through green lines) are a sure indication of avalanche chutes.

From abstraction to reality. You have a map and you can read it but now you're on skis. Let's talk about snow conditions and practical routefinding in several typical situations.

Lowland Flats, Forests, and Frozen Lakes

This is the sort of touring terrain one often finds in the East, in the Midwest and northern Midwest, in the foothills of the Rockies, and the western flanks of the Sierra. Flat-to-rolling terrain, made to order for Nordic skiing, but often with a general absence of striking, tall landforms to steer by. Here a compass can be important to orient yourself and your map. (I almost never carry a compass in Alpine terrain where orientation is easily done by looking at the shapes of mountains.)

Even with a compass you'll be looking for whatever land features you can find to guide your progress. Without the vertical relief of ridges and such, the next best thing is to ski with reference to streams and rivers—not next to them, which can be tortuous and messy (skis are not designed for bushwhacking), but parallel to them, often on slight ridgelets above. In featureless forest terrain, stream confluences can become major landmarks.

In some areas, near the arctic, skiing on top of frozen rivers is often the swiftest way to travel, but I've never yet found a river in the American West that I could actually ski on. Lakes, on the other hand, are highways and a delight. Frozen lakes, after the first few months of winter, and once covered with a respectable layer of snow, are almost always safe to ski on. In late spring they get shaky and if you have an uneasy feeling about the ice, better respect it. Who wants to drown on a ski tour? Even getting wet can precipitate a major crisis in midwinter. Stream crossings might well be considered the major objective hazard in such lowland touring. Most streams can be crossed on snow bridges, gingerly.

Snow on such flattish terrain is invariably safe, but it still runs the whole gamut of winter and spring conditions: more protected in the forest; exposed to sun crusting and wind erosion in open fields. About the most serious skiing problem you can encounter in such terrain is completely botching your wax.

Since climbing isn't a problem, wax for speed and add a softer kicker underfoot, as needed, to handle gentle hills. Deep new snow on flat terrain is, at worst, a chore. You can make it a less painful chore by changing the lead fairly often and using an upward kicking/pulling motion with each step to free the ski tips when breaking trail.

Subalpine and Steeper Terrain

We're in the mountains now, and the skier's landscape changes significantly as a function of steepness. Sun exposure becomes important. A tilted slope faces north or south, or somewhere in between, and the extremes of orientation do strange things to the snow. The snow researcher thinks in terms of energy transfer at the snow surface, but the skier immediately learns that northern exposures hold cold powder for days after a storm, while south-facing snow quickly turns into glop, cardboard, cement, or crust. Thus if you're skiing along a valley that's oriented more or less east-west, the snow on one side of the valley may be totally different from that on the other, and much better to ski in. In some areas, spring snow conditions arrive on south-facing slopes almost two months before they appear on the north slopes, because of the sun's action.

Snow depth becomes a good deal more variable as we move higher into more mountainous terrain. There may be deep, sometimes lumpy, areas of avalanche deposit at the foot of steeper slopes and chutes. Wind effects are more pronounced, as well. Don't expect continuous or steady winds throughout a mountainous region. Winds flow both up and down valleys and in from side canyons, curl over ridge tops, and bend and eddy around any number of obstacles. Wind patterns, in short, are local and terrain-influenced rather than general, and this in turn has profound effects on the snow cover. Wind, of course, transports snow, eroding but also compacting it on the exposed side of a ridge, and depositing large amounts of snow on the lee side—not only in the lee of high skyline ridges but of hills, hummocks, and gentle rounded lateral ridges and rolls in the terrain as well. As we shall see, this has important consequences for avalanche potential, but it also means that the backcountry skier will encounter different skiing conditions on the windward and the lee sides of any break in the terrain. Look for harder, semipacked slopes to the windward side, deep drifts to the lee. Occasionally you will also encounter grotesquely wind-sculptured snow (on the flats as well as on high ground) which goes by the Scandinavian name of *sastrugi*. These curiously corrugated wind carvings, etched with tiny lines like a contour map, make wonderfully dramatic art photos but are a real pain to ski over.

Routefinding up the valleys and canyons, and across the passes of higher, more mountainous regions is really a simple affair. Terrain features have more relief and are easier to see. You can orient your topo map with reference to obvious landmarks and go from there. One of the subtler map-reading arts is that of judging relative steepness. The eye looks for a change in the rhythm or pattern of contour lines: do they suddenly spread apart, indicating a flat bench in a sloping valley? Or do they bunch together, indicating a band of cliffs and waterfalls blocking the route? One of the niftiest features for touring skiers, because it offers an easy route of ascent, is a relatively flat bench that slopes up diagonally across an otherwise steep hillside—indicated on the topo map by a sort of diagonal dislocation of parallel contour lines.

The country I've been talking about here is mostly below timberline and characterized by moderately steep valleys and hanging valleys—either round-bottom U-profile valleys shaped by remote glacial action, or steep-sided V-profile valleys cut by river action. You'll be skiing either along a valley or perpendicularly up and down its flanks, and a simple awareness of which way the valley runs is enough to keep anyone from getting lost (if you know what valley or canyon you're in!). Routefinding in this situation is more a question of contouring around cliff bands and other obstacles than of finding your way from here to there.

This is also the zone—steep, but in the trees—where you'll find the best powder skiing. Not only does timber protect the powder from wind and sun action, it also aids visibility in stormy weather when powder skiing is often the best. Even in dense clouds or fog that would produce a whiteout on an open slope, tree trunks will give you an accurate sense of the vertical; they even seem to cast shadows in totally flat light, bringing out texture in the snow surface. Of course, touring in stormy weather, even for the sake of great powder, presents extra avalanche hazards. Tread lightly!

Another potential tree-skiing hazard, in any weather, are tree wells, gaping moat-like holes that often ring larger trees in deep snow. I know a number of skiers who have fallen head-first into these moats and been trapped for up to two hours, unable to release their bindings overhead, until someone found them and pulled them out. Worse yet, you can suffocate and die in this embarrassing position if loose snow packs in on top of you. A number of skiers have!

To prevent such unpleasantness, it's a good idea to have the best powder skier descend last, at least in situations where there might be some problem, not just in deep powder among trees, but whenever the snow is so deep and heavy that a fallen skier might have trouble getting up. This isn't too common, but it happens. Usually a fallen skier can make a platform to push up on by crossing his ski poles in an X, yet in three or four feet of new snow I've often seen fallen skiers unable to move. A helping hand is more than welcome.

High Alpine Terrain

The Alpine environment is a kind of ultimate challenge for the skier in terms of judgment as well as technique. In good weather you have no problem navigating above timberline because you can see so much farther. In stormy weather, watch out! Not only can low clouds obscure all your landmarks, but whiteout conditions above timberline can make it impossible to ski at all, and give you a good case of vertigo to boot. In a true whiteout you can't separate snow from sky, and, what's worse, you can't really tell whether you're moving or standing still. (I've experienced it both ways: falling off a small cliff after I thought I had come safely to a stop; and trying to keep on turning downhill only to find myself at a standstill.)

A lot of bad weather produces only partial whiteout conditions, but in a treeless, rockless landscape, you will lose your bearings pretty fast. As bad weather starts to close in, you should cast about for really major landmarks, especially dark-colored rock, that you can use to stay oriented once the clouds close in. If you find yourself on basically safe terrain, you can often keep on skiing, slowly and cautiously, using your ski poles much as blind people use their canes—tapping and feeling with your poles, but above all dragging them in the snow when skiing downhill to get a tactile sense of steepness.

On high Alpine glaciers, which become absolutely featureless in the clouds, your best bet is to stay put. Sit down, eat something, bundle up, and wait till the fog lifts. True whiteouts seldom last more than a few hours. This is often cited as one situation where a compass would help, but I don't agree. You may be able to steer a straight course, but you'll stumble into the first crevasse in your way. And crevasse rescue is always a pain.

I have particularly vivid memories of one such blurry situation. We had carried loads up to the head of the Kahiltna Glacier on Mount McKinley, and were just starting to ski back down to our camp, miles away, when the clouds moved in. We spent the next few hours snowplowing, hunched over and staring at the snow, keeping the barely visible tracks of our upward ascent centered between the two ski tips. That was all we could see: about three or four feet of our ski tracks and each other in a confusing, all-white world. We ultimately did get back to camp, with tired eyes and sore backs, but if we had lost our upward tracks for even a minute we would have been forced to sit where we were and wait for the clouds to lift (which they ultimately did that evening). I mention all this not because whiteouts are that common—they aren't—but rather to emphasize the importance of visual orientation in routefinding. You figure out where you are by looking at the landscape, not at the map: a map can only help you to look in the right direction.

Snow conditions, and hence the skiing, in high Alpine terrain can vary every bit as much as the visibility—from wide-open fields of "textbook" powder or corn snow, through claustrophobically narrow chutes, icy faces, and unskiable wave-like sun cups. In addition to sun and wind effects already mentioned, which are only accentuated above timberline, the effects of steepness become important for the backcountry skier. There's the steepness of the slope you're on, but, just as important, the steepness of slopes above and below you. Under some conditions, an inviting ski route becomes unreasonable when threatened by slides from steeper slopes above. And a very inviting slope may suddenly seem less so when you notice that it dead-ends in a band of cliffs.

Characteristic mountain features of importance to the touring skier include: *bowls*, nothing more than open, wide, treeless valleys. *Faces* are steep, broad, fairly uniform areas, often leading up from the sides of a bowl toward higher ridges. (The word is used for rock as well as snow faces.) Often snow does not extend all the way up to the high ridges of major peaks except as *gullies* or *chutes* cutting through rocky cliffs; moderately narrow chutes flanked by rocky buttresses are often called *couloirs*. Such snow gullies often reach a ridge crest at a small notch, a kind of mini-pass called a *col*. Typically, the ski mountaineer will select a ridge route to reach the top of a peak and, if possible, choose a broad face, bowl or gully to ski down. While high-mountain ridges can be broad, snow-covered flanks offering good skiing, they are often rocky and narrow, and are then called *aretes*, sometimes broken or barred by rocky towers known as *gendarmes*. Ridges are the most common scrambling and climbing paths to a *summit*.

Another ridgeline feature that looms large for the backcountry skier is the *cornice*. Cornices are wave-like or fang-like lips of snow, projecting out into space on one side of a ridge. These wind sculptures can be quite small or gargantuan; they can run along a ridge for a few meters or for miles; but they are always formed toward the lee side of a ridge by snow which is transported and packed in place by the prevailing wind. These ubiquitous high Alpine features are neither safe nor unsafe—in general, that is—although in different circumstances they can be a skier's playground or an alpinist's death trap. There are few moments in skiing more exhilarating than jumping off a cornice and landing comfortably on a steep, untracked slope below. Cornice jumping, by the way, is just as much fun on Nordic as on Alpine skis—although the landing can be a lot trickier. But you'd better be damn sure the cornice isn't going to collapse under you as you ski out onto it! Great prudence is in order when approaching the lip of a cornice, especially if you can't see how far out it extends. Standing back and stomping with your skis, whacking a slot in the edge with a ski pole to try to see through, going out of your way to find a safe viewpoint, or just giving the cornice a wide berth, are some of your options.

More important than the cornice itself is the

indication it offers about the direction of the prevailing winds. Only a small portion of the wind-transported snow passing over the crest forms the cornice; most of it is deposited on the slope below. Such wind-loading typically takes place in the upper reaches of steep gullies and bowls, which are natural avalanche zones, and as we shall see, this is one of the main causes of slab-avalanche hazard. Scoured, packed slopes to windward of a corniced ridge, on the other hand, are among the stablest of slopes.

Avalanche hazard aside, the important point for the backcountry skier is that skiing conditions are often amazingly different on the two different sides of a ridge. If you're struggling with crust on one side, the other side might just be hiding powder. The major external forces that affect the snow's surface—wind and sun—act differently on every high-mountain exposure, creating a world of surprises for the skier. With enough experience you'll be able to dope out the conditions before you meet them. But while we ski over the snow, mysterious things are going on inside it.

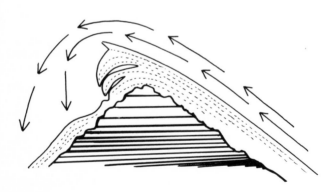

52. *Wind action in the formation of cornices, and the typical wind-deposited scarp of snow beneath the cornice on the lee side—a potential source of slab avalanche danger.*

The Secret Life of Snow

From the moment it falls, snow is involved in a perpetual process of change and transformation. It reaches the earth as millions and billions of tiny ice crystals, accumulates layer by layer into a more or less solid snowpack, and eventually melts away or else is compacted into solid glacier ice. It's a long, complex process with a multitude of curious steps. The terms used to describe these steps are no less curious. The change or transformation of snow is commonly referred to as *metamorphism*. This sounds suspiciously like scientific jargon, but you should get used to it. For one thing, this is the terminology used in an invaluable book, the USDA Forest Service *Avalanche Handbook* by Ronald Perla and M. Martinelli (Agriculture Handbook 489, available from the U.S. Government Printing Office). This is a dynamite book (pun intended) because it's at once very technical and very readable. If I could choose one other book to share your bookshelf with *Backcountry Skiing*, this would be it. And if your taste in touring terrain leads you to spend much time in or near possible avalanche areas, then reading (and understanding) this book could be the single biggest contribution to your eventual survival. The specialized language is held to a minimum, and this work is far easier to understand than previous technical manuals.

There are three main processes of change, or metamorphism, that affect the nature and stability of the snowpack. We'll look at each in turn, after first considering the lowly snowflake, or to be exact, the snow crystal.

Snow falls in innumerable forms. The form in which most people visualize snowflakes is the *stellar crystal* (star-shaped), but the most common is the *spatial dendrite*, a three-dimensional shape much like the jack of a child's jack-and-ball game. This type of crystal interlocks easily, producing a relatively compact, cohesive layer of snow. The stellar crystal and the less common *plate crystal* are not as cohesive and tend to produce the ultra-light, "bottomless" powder that is a skier's delight. Other snow crystal forms include a variety of regular, six-sided crystals, *columns* and *needles,* and also some highly irregular forms such as the lumpy, pellet-shaped *graupel,* which resembles hail. The beautiful multi-branched snowflakes that you can admire on your parka sleeve during a storm are really composed of a number of interlocked stellar crystals.

Once on the ground, all these different forms begin to change—in the jargon, to undergo metamorphism. The first form of snow metamorphism we'll look at occurs most typically in the mid-winter snowpack. It is called *ET metamorphism* (or equitemperature metamorphism) and it works like this: Newly fallen snow is seldom dense, for the branched ends of individual crystals and flakes keep one another at a distance, unless they are tumbled, broken, and packed together by the wind. Thus new snow is fluffy and unconsolidated, and it contains a lot of air spaces. Yet after a few days, two feet of new snow may have shrunk to no more than a foot; it's more consolidated, denser, and has begun to form a coherent, bonded layer. The compression is mostly due to the weight of each new layer of crystals pressing down on the snow beneath, but it's also due to a change in the snow's structure. As snow crystals pile up, they are pressed into contact with their neighbors and become mere *grains* of ice in an interlocking structure. Due to small but important differences in vapor pressure over different parts of this ice structure (the concave versus the convex surfaces of the massed-together grains) a remarkable migration of material takes place. This probably happens through *sublimation:* ice turning to water vapor without passing through a liquid stage, and then redepositing directly as ice. The redeposited ice tends to solidify and thicken the points of contact, or necks, between adjacent ice grains—this is called *sintering*—while simplifying and rounding the shape of individual grains. The actual mechanism is only partly understood but the net result is clear: the snowpack settles and grows stronger as individual ice grains pack and bond together into a more solid structure.

The reason this process is called ET (equitemperature) metamorphism is that it can only take place if there is *no great difference in temperature* across the layers of snow involved. If there is, a completely different type of metamorphism occurs. This is called *TG metamorphism* (for temperature-gradient metamorphism) and is particularly significant to the touring skier because it *weakens* the snowpack rather than strengthening it.

TG metamorphism is so called because its mechanism depends on a marked temperature gradient, or differential, between the top and bottom of the snowpack (or across a given layer within the snowpack). It works somewhat like this: early in winter, before the snow cover is very deep, air temperatures commonly fall far below freezing, so the surface of the snow is extremely cold. Yet since snow is a fairly good insulator, the interface of the snow and the ground remains around the freezing point (0°C/32°F). As an example, imagine only a foot of snow on the ground with air temperatures falling to -20°F. This gives a temperature differential, or gradient, of more than 50°F across only 12 inches of snow. Such intense differences in temperature create a strong vapor flow within the snow, from the "warmer" lower snow toward the colder surface. But unlike the more localized vapor transport in ET metamorphism, this strong flow of water vapor is redeposited on the bodies of snow grains, not on the necks that separate them. Thus the individual grains become larger and fatter, the bonds between them weaker. In its advanced stages, TG metamorphism produces a layer of incohesive, ballbearing-like snow known as *depth hoar*. Its sugar-like consistency in the hand gave rise to the term "sugar snow." Under a glass, the grains appear angular rather than rounded, and seem to be built up in shimmering geometric layers (like stacked polygonal plates)—curious and unmistakable.

One expects to find TG snow or depth hoar near the bottom of the snowpack, formed, as I've just described, when there is a great differential between ground and air temperatures. But local conditions can also create a marked temperature gradient between two layers within the snowpack, or between the surface of an older layer and new snowfall above. Such conditions produce a thin layer of TG crystals—some such layers can be less than 1 mm thick. They are difficult to spot, even for trained avalanche personnel who have dug a snow pit to investigate the different strata, but they are important, as they constitute a layer of very weak bonding in the snow cover.

TG snow is insidious, dangerous, and generally invisible, as it's ultimately hidden under successive layers of snow. As the snowpack thickens, the temperature gradient across any part of it decreases until at last ET metamorphism dominates and begins to consolidate and strengthen the snow. But the weak layer of TG depth hoar is still there, the perfect bed layer on which an avalanche may later break loose and run—a kind of buried land mine in the skier's universe. The danger presented by such snow is far from theoretical. In some parts of the Rockies, where early snowfall is scant and temperatures very low, weak TG snow layers are so prevalent that the steeper slopes in the backcountry remain deathtraps until spring. In maritime climates, such as those of the Pacific ranges, where early snowfall is deep and temperatures warm, depth hoar is less common— although often present on north exposures—and, as a result, midwinter touring on steeper slopes is somewhat safer there.

In springtime—luckily for skiers—a third form of metamorphism appears and generally takes care of any lingering instability in the snow cover. This is *MF metamorphism* (or melt-freeze metamorphism), and it produces the corn snow which is the delight of all touring skiers. With spring warming, all remaining temperature gradients disappear and the snow cover becomes *isothermic*, that is, uniformly of the same temperature, 0°C/32°F. As a result of extreme fluctuations in air temperature with which spring skiers are very familiar—scorching days and freezing nights—a melt-freeze cycle occurs within the snowpack, and the repeated refreezing of only partially melted grains produces larger, polygranular lumps: MF grains or "corn snow." This is the stuff that feels so velvety under your skis around 11:00 a.m. on a sparkling spring morning. The importance of melt-freeze metamorphism is that frozen water is holding the snowpack together. Such snow is extremely stable except on late afternoons, when free water from day-long melting can produce wet-snow avalanches. Nonetheless, the rule of thumb for spring snow is simply that if it's good to ski on, it's safe. If the snow is so wet and rotten that you don't want to be there, you probably shouldn't be.

But the small-scale, even microscopic, processes of metamorphism are not all that's going on inside the snow. Successive storms lay down successive layers of snow, and if you dig a pit down through the snow you can read on its walls a visual record of storm and metamorphism throughout the winter. The various processes of consolidation and bonding always work better within a given layer than between two layers deposited in different storms. But bonding between layers is very important in assuring the stability of the whole snow mass. TG depth hoar is not the only layer that provides weak bonding to new snow. The primary offenders are cold, unconsolidated powder, or "wild" snow; feathery surface crystals called *surface hoar*; graupel; and also slick surface layers like ice, rain crusts, and some hard windslab surfaces. There's no way a skier gliding on top of four months' deposit of snow can tell if there are weak or poorly bonded layers beneath his skis. Ultimately slab avalanches must break loose and slide along such weak layers; hence the usefulness of checking with Forest Service or ski patrol personnel (who have kept records and dug snow pits) about the stability of the snowpack.

Until something gives, however, the entire snow cover acts like a solid unit. More or less solid, that is, since snow behaves as a visco-elastic material: it deforms and flows, but has some resilience too. On flat ground, the action of gravity only compresses the snow. On a hill, one component of the snow's weight acts in a downhill direction, causing the snow to deform and flow, ever so slowly, and imperceptibly, down the hill. If only the upper layers move downhill, while the bottom of the pack remains anchored to the terrain, we speak of *creep* in the snow cover. This produces the beautifully or grotesquely overhung cornices on the eaves of Alpine chalets, as well as areas of tension in the snow cover. When the entire snow mass creeps

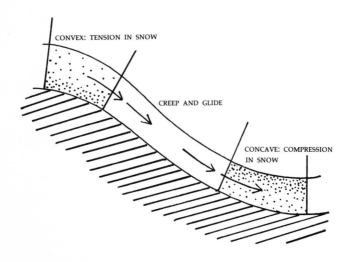

53. *The action of creep and glide on the snowpack. This extremely slow motion due to gravity produces regions of tension and compression in the snow.*

slowly downhill, we speak of *glide*. Such deformations of the snow cover can increase or decrease stress in its different layers, but more often than not it acts to redistribute and relieve mechanical stress. Snow is most viscous near the freezing point and this settling, stabilizing movement is more effective at such "warm" temperatures. In very cold, midwinter temperatures, snow becomes relatively brittle, or rigid, and mechanical stress (in wind-deposited slabs, for example) may remain high for weeks.

Obviously there's a lot more to the story of snow than I've put into these few pages. Turn to the Forest Service *Avalanche Handbook* for a far more comprehensive explanation of the many mysteries of snow. But armed with this very elementary theory, you should have a much easier time understanding the why and wherefore of avalanches.

Understanding Avalanches

Why avalanches? The simplest explanation is that a mass of snow becomes too heavy for whatever is holding it up, and slides away down the slope. This is a gross oversimplification, but a useful one because it suggests that there are really two different mechanisms for triggering snow slides. One involves an area of snow becoming heavier and heavier, as happens when a particularly heavy snowfall loads a slope beyond its capacity. The other involves the weakening or collapse of whatever is anchoring or holding the snow in place, as might happen when skiers' tracks cut or weaken a snow slab's attachment to the snow around it. Not surprisingly, the two types of avalanche release mechanism often occur together.

Avalanches can occur in all sizes, on just about any inclined terrain (although slopes from around 30 to 45 degrees are considered the most dangerous). They can involve just about every kind of snow and exhibit a bewildering variety of characteristics. They can be harmless or incredibly destructive and, of course, lethal. And they can be triggered either by skiers or by a host of natural, seemingly spontaneous, release mechanisms. To make sense out of this white chaos of possibilities, it's helpful to look at the usual ways of classifying avalanches. Broadly speaking, there are two main types: loose snow avalanches and slab avalanches.

Loose Snow Avalanches

Loose snow avalanches involve unconsolidated, usually newly fallen snow. They appear to start from a point and fan out downward from the spot where the snow first slipped. They begin when a very small patch of snow that has piled up past its maximum angle of repose slips slightly downward. This snow bumps into other grains of cohesionless snow just below it, lying at an equally critical angle, and a chain reaction is set off. Different snow types, at different temperatures, will have a different maximum angle of repose (think of grains of sand which you can only shovel up to a certain angle before they slide away), so it's hardly possible to identify in advance the slopes on which you should expect loose snow avalanches. They are quite common during and immediately after serious storms, but, fortunately, loose snow avalanches pose little or no danger to touring skiers. Most are small and are usually called sloughs (pronounced "sluffs")although some loose snow avalanches can attain truly threatening dimensions. They can also involve either dry or wet snow. The wet snow version is a somewhat nastier customer. I tend to think of loose snow avalanches as the mountain's way of getting rid of excess snow before getting down to the serious business of metamorphism and the creation of a solid snowpack—much the way a wet dog shakes off water droplets before trotting away.

Slab Avalanches

Slab avalanches are something else altogether, much more important, and more frightening, to wilderness travelers and skiers. In slab avalanches an entire, more or less cohesive, layer of snow breaks loose as a single unit. The slab of snow need not be a single layer deposited in one storm but may be made up of a number of successive layers bonded together over time. Slab avalanches are released by large fractures or cracks that often appear to cut the slope above the slab. But these fractures must actually run completely around the slab and *beneath it*, for the slab to slide away.

It's usual to make a distinction between soft and hard slab avalanches. A soft slab tends to break up completely in the course of its slide, while a hard slab fractures and breaks up into smaller, slab-like chunks and blocks. Actually a hard slab is just a more extreme case of the same phenomenon, composed of much more compacted snow. Before it releases and slides, a hard slab may be so dense that skis don't penetrate, but leave only thin edge tracks on its surface. In soft slab conditions, the snow may seem to offer good powder skiing. Slabs, in short, are not rigid masses of snow, but *relatively* cohesive areas of snow, which may fail and slide as a unit. What distinguishes them? How are they formed? And how can you tell when slab formation is reaching a critical or dangerous point?

Steepness is the first requirement. An entire mountain area may be covered with a deep, compact blanket of snow and yet present little danger of slab avalanche because the terrain is too flat. From about 30 degrees on up, the downhill stress component of a snow slab's weight becomes large enough that it may be able to cause a shear fracture across the bed surface (or bottom) of the slab, detaching it from the slope. On the steepest slopes, above 45 degrees, snow sloughs off before it can form serious slabs.

Next to steepness, the amount (weight) of snow

in the cohesive slab-like layer, is the critical factor. Rate of snowfall and wind action are the culprits here. In an unusually heavy, sustained snowfall, snow depth in likely slab areas increases without benefit of the continual settling action that keeps pace with a slower snowfall, redistributing and easing tension.

Wind action does the same thing, only more so. In the lee slopes of ridges and gully walls, wind-deposited snow often builds up at twice the rate at which snow is falling elsewhere. In addition, wind-transported snow is tumbled and abraded into much smaller grains, which consequently pack more closely together, forming an even more compact slab. The main difference between soft and hard slabs is the extent of wind action on the snow.

And to top things off, wind action, steepness, and terrain profiles particularly suitable for slab formation all occur together as often as not. Wind is stronger on upper slopes and ridges, which are typically steeper, and here one encounters both bowls and gullies, natural snow-catching areas which facilitate the buildup of thick slabs. Trees, especially dense forests, can help to anchor snow to a slope, as well as cutting and deflecting the wind. So the conditions for slab formation are most prevalent above timberline.

Any steep, open terrain, especially bowls and gullies on the lee side of a ridge, must be considered suspect. And indeed every major storm should be considered a potential source of slab danger. But when can you say for sure that a given slope is really dangerous? There's the rub. Most of the time it's impossible to say, with absolute certainty, that a slope will avalanche. I've seen avalanche control teams at ski areas toss one explosive charge after another onto a known avalanche slope that everyone swore was primed to go, with no result! You can, however, make a pretty good assessment of the possibility of a slide: negligible, moderate, or very high. But remember that the presence of skiers tends to make it higher, because a lot of potentially unstable slabs will never release unless their equilibrium is disturbed by outside forces—like you and your skis.

The buildup of large, slab-like snow layers alone is seldom sufficient to cause an avalanche. In addition to fairly cohesive snow lying at the right steepness, a weak layer underneath is necessary. In the cold continental climate of the Rocky Mountains, this is usually a layer of TG depth hoar. In the warmer climates of the coastal ranges, it's usually something else: a layer of incompletely metamorphosed new snow or a layer of wet, incohesive snow. In any climate a slick, icy, or crusty layer can do the trick, especially when lubricated by free meltwater in springtime. What happens is that the bond between the slab and the weak layer lacks the strength to resist the downhill pull of the slab's weight, and a shear fracture separates the slab from the slope. Or else a tension fracture at the top of the slab can weaken the peripheral boundary anchorage of the slope, causing the bed surface separation. In any case, cracks at the top, around the slab, and beneath it, all reinforce one another, and *poof*, the slab lets go.

During big storms, the buildup of slab weight can either release slabs or prime them for potential release. Then a slide may be triggered by outside forces such as a collapsing cornice, loose snow sloughing from above, a skier cutting across the slope, or even another avalanche in a side gully or on a nearby slope wiping out some of the anchorage or support for the slab. In the warmer maritime mountain climates, avalanche danger will be at a peak during storms and for about twenty-four hours thereafter, subsiding rapidly after that as the snow settles, deforms, and compacts, easing and redistributing the mechanical stresses which could have led to the slab's fracture. In colder continental climates, avalanche danger may remain high for weeks after a bad storm, if intense cold keeps the slab formations brittle and ready to crack.

So estimating avalanche hazard, particularly slab avalanche hazard, depends on local experience plus knowledge of what the weather has done recently (snowfall, temperature, and wind), as well as some sort of reliable information on the presence of weak layers beneath the surface, which you'll doubtless have to obtain secondhand from the Forest Service or ski patrol. Aside from hunches, that's all the backcountry skier has to work with in evaluating avalanche potential. But don't disregard hunches, at least not negative ones. When the hair on the back of your neck rises up, and a little voice inside is shouting: no, don't do it!—don't.

Wet Snow Avalanches

These slushy devils deserve special mention although they can occur both as loose-snow and slab avalanches. They are mostly springtime happenings and the weakness that triggers them comes from excessive free water in the snowpack. This free water saturates the snow until it loses all cohesion, or percolates downward to a solid crust and lubricates it so that the snow above can slide. Unseasonable rain can saturate the snowpack and produce devastating wet-snow avalanches. But most free water is produced by the daily melt cycle, so avalanche hazard builds toward evening while spring mornings tend to be quite safe, with the snow usually hard frozen. Logically, wet snow avalanches in spring shouldn't be a problem for skiers since they don't occur during the hours of good skiing. But we all make mistakes, climb a peak slower than we planned, and sometimes wind up skiing down in deep, rotten, wet junk snow. The danger still shouldn't be too high since most spring slides are slough-like, and even the big ones tend to move quite slowly, often giving ample time to ski out of the way. But you must take them seriously! Wet snow is like cement and can trap a skier even if it only piles up around his knees. If it buries you, there will be bone-breaking forces, no air spaces, and a good deal less chance of survival than in other cases.

The Anatomy of Avalanches

Avalanches don't just break off and sit there, they can go a long way. So it's natural to distinguish the *starting zone,* the *track,* and the *runout zone,* the whole lot being collectively known as the *avalanche path.* The starting zone has some nifty nomenclature of its own: the *crown* surface is the wall of snow (always perpendicular to the slope) left at the top, where the slab pulled away from the snow above; the *flank* and *bed surfaces* are self-explanatory; and the lower boundary of the original slab is called the *stauchwall* (the Swiss, who were looking at avalanches long before we were, contributed this term).

The mountains are full of rather obvious avalanche paths, especially treeless gullies extending from high, open bowls down into heavily forested zones. These big gashes are scoured from time to time by really monstrous avalanches. Such macro-chutes often drain high-altitude starting zones that may cover a few acres. Major avalanche chutes, indeed, are so evident, and the avalanches that periodically roar down them so great, that there is little likelihood of a touring skier being caught in one. Small- to medium-sized avalanches present a more real threat to backcountry skiers, especially above timberline where there are far more potential starting zones: the tops of gullies and bowls, the cushion or scarp of wind-blown snow beneath cornices, and indeed the lee side of almost any ridge. Coping with this threat is of far greater concern to the backcountry skier than simply understanding it. That is our next topic and a most important one, indeed.

Coping With Avalanche Danger

I hope you will read this section as more than

just a series of *don'ts*. It does contain a few grim
scenarios. But I'm convinced that with a little hard
knowledge, and a lot of common sense, you can
reduce avalanche hazard in the backcountry to
reasonable and manageable proportions, and do a

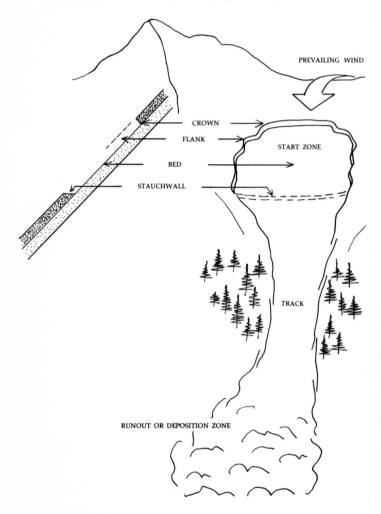

PREVAILING WIND

CROWN

FLANK

START ZONE

BED

STAUCHWALL

TRACK

RUNOUT OR DEPOSITION ZONE

54.   *Anatomy of a slab avalanche: slab formed on high slopes by
wind-deposited snow. In this case the avalanche track is confined by
the walls of a gully, but of course this is often not the case.*

hell of a lot of all-terrain touring with virtually no avalanche risk whatever. You cannot, however, ski every tour every single day of the winter, and get away with it. It's worth repeating something that's been implicit throughout this chapter: *avalanches are the most unique, the most insidious, and probably the biggest danger facing the adventurous backcountry skier.* In this section we'll see how to improve the odds in your favor, even in the worst cases.

Evaluating the Risk

The first step is to avoid avalanche conditions as much as possible by recognizing them and by skiing routes and lines that keep you off, or out from under, dangerous slopes. You will occasionally face a period of *generalized avalanche danger* in the high country, the result of an extended storm cycle or unusual temperature trends. In many areas of the Rockies, the Forest Service will put out generalized warnings through a number of media, and it's utter folly to disregard them. Simply change your plans and go touring in low, flat country—one of the great beauties of the Nordic option is that you can always find good skiing somewhere! As cross-country touring grows in popularity we'll surely see a lot more avalanche information made available to skiers. In Switzerland, for example, you can get fairly reliable avalanche forecasts on the telephone.

Most of the time though, you will be concerned with only *local avalanche hazard* on specific slopes or exposures. You already know something about snow and avalanches, and where to find more detailed information, but all the theory in the world will not help unless you can read the signs in front of you, in the snow. Becoming sensitive to snow is the first step. Because of their interest in waxing, Nordic skiers generally know a lot more about snow than Alpine skiers do. You can go one step further in your study of snow by going out of your way to look for examples of change and metamorphism in the snow cover. Try to relate the theory of snow to the snow you actually ski on. At the same time, tune in to terrain. Start looking for potential avalanche gullies, starting zones, exposed passages—even when you know the snow is safe. In short, pay attention!

Avalanche conditions are not random. There is a general pattern of stability and instability throughout the winter as well as very specific, local avalanche patterns which each tourer must learn about in his or her own area. Early in winter (November through January) the snowpack is unconsolidated and avalanche danger relatively high. Weak TG snow is common, especially on shadowy, cold, north-facing slopes; south-facing slopes tend to be safer but instability can last for weeks after a storm. As a general rule of thumb, avoid steep slopes (30 degrees and over) during this period. There's plenty of exciting powder skiing to be had on gentler slopes of 20 degrees or less. Fortunately, the coldest regions, where early winter instability is greatest, also have the lightest powder—which allows fast and graceful skiing on very gentle, safe slopes because this light snow offers so little resistance.

Midwinter to spring (February through April) is a period of increasing consolidation in the snow cover. Slab danger decreases within a few days after a storm, and steeper slopes can be skied—with caution! Finally, in spring (which, depending on exposure and altitude, may arrive in April, May, or even June), the snow becomes dense, isothermal, and quite stable. The steepest slopes are inviting—and safe. Slabs stabilize in a couple of days after a storm, while wet-snow avalanches are predictable and avoidable. But remember that this general "timetable" will be modified by the local climate (temperature and humidity) of your region, as well as by individual factors from slope to slope, valley to valley—in particular by prevailing wind patterns.

If you suspect avalanche conditions on a tour, try to confirm your suspicions by *test skiing*. Not, I hasten to add, on big slopes where you could be swept away, but on smaller, safer slopes of the same exposure. Cut the suspected slab in a steep traverse, using plenty of heel thrusting and bouncing in an effort to dislodge the snow. If nothing slides, that's still not a guarantee that a much higher slope will be safe, because wind-loading patterns could be completely different. But it is an indication. Occasionally you may feel that it's safe to use test skiing at the top of a serious slope, traversing rapidly toward a presumed safe spot. But this is a questionable procedure. And under certain circumstances test skiing the top of a slope might be far too dangerous.

Staying Out of Trouble

Once you have reason to suspect that certain slopes or certain exposures are touchy, it's time to take evasive action and go around. This means using timbered slopes rather than crossing open bowls, and skiing on ridgelines where you can. Basic routefinding! Don't get so paranoid that you start avoiding all open slopes in the high country; that's often where the best skiing is found. It's only a question of avoiding them when you feel that avalanche conditions are present. In some areas, on some slopes, that could be all winter—it all depends.

You should take special care when skiing *below* threatening slopes. Steep, V-shaped valleys are the worst offenders in this regard because the valley floor is often too narrow to let skiers avoid the mouths of obvious avalanche chutes coming down the flanks. You're always in a runout zone. Acute avalanche conditions—which you might surmise from visible natural releases on surrounding peaks—call for abandoning such canyon-bottom routes. If the hazard seems low and the canyon bottom is not threatened by too many ugly side gullies, you may elect to ski past them as fast as possible. The classic scene is that of a group of Nordic beginners, who have toured along a gentle road in the bottom of such a steep canyon, sitting down to a carefree picnic in the runout zone of a monstrous avalanche gully. Fortunately, their guardian angel is usually present at the picnic, too.

In the last example I wasn't talking about skiing across a slope which might slide, but about skiing past a spot that seemed threatened from above. Skiers are hardly likely to trigger an avalanche many hundreds or thousands of feet above them. And yet, if you tour a lot in high-mountain terrain, you'll someday find yourself in a position where you have to ski on a dangerous slope, or else you're mighty tempted to. What then?

If You Must Ski It . . .

The Forest Service *Avalanche Handbook* gives a very logical list of mitigating strategies—ways to make the best of a bad thing—which I'll try to summarize:

1. Cross a suspected start zone as high as possible; you have a better chance of fetching up on the surface if the slab goes.

2. Ski the side rather than the center of a suspect slope. Snow from the side tends to be deposited on top of snow from the center of a slab.

3. If you have a choice, slabs with a flat runout zone are preferable to those that feed into gullies (with deeper potential deposition).

4. If depth hoar is present, choose sun-exposed sections to ski.

5. Realize that crown fractures spread between anchor points—like trees and rock outcrops—and plan traverses to take you above the likely fracture path.

If you're going to ski a potential avalanche slope, it should be a well-considered decision. The temptation should be worth it, or the need should be overwhelming. And aside from the route-finding decisions described above there are a number of other precautions to take. But do think it through. Not just at the moment of choice, when you're fairly drooling at the thought of the untracked powder below, but right now, at home, because statistics overwhelmingly indicate that *most skiers killed in avalanches started the slide that got them.*

I don't want to get too preachy here because I've often accepted what I judged to be low-level avalanche risks for the sake of fantastic skiing. I've even been swept off my feet a couple of times by strong but harmless sloughs that I've set off. But knowing my own predilection for skiing in marginal situations, I've taken great pains to learn all I can about snow, and faithfully to carry and use all the avalanche safety gear I'm about to describe. I've also worked out my own skiing priorities in terms of two basic rules for skiing potential avalanche terrain: *expose yourself for as short a time as possible,* and, perhaps most important, *expose only one member of the party at a time.*

This translates into never climbing up across an avalanche area, since progress is slow, and the whole party can easily get strung out across a dangerous area. Always find a way around on the ascent! And on the descent, ski one at a time! Long traverses on touchy slopes are more likely to "cut" and release slabs than skiing in the fall line (remember test skiing). So for weaker skiers, who will find it difficult to ski the fall line, it's especially important to consider skiing or climbing around to a safer route somewhere else. In any case, once one skier is committed on the suspect slope, all the others should remain in a secure position and *watch*, so that in case of a slide they can see roughly where their companion is swept. If he disappears beneath the snow, they can fix *the last seen point*, critical for any rescue effort. And just because the first skier makes it down, or across, a suspect slope with no problem, everyone else should not pile in behind. Delayed releases aren't uncommon, and each skier could well weaken a slab's attachment, until the last one sets it off. If there's any hint of slab avalanche hazard you simply *must* expose no more than one skier to it at a time.

Other basic precautions: Take the pole straps off your wrists, so you can use your arms to stay on top if you're swept away and to protect your face and make a breathing space if you're buried. Keep parkas and clothes fastened to keep snow out (they probably already will be if you're skiing in deep powder). Some authorities have recommended releasing the runaway straps of your skis, but most avalanche control workers I know don't do this. They reckon that once the slide is over, they're going to need their skis to ski out, and that without runaway straps, the skis will be irretrievably buried in the avalanche debris. Their confidence that *they* won't be irretrievably buried is based largely upon a number of items of avalanche rescue equipment that they not only carry but have practiced using. And so should you!

Gear That Can Help

If there's a real possibility of skiing hazardous slopes, you should carry all the standard avalanche rescue equipment: ski poles that knock down and fit together to make a long probe pole. (In this country, Life-Link and Ramer make effective models for both Nordic and Alpine styles.) At least one snow shovel per party, best carried by the last skier, never by the first. (I've already mentioned that Life-Link makes the best snow shovel I've ever seen: light enough that you won't be tempted to leave it at home, strong enough to do the job.) Probe poles allow people on the surface of an avalanche to pinpoint a buried body and, of course, the shovel is to dig it out. But if a buried skier hopes to be found, he or she had better be wearing an avalanche cord (at the very least) or an avalanche radio beacon (much better) or both (best).

An avalanche cord is about 20 meters of bright

red twine tied to the skier's waist and allowed to trail along the snow behind, with small markers every few meters pointing toward the skier's end of the cord. In theory, at least part of the avalanche cord may be visible if the skier is buried and can then be followed to the victim. This is far from certain, but better than nothing; and such cords cost and weigh very little.

Infinitely better is a personal radio beacon, often referred to as a "beeper." This is a tiny radio, not much bigger than a cigarette package, which both transmits and receives. In hazardous terrain, every member of the party wears a beeper *inside* their clothes. All are set to transmit and switched on, and each emits a steady "beep beep beep . . ." signal. If one skier is buried, his companions switch their sets to receive and, using a fairly simple right-angle search pattern, can usually locate the victim in short order. The radio signal itself is not directional, but the receivers are very sensitive to distance; the searchers use relative volume (loud versus soft signal) to zero in on the buried transmitter. Simple as it sounds, it's nonetheless essential to practice with these units—locating a buried radio (not a body) according to the specific instructions that come with the beeper—before you ever have to use them for real.

The first such units were the *Skadi* transceivers, a very fine piece of electronics, designed and manufactured in the U.S. for professional avalanche control teams at ski areas. They've been around for a decade, but their high cost kept them from being widely adopted by backcountry skiers. The *Pieps I* beeper, manufactured by Motronic in Austria, is a less sophisticated but equally effective unit that sells for under $100 and has been widely used by touring skiers. (It is currently being replaced by the Pieps II, which costs almost as much as the Skadi.) Most recently, Paul Ramer has designed and produced a significantly less expensive avalanche beacon that he calls the *Echo*. (The latest model is called the Echo II, but expect more Roman numerals, as Paul cannot resist improving a good thing.) Ramer managed to cut costs by eliminating the volume control, but his tests seem to indicate that you can find a buried unit just as fast. All these units have a range of 30 meters or so, and fortunately all operate on the same frequency, making them quite compatible. (Other brands, likewise compatible, are manufactured in Europe but seldom seen in this country.) It will still cost you over $100 to get a pair of beepers (a single one is obviously useless), but if you plan extensive touring on high steep slopes, especially in mid-winter, you should think of your avalanche beacon as your cheapest piece of equipment!

If You Are Caught . . .

Since we've begun to talk in terms of buried skiers, let's plunge fearlessly on. You've taken your precautions, made your own evaluation, but guessed wrong. Is it all over? Emphatically not! Getting caught in an avalanche doesn't automatically mean getting swept away, or buried, or killed. What happens?

There isn't a lot of warning. Avalanches don't start with much noise—a dull thud at most—so your first clue will likely be some kind of motion in the snow around you. If you're at the very top of a slope which is avalanching away beneath you, dig in! Cling to the slope as best you can with poles and skis, and you may be left high and dry as the avalanche recedes. If the slope breaks above you and you're in some kind of ready-to-ski position, it's always worth trying to ski out to the side. You may not make it all the way, but the debris will be less deep near the side. If it's clear that you can't ski out, you can still make vigorous efforts to stay on your feet: a small avalanche that is only a few feet deep may cover and trap you if you fall over.

A big avalanche, of course, is going to knock you down and sweep you away. Then it's time to try the famous "swimming movements" of the arms in an effort to stay on top. Like avalanche cords, their effectiveness is questionable, but it's better to do something than nothing. It might just work. Finally, as the whole thing starts to slow down, *thrust one hand straight up*, as high as you can. Some victims have been spotted by a protruding glove. And at the same time, protect your head and chest with the other hand and try to create a bit of a breathing space.

Then it's over. You'll know in a few seconds whether you're completely trapped or if you can move. If you can, scramble, dig, and flounder up out of the debris. In most cases, the snow will set up like cement, even if it was light powder to begin with (probably due to the kinetic energy of motion being transformed into heat as the avalanche stops). At this point it's out of your hands. To give your friends as much time as possible to find you, stay calm and don't struggle. This will save oxygen and prolong your survival time. Put your thoughts in order, trust in your stars, and wait.

The Rescuer's Role

Meanwhile, back on the surface: your friend has been caught, swept away, buried. Time is precious and you have a lot to do. After half an hour, a buried victim's chance of survival is at most 50/50. After that it drops radically, yet with an electronic transceiver it's generally possible to locate a victim in ten minutes or so.

With or without avalanche radios, there is a basic rule: *always start a search, never just leave to get help.* Realistically, if you're ski touring you're probably too far from help anyway, but a quick, rough search gives the best chance of recovering your companion alive.

The sequence of steps in an avalanche rescue goes something like this: *mark the last seen point.* The search will take place below this point, but it's easy to lose track of it, especially if it's snowing. At the same time, look around carefully to see if you and the other rescuers are threatened by a second avalanche. Then *make a rapid surface search*. With luck, you could spot a hand, leg, ski, or avalanche cord breaking the surface, which would lead you immediately to the victim. Next, if the party is equipped with beepers, *walk a search pattern downhill from the last seen point with radios on receive*. This involves walking down several abreast, up to 30 meters apart, to cover the whole surface of the avalanche. If there's only one rescuer, he can cover the surface in a zig-zag descending path. Volume controls are initially set on maximum, and when the victim's beeping signal is heard, the surface party can locate his position by means of a right-angle search pattern (described in detail in the operating instructions of avalanche transceivers, and practiced beforehand).

If the party isn't equipped with radios, *begin probing*. This will be a very "coarse" probe, with all available skiers standing in a line across the slope and working down the avalanche path together. If there are very few of you (which is probably the case) you should maximize your efforts with some intelligent guessing about where a body is likely to fetch up: flat benches in the avalanche path, the curving outer wall of a gully, a partly buried stand of trees. Start probing in the likely spots, and if you don't find your friend soon, start again below the last seen point and do as thorough a job as you can. By this time, of course, you're cursing yourself for not having bought avalanche beepers, and well you may! Next to good judgment—that is, discretion and prudence—these cunning radios are the best defense against becoming an avalanche fatality.

In any case, even if you don't find your buried friend immediately, *don't give up*. Statistics are one thing, but there are also incredible tales of survival after many hours, even days, under the snow. You owe it to your companion not to give up the search in discouragement, no matter how long the odds may seem.

When you do find the buried victim, the rescue becomes a first-aid operation. *Do not* wait until you have dug the victim out before checking his condition. Check for breathing as soon as the head is exposed and, if needed, clear an airway and start mouth-to-mouth resuscitation right there while someone else continues to dig the victim out. No matter what other injuries the victim may have sustained during his white tumble, you'll have to warm him up and treat for shock. But with that we're back to a more commonplace subject, mountain first aid, which is part of the next chapter.

I hope, I truly hope, that no one reading this book ever has to live through what I've just described, either as rescuer or victim. Although I know several skiers who owe their lives to their beepers, I've never had to dig someone out. I can assure you, practice sessions are sobering enough. If you take the danger seriously enough to prepare for it, your chances of getting "chopped" in an avalanche are reduced immeasurably. But the question remains: just how serious is all this?

It all depends. In many parts of the country touring skiers never have to contend with avalanche hazard. Ten years ago I would have said that most Nordic skiers didn't. No longer. The adventurous spirit behind the three-pin telemark revolution is tempting more and more Nordic touring skiers into ever steeper, ever more challenging terrain. If your personal backcountry is both high and steep, you'd bloody well better take avalanches seriously. For all that, the high country is not really a minefield of hair-trigger avalanches waiting to gobble you up. Far from it. But only by learning about avalanches can you put them in perspective—one more mysterious element in a mysterious white world. A lot of purple prose has gushed over "killer" avalanches. But we can look at them another way: by making us more alert, they make us more alive.

10

Day by day the subtle drifts
extend their sway, deeper
still & higher, while we play
at skiing or at flying on skis,
far from crowd, track, trail,
& floating above the earth find
new ways of stopping time.

The mind too begins to grow
subtler day by day, night
after night, pale gray
thoughts on paler white.
Only the mind can fly & then
when skis & skier fail
bring us back to earth again.

10

Self-Reliance

***B**ackcountry skiing,* we've seen, is an elusive concept to define, an elusive sport to pin down. Not exactly synonymous with cross-country skiing, but rather something that happens whenever and wherever skiers strike out on their own. It's no exaggeration to say that self-reliance, more than any other quality, distinguishes backcountry skiers from skiers of any other stripe. All too often in modern skiing, downhill or cross-country, we let other people take responsibility for a large part of our experience—ski patrol, packing crew, track setters—but backcountry skiers can't afford this luxury. We neither need nor want other people to guarantee our comfort and our security, to guarantee that we won't get lost, or won't get hurt. And it's a good thing, because there's no one around to do it.

Everyone's all for self-reliance, just like motherhood and the flag, but in practice it requires a mixed bag of attitudes, knowledge and skills. We'll track this theme down from the general to the specific, looking at general safety principles, emergency shelter, winter first aid, and evacuation.

States of Mind

Sometimes it hits you with the force of revelation: you're fifteen miles from the roadhead, sitting up, bruised but unhurt from a nasty tumble—*what if?* What if I'd sprained my ankle on that last eggbeater? Nothing fatal, hardly serious, but . . . no ski patrol, no toboggan, no snow cat to pull me out. Just a couple of friends with tired muscles, and a lot of miles between us and the doctor. What if? . . .

Too many "what-ifs" can ruin any experience, but after you ask the question, you'll have a better sense of where lies the real security in backcountry skiing. As near as I can make out, ski-touring safety rests on a few key points. Adequate preparation before the tour. Skiing reasonably, which means well within your technique, and not at its very limits. Seriously looking after your companions' welfare on the tour, and trusting them to do the same for you. And finally, if something goes wrong, keeping a relaxed, cheerful attitude while you attempt to deal with it.

Before the tour. Pre-planning and preparation for a long ski expedition is an art in itself, one we'll cover in the next chapter. But every ski tour, even the casual day trip, requires a minimum of preparation. You can save yourself a lot of grief by making sure that your equipment is in good shape—bindings, edges, boots, laces, waxes. Five minutes here can eliminate a lot of cursing on the trail. Gathering information about the tour before starting is usually a must. It may be only a topo map, a guidebook description, or just a quick chat with someone who skied out that way last week. And don't neglect that most reasonable of all preparations for wilderness travel: letting someone know where you're going and when you expect to return. None of this is difficult or onerous.

Skiing reasonably is a different proposition for different folks. You simply have to develop a sense, almost a sixth sense, of what you can and cannot ski safely. And then you must be modest enough, or un-macho enough, or maybe just smart enough, to back off when you find you're in over your head. This doesn't mean abandoning the tour. If you're standing on top of a long slope of breakable crust that's obviously too hard and too dangerous for you to ski with rhythmic turns, you can still get down by using those old standbys, traverses and kick turns. It's only a question of being honest about your skiing limits, and then modifying your skiing strategy accordingly.

As an example, in more than fifteen years of backcountry skiing I've never once had a ski injury on a tour, and neither have any of my touring companions. (Knock on wood!) This isn't because I'm an infallible skier, but rather because the farther out I get in winter, the more conservatively I tend to ski. On the other hand, I've participated in a number of rescues and evacuations of touring skiers who managed to damage themselves quite badly. Every one of these cases was a matter of the skier "going for it," at excessive speeds in difficult snow or terrain. It isn't worth it—for you or for the skiers who will have the job of bringing you out. On a long, expedition-style tour, a skiing injury is unthinkable. You have to ski within your technical competence, period!

Skiing injuries of any sort are less likely on Nordic gear with flexible pin bindings than on Alpine equipment, which is one of many reasons I've weighted this book toward Nordic touring. But don't rely on pin bindings and soft boots to save you from a broken leg or sprained ankle. Skiing under control has an altogether different meaning in the backcountry than at ski areas or on prepared tracks. In the last analysis, it's not even an option. It's an absolute necessity.

Mutual responsibility of all members of a touring party for each other's welfare is another key factor. I don't hold with the idea of a trip leader. It's just a way of shuffling off individual responsibility, a common excuse for other members of the party to be less alert. You forget to notice that someone is falling behind because, well, you're not the leader. No good. I'm not advocating that all decisions be made by the whole group, because often one person's experience or prior knowledge will prevail. I'm talking about a situation in which every skier of the group remains actively concerned about, and alert to, what everyone else is doing—how they're feeling, how they're moving, how many hours the group has been skiing and how long it has to go, what the weather is doing, how the snow is changing. All those details, in short, that add up to a successful trip—or to a disaster in the making.

Knowing your companions, and trusting them, is the only way to achieve such a situation of shared responsibility. Most backcountry accidents, in mountaineering as well as in skiing, occur in oddly assorted, sometimes hastily assembled groups, whose members don't know each other well. Strengths, weaknesses, skills, and limits are all question marks, and confusion can be rampant. (A touring instructor or guide deals with this situation daily, but generally on familiar terrain, and always with a lot of extra attention to spotting and taking care of the weakest skiers.) The more touring you do, the more important it becomes to find a group of ski-touring friends you really trust.

I'd hate to set down rules about the number of people to ski with. Three or more in the party do give an extra margin of safety (since you wouldn't have to leave an injured skier alone in order to go for help). Yet many of my most magical days on skis have been with only one other person. And I'll confess to touring by myself on occasion—hardly to be recommended, but still an option if you can accept in advance the total lack of back-up support and act accordingly.

The final point is *keeping your cool* when things finally do go wrong, as they surely will, sooner or later. Sometimes I wonder if the ability to cope with stress and crises can be learned at all, or whether some individuals are born with it and others not. Who knows? For the backcountry skier, anyway, a calm, cheerful attitude is really the ticket—in the face of minor frustrations like a wax that won't grip, or major disasters, like a bleeding skier lying unconscious in the snow. An angry, nervous, or frustrated reaction to trouble on the trail almost guarantees that your countermeasures won't work. Consider the classic crisis: an unplanned night out with no winter camping equipment.

Long Nights, Welcome Dawns

You didn't plan it that way, but your easy day ski tour has just become an overnighter. What happened? A broken ski tip slowed you to a snail's pace? You took a false turn and skied up the wrong valley for two hours before you realized your mistake? You couldn't find that touring hut by the frozen lake because it was completely snowed in? Or maybe you were looking around the wrong lake. They've all happened, and most of the time the reasons are far more improbable. What now?

Alpinists have a great word for what you're about to do: bivouac! But bivouacs—unplanned nights out in the high mountains, often on tiny ledges, sometimes in raging storms—strike mountaineers as a romantic, not a regrettable, part of their experience. This is the kind of attitude I was alluding to above. Sure you're going to be cold, wearing only a sweater and wind shell, or whatever you've got, as the temperature drops well below freezing. But let's make the best of it. Set about creating a shelter with a cheerful attitude and you'll make it, for sure. Treat this touring emergency as the end of the world, panic, and it's all over.

Snow Shelters

Of course, a positive attitude alone won't keep you warm. What you need is insulation, and the

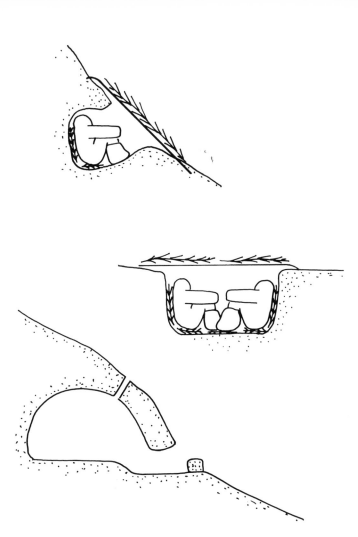

55.   Snow shelters, from the simple to the palatial. Top: a small
snow hole dug into the side of a drift, large enough for one skier
(maybe two side by side). Center: an improvised snow-trench
bivouac, dug directly into flat terrain and roofed with skis and
branches. Bottom: a large snow cave for more luxurious winter
camping. Note the circular or domed cross-section for strength and
an extra air hole pushed through to the surface. The variations are
endless; there is no "right" way to make a snow shelter.

snow will provide it. Snow is a remarkable insulator. We've already seen that the snow/ground interface stays just at the freezing point all winter long, no matter how cold the air temperature becomes. So once you put a few feet of snow between you and the night air, the temperature of your bivouac shouldn't drop below freezing either. In the right kind of snow shelter, a small candle flame, or even your body heat, will suffice to keep the temperature just above freezing—remarkable!

So the idea is to dig in—which can be a challenge if you don't have a snow shovel. In that case, use what you can. The curved, shovel-like tips of your skis, although not ideal, can be used for creating, enlarging, or improving snow holes. If you have nothing better than your skis to dig with, begin by looking for a natural hollow in the snow; a deep tree well is ideal. If nothing presents itself, look for a slope or inclined snow bank you can burrow into. Firm, consolidated, but not icy, snow is ideal if you have a choice; really soft snow must be packed to keep it from collapsing in on you all night long. Even on flattish or gently rolling terrain, a cornice-like drift of windblown snow will often give you just the right surface for digging into. If the snow is totally flat, the best you can do may be a trench, scooped straight down into the snow, three or four feet deep, just wide enough to sit in and long enough to accommodate all the skiers. The advantage of this trench shape is that it can easily be roofed with an improvised covering of branches, skis and poles, and more snow. Of course, if there are a lot of hands to dig, you may be able to produce a more clever shape.

The ideal snow shelter is a cave. At its most primitive, this is a burrow-like hole scarcely big enough for one person to crawl into, out of the wind. At their fanciest, snow caves can be palatial, especially when used as permanent camps on expeditions. Overnight emergency shelters will necessarily be modest, but if you have a snow shovel (and you should) you can do a really good job.

Make a fairly small entrance, dig straight back into the hill, and once you're a couple of feet in, start enlarging the hole. Not too big, as you'll wind up with a larger air space for your body to warm up! A round dome-shaped ceiling is the strongest for supporting the snow above—an important point, since you don't want to be buried in your own snow hole. If the snow is so loose that you really can't dig a cave, try packing it first with skis, then with boots. If nothing works, a boxy sort of hole or trench cut straight into the slope is better than nothing and can perhaps be roofed over with some ingenuity (a small tarp or bivvy sac works well). With a good shovel, it shouldn't take long to dig a minimal cave or similar shelter. In half an hour or so you should be inside the snow, and at least you'll start the night warm from your exertions.

Before settling in for the night, take great pains to seal your snow hole from the outside air, improvising a door to the cave or a roof for the snow hole. And stack up as much insulating material as you can to sit on; snow insulates you from colder outside temperatures but drains off your own heat. Tree branches are probably best (don't worry: the forest gods will forgive you for breaking them off!); rucksacks and skis are possible. The shovel will make a good seat for one person, and some packs have a removable piece of foam to pad the back that makes an ideal seat. At any rate, don't sit on the snow. Notice, too, that I said "sit." Bivouacking on a lot of climbs has taught me that one stays much warmer when sitting scrunched up, or curled into a ball, than stretched out at full length.

And that's all. Get real cozy with your companions to pool your heat and settle down for a long, cold night. Telling stories helps, humor too, but after a while you'll probably fall into a kind of stupor, which really helps time to pass. If you're lucky, you might even get some sleep. There's an old canard, still bruited about, that if you let yourself fall asleep in such situations you'll freeze to death. Utter nonsense! This idea added tension to a number of fine Jack London stories, but it has no basis in fact (unless someone is in the very last stages of exhaustion and hypothermia). Your own shivering would wake you up long before you were in serious danger. The point I want to make is that you're *not* in serious danger, as long as you keep your wits about you.

I saw a perfect example at a ski area where I worked a few years back. Two young kids (I don't think they were more than twelve or thirteen) took off for some out-of-bounds powder skiing on the backside of the mountain. Late in the afternoon, they became completely lost in a blinding snow storm, and didn't return home to the village that evening. The whole adult population panicked: ski patrol, anxious parents, and worried volunteers spent the whole night in fruitless searching. The boys meanwhile had crawled into a deep tree well when it got dark, covered themselves with branches, and spent a reasonable though slightly uncomfortable night. With improved visibility the next morning, they skied on home. I was impressed that they had done so well in a situation where many of their elders would have totally lost it. Not only did they do the right thing, but they didn't make a big deal out of it. The resourceful, cheerful spirit scores again.

Lest you think I'm laying too much stress on *attitude* in coping with backcountry emergencies, here's one more example, a counter-example really, and from the world of climbing rather than skiing, but one which dramatizes the point. In the summer of 1965, two French climbers and I were caught in a monstrous week-long storm, halfway up the west face of the Petites Jorasses, near Chamonix. Our retreat took nearly three days, but after the first day and a half of struggle, one of my companions gave up. He had become convinced that we weren't going to survive, and within a few hours of this decision he began to lose all his strength, alertness, and coordination. Ultimately we made it, lowering our nearly unconscious companion like a dead weight. Afterward he was hospitalized for a week with frostbite and exhaustion, while we felt fine after a night's rest. Yet he had been the strongest of the three, and we were all well equipped and warmly dressed. Hypothermia didn't get him, his mind did. And in a sense, it was our irrational but unshakable optimism that actually got us out of a lethal situation.

Ski touring emergencies seem a lot tamer, but the same principle holds true: deal with emergencies as matter-of-factly and cheerfully as you can, and you'll do all right. And don't close yourself off in frustration to the unexpected humor and beauty to be found in bad situations. When the long, cold night is over, you'll feel stiff and cramped but glad to be alive. And how many mornings do you actually get up early enough to see such beautiful dawn colors as you hit the trail?

Winter First Aid

When someone's hurt or hurting you administer first aid, right? True enough. But the backcountry situation imposes a special burden. Traditional first-aid training (that given in Red Cross courses, for example) stresses care of the victim until a doctor arrives. On a ski tour the doctor simply isn't going to arrive. The easiest situation will probably require several hours of difficult evacuation to transport a hurt companion back to the roadhead, and then to proper medical attention. On a multi-day ski trip to a remote area, an injured skier may be more than a week from real medical care. The distinction between first aid and emergency medical care becomes very vague in a backcountry accident, and you should be prepared to give either or both.

This isn't a first-aid text, or even a first-aid chapter. There's too much to cover and other people have done too good a job. What I can do is suggest a few ways to increase your first-aid knowledge, and discuss a few medical problems that have a special importance for touring skiers.

If you have no first-aid training, start with a standard Red Cross first-aid course; these are offered periodically in just about every city in the country. But the information you pick up in such a course is almost too elementary to be of much use in the backcountry, so go right on and take the Red Cross advanced course. This time, look for a course given in cooperation with the National Ski Patrol, and designed especially to train volunteer patrol personnel. Such courses are given in early fall in cities near major ski areas. They are oriented toward common ski accidents and winter first-aid problems, and they usually end with a practice day at a ski area, which includes transporting volunteer victims down easy slopes on rescue toboggans—invaluable! Even so, the patrol's responsibility stops once they've got an accident victim down the hill (and at Nordic resorts there's usually a snowmobile standing by to pull people out on a sled). So if you're heading very far off the beaten path, you'll need still more information. You can only get it in two ways: from more specialized texts, or from a doctor friend who understands the seriousness of backcountry situations and is willing to share some basic medical strategies with you.

Fortunately, there are a couple of great books to read. *Medicine for Mountaineering* by James Wilkerson (The Mountaineers, Seattle) has been the standard work since it first appeared in 1967. A newer book that may be even more useful is Peter Steele's *Medical Care for Mountain Climbers* (published in England but widely available in the U.S.). This is a slimmer volume, and its pragmatic style and organization make it easier for most laymen to follow. Both these books treat the wilderness adventurer as an intelligent, alert human being who may someday have to play the role of doctor without the formal training. Miles above the level of the classic first-aid textbook!

The second option is just as valuable. Over the years, my good friend Dr. Gil Roberts has played the role of medical guru for me. Appropriately, Gil is an emergency room physician as well as a climber, ski tourer, and sometime Himalayan vagabond, and he served as expedition doctor on the first American climb of Everest (West Ridge, 1963). Over the years, I've checked in with Gil before every major expedition I've gone on, to chat about the latest ideas in the treatment of mountain illnesses and trauma, and to replenish my first-aid kit with some very important, prescription-only drugs. In at least one case, this saved the life of one of my companions. I mention this mainly to encourage you to find a sympathetic M.D. who can help you prepare to deal with medical emergencies far from the road. "Far from the road" is a poetic image, but it changes everything. Gil has often pointed out that if you were in a position to apply some of the standard remedies (thawing frostbitten feet in 105°F water, for instance), then you wouldn't be in trouble in the first place. His pragmatic approach to mountain medicine has certainly conditioned my thinking on the subject, and I would say that Gil is mainly responsible for any useful information you find in this subchapter.

Medical problems you might have to deal with on a ski tour include problems due to cold, both hypothermia and frostbite; problems due to altitude, from mild mountain sickness to pulmonary edema; classic ski-related injuries; and less dramatic, but more frequent, problems caused by intense sunlight. Let's look at each in turn.

Problems Due to Cold

Hypothermia is a rather well-known outdoor hazard these days. The word comes from the Greek for "too little heat," and is the medical term for what used to be called "exposure." It describes the extreme cooling or chilling of the body's central core.

Hypothermia is particularly insidious, because it can occur when the air is above freezing; it's not the ambient temperature, but the body's heat loss that counts. And it's definitely a potential killer. Dampness and wind greatly speed up the body's heat loss through evaporative cooling, so cold, wet and windy conditions are more dangerous in this regard than extreme dry cold. Wind alone dramatically decreases the effective temperature (the so-called wind-chill factor). But heat loss by itself doesn't result in hypothermia. It's also a question of the body's inability to produce enough heat (through metabolism, shivering, or exercise) to keep things in balance and maintain the central core at a stable temperature. If a skier is physically exhausted, psychologically discouraged, or even just hungry,___ he'll be less able to keep up with heat production in severe conditions and more likely to go into hypothermia.

The first signs of hypothermia are poor coordination, thickness of speech, intense shivering and muscle tensing, and a feeling of deep, numbing cold and fatigue. But far more serious than these symptoms is the impaired judgment that invariably accompanies them. The hypothermia victim, even in the initial stages, just can't look after himself and take the necessary action to get warm. Everything seems to be "too much" or "too complicated" for the chilled skier to cope with. Fatigue is always present, and contributes to the impaired judgment and inability to cope.

Thus even the earliest stages of hypothermia (core temperature 93–95°F) are very serious. It is up to the victim's companions to spot the onset of hypothermia and to act fast. You can easily spot hypothermia in a friend by its most obvious symptom, ataxia (medicalese for "the staggers"), typified by a broad-based gait and a slow and stumbling pace. If in doubt, try a highway patrol sobriety test: ask the victim to walk heel to toe along a straight line. Or use the Rhomberg test: standing in place, feet together and eyes closed, a hypothermia victim will sway and lose balance.

At this point things haven't gotten out of hand. Stop immediately and warm the victim up: get him out of the wind, take off his wet clothes, add more dry ones, prepare hot drinks for the victim, and make him eat to keep his blood sugar up. But you have to act quickly, because once the core temperature drops into the range from 93–90°F, hypothermia is a whole different ball game. This is a very serious case. The body can no longer produce enough heat to warm itself up, even if placed in a sleeping bag. Shivering stops, muscles stiffen, behavior, if any, is irrational. Eventually, as the core temperature drops below 90°F, coma leads to death through ventricular fibrilation (erratic, ineffective heart beats). A grim scenario—and one that should never take place if you're reasonably well equipped and alert.

If someone does slip into advanced hypothermia, you must rewarm them with outside heat. The ideal rewarming procedure is to put the victim in a tub of warm water—hardly a possibility on a remote tour, but I mention it because you could conceivably be close enough to a farmhouse or a ski area to save someone this way. Leave the victim's arms and legs out of the water to avoid robbing the core of needed circulation. And use only comfortably warm water. As Peter Steele says, "If the baby turns red, the water is too hot for your elbow."

On a more practical and primitive level, in a backcountry situation, you still have a number of effective options for rewarming an advanced hypothermia victim. Give hot drinks and apply hot-water bottles (easily prepared with a camp stove) to the groin, armpits, and neck, where major blood vessels are close to the surface. If the victim is unconscious, you can administer warm enemas (not above 100°F). Do not just put the victim in a sleeping bag (he can no longer heat himself); put one or two warm, healthy people in the sleeping bag next to him. These may sound like Draconian measures, but they are absolutely necessary in the advanced stages of hypothermia. If you don't warm the victim's core, he'll probably die.

And finally, if you are confronted with a pulseless victim in the very last stages of hypothermia, simply do your best to rewarm the core but avoid any attempt at CPR treatment, which could bring on fibrilation and guarantee death.

In actual practice, it is extremely difficult for lay people to distinguish mild from extreme hypothermia (without a subnormal-reading thermometer), so assume that there is no mild case and actively warm any hypothermia victim.

Better yet, don't let it happen. With today's efficient mountain clothing—especially breathable, yet waterproof, outerwear, a skier or climber has to be just plain stupid to get hypothermia! It will only be caused by distraction and impatience to finish the tour in a hurry, to get somewhere by a certain time, or by trying to ski farther than you reasonably can in bad weather. My basic assumption is that backcountry skiers (like certain spies) are smart enough to come in from the cold, figuratively at least, and I'm sure I'm right. A good system of layered clothing is worthless if it stays in your pack when you should be wearing it.

Frostbite might be looked on as one of the body's own defenses against hypothermia. Technically it is the freezing of tissue. In practice, only extremities like hands and feet suffer frostbite. In extreme cold the body shuts down circulation to these extremities (through capillary constriction) in order to pool blood, and the heat, oxygen, and nutrients it carries, in the central core. Nordic skiers are much less susceptible to frostbitten feet than are Alpine tourers or mountaineers, because their feet are in constant motion inside their flexible boots. Skiers' hands, too, are quite active, gripping and using the poles, which maintains circulation and reduces the likelihood of frostbite.

Circulation evidently is the key. It is the major heat transfer mechanism within the body, which means that different people, with differing circulatory efficiency, may have very different responses to the identical cold. More women than men suffer from weak circulation in the extremities—though this is a hazy generalization at best. But once a skier has realized that he or she is always bothered by cold hands and feet, then it's a simple matter to start skiing in mitts instead of gloves, and using insulated overbooties on top of Nordic boots. Double Alpine touring boots are much warmer than the single mountaineering boots that have often been used for ski mountaineering, and insulated overboots and "super gaiters" are available for them too. A classic saying tells the mountain traveler: if your feet are cold, you should put on another sweater. Good advice: insulating the central core and the head is a good way to stave off circulatory shut-down in the extremities.

Despite your best precautions, slow movement in searing midwinter cold, augmented by high wind-chill, can certainly expose you to frostbite danger. The first symptom is an absence of symptoms: you lose feeling in toes, feet, or fingertips. *Don't wait.* Stop right then and there, and warm them up. Loosen your boots and massage your toes; swing your arms in circles; do something! Don't wait another mile till you reach camp. Don't just keep skiing. Don't be lazy. Rubbing, massaging, even stomping up and down in place will usually do the trick. You'll feel a mildly painful tingling as sensation returns to numb toes and fingers but you'll be fine if you take action at this "frostnip" stage. Numb fingers and toes just aren't that serious if you respond right away.

If the affected part has been numb and frozen for several hours, you have a real crisis on your hands (or feet). The optimum treatment is immediate thawing in warm (105°F) water. But after thawing, the frostbite victim mustn't walk on his thawed-out feet and will have to be evacuated on a litter. If it's possible to ski out, however, one can go some distance on already frozen feet without inflicting further damage, provided the feet stay frozen. *Don't ever rub or flail the frozen part*; this will cause extensive tissue damage. In such bad cases, abort your tour, evacuate the frostbitten skier and get him to medical attention as soon as possible. The whole cycle— white, frozen skin blistering, then turning black, dead tissue separating from live tissue and sloughing off—is long and painful, and the proverbial ounce of prevention is worth far, far more than all the pounds of bandages and antibiotics and pain involved in the "cure." If you pay attention to your feet in cold weather there's simply no excuse for getting frostbite. Yet some touring skiers do, every winter! ("Many are cold, but few are frozen.")

Good, rather detailed information on this problem is available in a well-known pamphlet, *Frostbite*, by Bradford Washburn (The Museum of Science, Boston). And while we're at it, let me recommend another pamphlet-sized book, *Mountain Sickness, Prevention, Recognition and Treatment*, by Peter Hackett (The American Alpine Club). Dr. Hackett covers the whole spectrum of altitude-related illness, from that hazy collection of symptoms known collectively as mild mountain sickness through the most extreme and lethal forms, high-altitude pulmonary edema (HAPE) and cerebral edema. His observations are based on years of work in a high-altitude clinic on the trekking route to Mount Everest and present the state of the art in the prevention and treatment of altitude problems. This small book completes your home library on mountain first aid, and brings us to our next topic.

Problems Due To Altitude

Is altitude a serious factor in backcountry skiing? Most of the time it isn't, since the various forms of altitude sickness normally occur only above 10,000 feet—and few touring skiers in the lower forty-eight states spend long periods above this level. In Alaska, however, high-altitude skiing is common, and every year we see more ski mountaineering expeditions to still more distant Andean or Himalayan ranges. In ski mountaineering situations that involve days, not hours, above 10,000 or 12,000 feet, the chance of acute mountain sickness, or worse, is very real. In fact, mountaineers on skis run the greatest risk because they can move so fast. All forms of mountain sickness involve incomplete acclimatization, which comes from going too high, too fast. No one is more tempted to do this than skiers, for whom rapid movement is both a possibility and a pleasure.

Acute mountain sickness is more than anything else a kind of general malaise that can be treated with aspirin, rest, and forcing fluids. High-altitude pulmonary edema (HAPE), however, is the blacker side of altitude illness and can kill you in twenty-four hours if you don't recognize it and descend to lower altitude. It is basically an expedition problem, deriving from hard physical work, rapid ascent, and days spent over 10,000 feet. (A few hours' ascent, to a 13,000- or 14,000-foot summit shouldn't cause anything more serious than momentary shortness of breath.)

HAPE symptoms include persistent shortness of breath—especially at rest, or at night, when sleeping may be difficult in a prone position, making the victim want to sit up; a feeling of pressure in the chest; restlessness and anxiety; and a hacking cough. Later, you will hear noisy respiration (rales), and then a gurgling sound in the lungs (difficult but not impossible to hear without a stethoscope). There will be a sudden onset of weakness, a frothy red sputum will be coughed up, and if action isn't taken quickly enough, unconsciousness and death will follow. There is only one treatment: descent, descent, descent! Three or four thousand feet lower, the patient will experience great relief and should recover with rest. In no case should you wait for outside help before starting to evacuate a HAPE victim to lower altitude. Even giving pure (bottled) oxygen doesn't work. The victim must descend, or be carried down, immediately.

What is the mechanism of HAPE? In the absence of sufficient oxygen, the body tries to compensate by sending more blood than normal to the lungs (in order to pick up more oxygen) in a process called "selective hyperprofusion." Some people don't tolerate this mechanism well at all, and the small capillaries around the lungs become leaky, filling the alveolae (the tiny air sacs in the lungs) with fluid. Ultimately, the patient can die from a kind of drowning, much like a pneumonia victim.

To keep a stricken skier or climber going during the mandatory descent—the only possible treatment!—it has been common to administer Lasix, a potent diuretic, which was thought to reduce the amount of liquid in the system that could be forced into the lungs. Its positive effect probably comes more from its action as a selective vasodilator, affecting the peripheral circulation more than the core, and thus keeping excess blood volume out of the chest/lung area. But Lasix can also cause blood pressure to drop too quickly, producing shock, which makes an already bad situation worse.

A more promising approach involves a drug called Diamox, which is a respiratory stimulant and a mild diuretic. Diamox has been shown to reduce the incidence of mountain sickness and HAPE when taken prophylactically—that is, before the fact—by those forced to make rapid ascents without adequate acclimatization. Hence, it's a useful aid for mountain rescue teams. In this sense, Diamox works chemically to pre-acclimatize the body, but it is no substitute for the real thing: the body's slow and effective adaptation to altitude. It may even make things worse by tempting people to exceed their limits. In any case, Diamox is only really useful prophylactically and not therapeutically, once an expedition member has HAPE.

Altitude sickness is not an abstract danger, and expeditionary skiers are particularly threatened, because they move so much faster than the climber on foot or on snowshoes. The strongest skier on our ski-climb of the West Buttresss of Mount McKinley fell victim to pulmonary edema, primarily because he had only one speed on skis: maximum! Short breathing began at night around 10,000 feet. A day and a half later, at 15,000 feet, my friend's astonishing mental ability to push his sick body forward evaporated in the face of growing weakness and increasing respiratory distress. Finally he confessed the extent of his symptoms, which for several days he had regarded as inadmissible weakness. By this time, his lungs were gurgling like an old radiator. We barely got him back down to 10,000 feet while he still had the strength to walk, but not enough strength to carry a pack or control his skis. End result: while he made a complete but slow recovery, my friend lost his chance at the summit, and we all learned a lesson about the consequences of being too "macho" in the high mountains.

Ski Injuries

Ski injuries are positively routine compared to the esoteric problems we've just discussed. Skiers ski with their legs, and as a consequence, skiers' legs are most likely to be injured. Typical ski injuries include sprains, strains, and, alas, broken legs.

Normal first-aid procedure for a fracture is to splint the limb, then evacuate the victim. On a backcountry ski trip you may often have to do more, especially if a deformed-looking limb indicates that the ends of the broken bone have shifted. In this case, first relieve pain (with appropriate medication), and then *before splinting*, pull *steadily and gently* on the injured limb to make it look like the other one. "No one was ever injured further by constant gentle traction along the long axis of a broken bone," says Dr. Gil Roberts. And he adds slyly, "God must have anticipated this sort of do-it-yourself orthopedics by giving us the other side of the body to compare with the broken limb."

This procedure—*traction before splinting*—is nowhere more important than in the case of a fracture-dislocation of the ankle, a not uncommon ski injury. In such an injury, both malleoli (the knobby ankle bones) are broken, and the foot appears to be off to one side. The talus, or heel bone, has actually slipped to one side. Such a position can cut off all circulation to the foot, and tissue death will take place in about an hour. Yet the foot will go back in place easily with about fifteen pounds of traction. Otherwise, the injured skier may face an amputation!

Beware, too, of overzealous splinting. With consequent swelling of the injured limb, a splint can become a tourniquet—a potential disaster in cold weather, where reduced circulation can lead to frostbite. Once you've applied a splint, continually monitor the color of the flesh and the pulse below the injury, and loosen the splint attachments as needed.

A very reasonable proposition, and better by far, is to ski in control and avoid broken legs altogether.

Minor sprains are more likely, especially sprained ankles in low-cut Nordic boots. They are only bothersome, and, if taped well, a sprained ankle can still get you up and down a lot of terrain. Dislocated shoulders and sprained wrists can be avoided by taking ski-pole straps off your wrists when skiing in trees (the baskets have an annoying habit of snagging on anything green).

Sun-Related Problems

These range from annoying but trivial cold sores on the lips, to incapacitating snow blindness, and all are easy to avoid. An evil alchemy seems to unite high-altitude sunlight and the herpes virus in the creation of enormous, disfiguring sores on skiers' lips, each and every spring. The time-honored defense is a white lip cream called Labiosan. Most lip preparations, like Chapstick, don't seem adequate in late spring. Plain zinc oxide is less expensive than Labiosan and probably does as good a job. And there are several anti-herpes preparations, such as Afil Sun Stick, available at drugstores.

The same intense spring light almost requires some kind of sun block for your face. PABA gels seem to be the best defense against high-altitude sunburn. I wouldn't mention sunburn at all, except that I've seen touring skiers almost crippled by bad sunburn when they forgot to take sun protection on spring tours. One of the best tips for long tours is to avoid washing your face for a few days beforehand so that dirt and grease, along with sunscreen, can form an effective protective layer. This sounds gross, but every time I wash my face in a high-altitude situation, I burn badly.

And finally, snow blindness. I don't think anyone reading this book is nuts enough to go skiing without eye protection, and most touring groups carry a spare pair of glasses for the party. What gets people into trouble are cloudy, foggy, overcast days. It seems too dark, so you take your glasses off, and later that evening it feels as though someone had poured sand into your eyes. Photographers soon learn that in total cloud cover you lose less than half an f-stop of light. In other words, it's still plenty bright; and clouds don't stop harmful ultraviolet radiation at all. Good yellow-brown lenses will reduce the temptation to take your glasses off when the light appears low. The treatment for snow blindness is darkness: either bandages or double goggles, as well as ophthalmic ointment and wet compresses to relieve the itchy sensation. But as with every single condition we've discussed in this section, the real ticket is to avoid it.

I think I'm going to end this section on winter first aid with a mystery—the question of what to put in your first-aid kit. It's really a question of what you feel competent to use, balanced against the weight and bulk you're willing to carry. I heartily recommend that you don't shy away from using sophisticated medication in the backcountry, especially in remote situations. But, of course, you'll need the help of a doctor who really understands such situations both to obtain appropriate drugs, and to learn how and when to use them safely. You won't want to carry the same kit on all ski tours. For a one-day tour, I take very little; for a two-week trip through remote country, I want to be ready for most anything.

Evacuation

The very thought of hauling an injured skier out of the backcountry is enough to make your heart sink. It's a hell of a job and no amount of skiing experience can make it easy. It's so hard, in fact, that you should make every effort to help an injured skier get out under his own power before resigning yourself to treating him as a basket case (for one thing you have no basket!).

With many minor injuries, like a sprained ankle or a pulled shoulder, the tourer can still ski, if his companions take his pack and divide the weight up among them. Sometimes one or two other skiers can ski alongside, offering physical as well as moral support to a hurt companion. Maybe someone has wrenched a knee, which makes it particularly painful to turn and steer the skis downhill, and yet can shuffle along fairly well on uphills and flats. A strong member of the party can carry this person's skis, and break trail if needed, while the injured one walks straight downhill, moving slowly, supported on his ski poles. Should one member of the party become simply too exhausted to control his skis on moderate downhill stretches, try the *wedge carry*. A strong skier assumes a wide, braking-wedge position, and the exhausted one wedges up behind him and hugs his

56. *The wedge carry.*

waist. (See Figure 56.) In this position, the front skier can easily control the pair's speed and downhill direction as long as the slope is not too steep.

But those are the lucky cases. If a hurt skier can't ski out, you'll have to haul him out. And that means, first of all, improvising a rescue toboggan or sled from the victim's own skis and poles. Actually you need more than that. Broken branches lashed across ski tips and bindings make good cross pieces, while the poles can either serve as diagonal bracing or be hooked to the front as pulling devices. Most of the specialized Alpine touring skis described in Chapter 5 have holes pre-drilled through the tips, which greatly facilitate lashing some kind of a sled together. One way or another, you can come up with something that works, given a bare minimum of mechanical ingenuity, and some light cord, tape, and tree branches to work with. Nylon drawstrings from your rucksacks can be used, if you have no other cord. And spare clothes and packs can supplement broken branches as padding for the victim. A few ski companies manufacture and sell relatively

lightweight kits to transform a pair of skis into a
rigid sled with a kind of canvas stretcher on top.
These are carried by the helicopter powder guides in
British Columbia, and are useful things to store in a
ski hut, but they are still far too bulky and awkward
to ever be carried by touring skiers.

57. *A rescue toboggan made from one pair of skis. More efficient
(and more comfortable) toboggans can be made out of more than one
pair of skis, an option if those pulling the sled out can walk on a
hard snow surface.*

Once some kind of a sled has been improvised,
the victim should be wrapped in a sleeping bag and
a waterproof tarp or tent (if possible), and tied or
somehow secured to the sled. Then the long haul
begins. Improvised sleds don't slide or track as well
as regulation ski patrol rescue sleds—which are
themselves quite difficult to pull across flats. So pace
yourself for a long and frustrating effort. Perhaps the
worst sled hauling situation is an ascending traverse,
where it may be necessary to pull the sled straight
up, then traverse straight across, rather than follow
the diagonal line. If the party has a rope of any sort
(not too likely unless you're on a real ski and
mountaineering trip), you may be able to use a
simple pulley arrangement to drag the sled uphill,
and you will gain a little security by belaying it from
behind on the downhills. Mostly, though, it's just a

matter of bodies wrestling with a sled.

Improvised evacuation of a backcountry injury is so difficult that you should immediately consider the option of going for help if you're within any kind of reasonable range of a ski area, or of a roadhead. Snowmobiles (which backcountry skiers quite rightly despise for their smoky, noisy intrusion into the silent winter scene) can look mighty good when they arrive to tow out an injured skier. In some areas, helicopter rescue is a possibility. The Forest Service, highway patrols, power companies, and military units have all participated in helicopter evacuations of badly injured skiers, both at ski areas and in the backcountry. But I wouldn't count on it. First aid, like avalanche rescue, is something that the skiers on the spot *have* to handle, right then! Evacuation, on the other hand, is inevitably a slow process, and I would send someone for help if the prospects looked at all reasonable. At the same time, get ready to do your best, in case no help is forthcoming.

And what of self-reliance? It's still part of the equation, even when the skier has made every mistake in the book and has to pay for it. Skiing, especially backcountry skiing, is potentially dangerous. We can't make it safe just by pretending that it's safe. But we can make it a lot safer, by taking pains to understand its dangers, and our motivations, a little better. Danger is, in fact, one of the attractions of backcountry skiing. Not exclusively, but it does add spice. Our goal is not to eliminate risk, which is (and I think should be) part of any wilderness adventure, but to reduce risk to a manageable level. To do this and still enjoy outrageous, free, spontaneous skiing adventures requires a fine blend of daring, prudence, and preparedness. In short, self-reliance.

11

Alaskan dawns
     endless daylight
shadow skiers
     sliding silent
two days down
     deep in powder
downglacier gliding
     down the Kahiltna
long straight tracks
     taking us home
under gray shadow
     of gray ice cliff
cold snow brushes
     cold air bites
high in the sky
     summits on fire
Alaskan dawns
     endless delight

11
Skiing the Back of the Beyond

How far back does the backcountry go? No use saying it's just a state of mind, especially not when you've just skied to the top of one snowy peak and you stand there hypnotized by range after range of frozen white crests, disappearing into a hazy blue distance. It's all a matter of scale. An astronaut floating overhead might disagree, but to a handful of skiers, dwarfed by so much winter, the snowy backcountry seems infinite, endless. It's hard to avoid thinking of winter as a separate geography, as though somehow the skiers' snowcovered world had no connection whatever with the more familiar land and life forms that melt out every summer. A separate landscape, a moonscape.

To me, the backcountry stretches farther back in winter. Skiing into it, I leave civilization farther behind than the number of kilometers covered would seem to indicate, and I'm not the only one to have felt this. Because wildness, isolation, natural forces seem so much greater in winter, the attraction of long trips is greater, too. What a temptation! To keep on skiing, day after day, across this surreal landscape, peak and pass, pass and peak, white on white upon white. . . .

Multi-day trips, from simple overnights to month-long treks, are somewhat trickier than their summer backpacking counterparts. But not that tricky. The main obstacle that keeps most people out of the mountains in winter isn't the cold or the inconvenience of winter camping, but just the problem of getting around—and, as a skier, you have that one licked. If you're already comfortable on self-contained summer backpacking trips, then winter camping should involve only a few modifications of your usual style of wilderness living. As to the range of possible trips—the where and when of it all—not only are the possibilities enormous, but you won't have to travel as far to experience remote, savage, high-mountain conditions. Winter tours in Montana or the Sierra may offer the same ambience, the same feeling that you would have to travel to Alaska to get in summer. Yet not every multi-day trip need involve the preparation and commitment of an expedition. Once you have your gear together, two- and three-day trips can be enjoyed at the drop of a hat, and with moderately light packs.

So that's our program for this last chapter: to consider the few important differences between winter and summer camping, winter and summer packing; to talk about planning and organizing longer ski trips; to stretch our personal backcountry skiing horizons a bit further.

Winter Camping

One could write a whole book on this subject, and I don't plan to. A very good one, however, among several I've seen, is *Ski Camping* by Ron Waters (Chronicle Books, San Francisco). This is a large-format paperback, beautifully illustrated with touring photos, which covers the minutiae of winter camping comfort with thoroughness and wit. Another good source of basic backpacking know-how is a Sierra Club outdoor book in the same series as *Backcountry Skiing*, called *Walking Softly in the Wilderness* by John Hart. Rather than competing (in vain) with either of these splendid books, I'm going to assume that you're already pretty comfortable with overnight and multi-day backpacking, and just share with you the personal tricks that I've worked out to adapt my summer kit to winter ski trips.

Packs

First things first. Longer trips mean more gear, which means more weight, which means *bigger packs*. No getting around this one. But that old Kelty pack in the closet just won't do. Rigid packframes are generally rejected by touring skiers, and with good reason, because they carry the weight too high over the shoulders, and tend to sway from side to side during typical skiing movements. Large soft-packs—some designed for mountaineering, some just for hiking—have become very popular in recent years and are generally splendid for skiing. Many of these, especially the Jensen-style wraparound packs, have solid, wide waist belts that not only support some of the load but do an effective job of controlling side-to-side sway. Climbers are prone to select very simple packs with no outside pockets that could catch in chimneys or cracks, or against overhangs; but skiers would do well to choose soft-packs that do have outside pockets—ideal for extra wax, water bottles, trailside snacks, and the like. Check to see that the pockets, when filled, don't interfere with arm movements.

Most completely frameless packs have very definite weight versus comfort limits, and can't really be recommended for much more than a short (up to four-day) trip. My preference for a week or more of skiing is an internal-frame pack. Such packs look like large, rather squarish soft rucksacks, but they have cleverly designed internal supports—most commonly, two thin, springy, metal strips either vertical and parallel, or else forming an X—which manage both to support awkward loads and to keep them comfortably away from your back. Not all internal-frame packs are equally stable, but come very close to being a perfect compromise between the load-carrying capacity of an aluminum packframe and the stability of a good soft-pack.

Savvy shoppers have learned to load a packframe-packbag combination with thirty or forty pounds of weight and wear it around the shop before buying. This is even more important when buying an internal-frame pack for ski touring, because it will almost always need a lot of adjusting to customize the fit. Go one step further, and run, don't walk, with the loaded pack on your back before buying. Use a long, swinging stride to simulate the movements of the diagonal stride, and run rapidly around corners, furniture, etc., to test for stability on turns. The ideal pack will seem to cling to your back during such eccentric behavior. Even in the shop, it will be obvious to you that a large pack, no matter how well balanced, is going to take its toll on your agility on skis. The first time you try to turn in deep powder with a fifty-pound pack on your back, you'll swear it can't be done. But everyone adjusts, and in the end it seems a small price to pay for a really long trip. (You can limit the weight to far, far less than that, when you go out for just a few days.)

For hauling enormous loads (of over a hundred pounds, for example) on long, remote expeditions, backcountry skiers may prefer to haul a sled, rather than relaying multiple loads in a conventional pack. A special Scandinavian sled, called a *pulk*, exists for this purpose. It is runnerless and resembles nothing so much as a shallow fiberglass tub for bathing infants. But this is a special measure for very special circumstances and is not a good replacement for a pack. Such sleds only work well on rather flat terrain. They have been used with great success on Arctic ski expeditions.

A fine substitute pulk for occasional expedition

hauling is a $15 red plastic sled, commonly found in the toy department of K-Mart and similar discount stores. It has become standard Mount McKinley gear in recent years. And finally, I have heard of packs which convert to sleds (and vice-versa), but have yet to see one of these wonders.

Warmth and Shelter

Sleeping arrangements are next on the list—sleeping bags, pads, and tents. Not too much new here. For a number of seasons I completely gave up on using a down bag in winter, because it was always getting damp from condensation in the tent, and daily efforts to dry it out in the morning sun never seemed entirely successful. Down still represents the best warmth/weight/compressibility package in sleeping bags, and with a better tent (a small-sized Gore-Tex model) I've gotten back into the habit of using a down bag on short trips. I still look on a fiberfill bag as a kind of extra survival-insurance policy, since you can crawl into a soaking-wet synthetic bag and spend a warm night. The construction of fiberfill bags, and the different synthetic fibers used in them, have both come a long way since they first appeared. I would definitely recommend one of the lighter designs for long and serious ski treks where you can't afford a wet bag. Perhaps the ultimate is a Gore-Tex-covered down sleeping bag—for those who can afford it!

And don't overdo it! Ski touring isn't the same as climbing Mount Everest. I find most so-called "winter weight" sleeping bags to be total overkill. The lightest, summer weight bags are usually very narrow-cut, which means you have less dead air space to warm up and less weight to carry. And on the coldest nights you can wear your down jacket to bed—instead of sweltering under ten inches of down on average nights. But that's only a personal view. I'm blessed with pretty good circulation and seldom suffer from cold. (No one as far as I know has ever written a pamphlet entitled, *Hyperthermia, Killer of the Overprepared!*)

Sleeping pads are an absolute necessity for snow camping. You might even consider a longer one for winter than for summer, otherwise you'll have to pile packs and equipment under the foot section of your bag, to keep it off the cold tent floor. Ensolite foam pads have been the standard for years, but a more efficient material is now available. EVA (ethyl-vinyl-acetate) pads are closed-cell foam, like ensolite, but less compressible, so that they maintain their full insulating value trip after trip. (They come in brighter colors too). Three-eighths-inch is the common thickness and is quite adequate, but some touring skiers like to construct custom sleeping pads, with a double thickness of insulation under the hips and shoulders.

And what about tents? Ultimate nomadic symbols, tents have been around a lot longer than skis, but in the last ten years mountain tents have undergone a complete metamorphosis. The first mountain tent I ever used was an Army-surplus classic that kept water in better than it kept snow out. This simple A-frame model was refined using rip-stop nylon, with a flysheet that really worked and appropriately cheerful civilian colors, and became the standard high-mountain shelter of the sixties. But the low, triangular cross-section was bloody cramped at best and I'm glad to announce that it's as good as gone forever. In its place, the seventies produced an explosion of dome-shaped and other unconventional, rounded designs. Most of these utilize fiberglass-wand tent poles, bent into hoops, to support the structure. Their hoop-shaped cross-section spills the wind, yields more useful space and more headroom, and provides nearly vertical sidewalls, which don't collapse on top of you at the slightest weight of new snow. Bravo!

For touring parties of three or more skiers, I'm really enthusiastic about almost any of the larger dome tents. (Most aren't true domes, but close relatives, with large, rounded shapes.) A very few are so complex that their geometry would probably give Buckminster Fuller a headache and—more important—would be very hard to erect in a high wind. Simplicity is always the hallmark of good design. The larger dome-like tents may seem to weigh a lot, but divide the weight by three or four skiers and you realize that they weigh less than a couple of small tents. In addition, one large tent simplifies cooking chores and makes camp life more congenial.

For parties of two, my favorite tent is a little Gore-Tex masterpiece called the Winterlight, made by Early Winters, in Seattle. I was even more skeptical about Gore-Tex for tents than for clothes, but I can report that in small-volume shapes it really works—even in winter. Part of the tent's remarkable dryness seems to come from the fact that warmer air

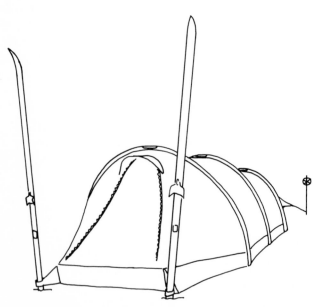

58. *An efficient ski touring tent for two.*

inside actually drives moisture out through the semipermeable membrane, before it can condense against the inside. Of course, at extremely cold temperatures there will be condensation in any tent. And in larger three- to four-person tents, a traditional breathable nylon fabric, with an optional waterproof flysheet, works far better than Gore-Tex. A number of small two-person tents are available that are similar in design to my Winterlight, that is, with a half-tubular shape supported by fiberglass hoops. In my opinion they beat conventional A-frames hands down, both for camping convenience and for stability in high winds.

Most of the time you will choose to leave tent pegs and such at home and use skis and poles to anchor the tent. In a situation where you plan to set up a skiing base camp, and will need your gear during the day, special snow anchors and wide-flange pegs are available. Skis also come in handy to stomp out a solid tent platform before you ever take the tent out of its sack. Ski-pack a platform as hard as you can, and then complete the job with foot-packing. Someone else can be setting up the tent as you finish packing a platform, because most of these dome-type tents are self-supporting and can be carried or moved around into position without collapsing.

The final shelter option is to dig a large snow cave, or even to build an igloo. Both are luxurious, relatively warm, and completely weather-proof. They can also take a long time to dig or build. So your decision on whether or not to make a snow shelter depends on the number of hands to help, the hours of daylight left, how solid the snow is, and so on. If it's a rest day, or a base camp situation, and time is no object, then constructing a snow shelter can be marvelous entertainment as well as highly practical. In howling windstorms, I've sometimes built a curving wall of snow blocks as a windbreak for the tent. One way or another, you'll get plenty of use out of your snow shovel around camp, if only to heap up fresh snow for melting water—which brings us to the next subject.

Food and Drink

Once your shelter's up (and often before) thoughts turn obsessively to dinner. Camp cooking, as usual, will be a passion or a distraction to some folks, a chore or a bother to others. But about the only problem you'll encounter is that of water. "Water, water every where nor any drop to drink." Backcountry skiers have it easy, compared to sailors; we only have to melt water, not distill it. But it's a long slow process, so as soon as the tent is up and the packs are unpacked, someone should fire up the stove and start melting snow.

The importance of a good stove is obvious. Without it, no eats, no drinks, and you can't ski far, chewing snow. A lot of people hate butane cartridge stoves, but I confess that I became addicted to them in the Alps. Contrary to popular myth, they work rather well in the cold, and they are both easy and safe to start inside a tent (reliable, too). But the weight of the gas cartridges is a disadvantage. Since melting water to drink and cook with uses a lot of gas, for this reason I use butane cartridge stoves only for overnight tours. A number of touring skiers have concluded that the advantages of butane outweigh the weight penalty, and use cartridge stoves even on the longest ski tours.

White gas stoves are the standard choice for long tours, and models with pumps for building up pressure are preferred. By far the most ingenious stove is the MSR, which has a separate burner unit that attaches to a common fuel bottle. But this lightweight wonder doesn't have the reputation for reliability of some of the more traditional stoves, like the Optimus, Primus, or Svea. You will need a minimum of one pint of fuel per day for a party of four.

A factor worth considering is the stability of the

stove, which depends upon the width of its base, the way a pot is supported on it, and the size of the pots you'll use. A combination windscreen and pot supporter is useful, and wide, rather than tall and narrow, pots speed the task of melting snow. Another trick to speed melting and avoid scorching your pots is to pour a little free water into the pan full of snow. It's hard to imagine "burnt" water, but a scorched pan makes water taste burnt. Light powder is the most frustrating snow to melt, as it seems to require a bushel basket's worth to produce a one-liter pot of water. Once you've begun melting snow, don't stop until every possible container is filled. And at night, put your bottles between or inside your sleeping bags, to keep the water from freezing.

With water made and the stove fired up, cooking great meals is no problem. In the backcountry, it seems as though a filling meal is automatically a great one. Cooking in a cramped tent, plus the importance of drinking the water you've melted, rather than "wasting" it on needless pot washing, make the one-pot meal an obvious favorite. I blush to say that my winter meals aren't very creative, and over the years, my resistance to ready-made freeze-dried dinners has all but evaporated. The only thing the backcountry skier needs to remember about menu planning is to go heavy on the carbohydrates. Of course, despite dehydrated foodstuffs, the weight of food you carry is the weight of the nutrition you receive; the rest, after all, is only water. So don't cut it too fine. Your body will process this food to supply warmth as well as work. I often double the suggested servings for midwinter touring. As to the details, every group, every touring skier, has a few favorite meals: *de gustibus non disputandum est.*

And there you have the basics of winter camping, which in turn provide the basis for long, multi-day ski tours. As in so many other situations, your best bet is to avoid making a big deal out of it. Sure there are five feet of snow on the ground, but that doesn't mean your sleeping-bag zipper will work differently. It's the same old game of wilderness walking, with the difference that instead of walking, a lot of the time you'll be flying. *Vive la différence!*

White Horizons

The question of where to go, and how to decide where to go, is even simpler than the subject of winter camping. Anywhere there's snow, anywhere you feel like it, you can probably create a ski tour. Create is the right word, too. There's no *a priori* correct way to get from point A to point B, since the snowpack covers both trails and trail signs. And since even the deepest ski tracks are routinely effaced, time and again, throughout winter and spring, you literally create each tour anew.

There are a number of basic strategies you might consider as you approach longer backcountry ski trips. The most obvious one is to start slowly, enjoying a number of overnight tours, before you pack up and take off for a week. In some areas you'll find huts to tour to, but they are the exception, not the rule. And because there are so few touring huts in this country, they're apt to be crowded with skiers on weekends—not exactly ideal. So your first few overnight ski tours will be experiments in self-contained travel. Treat them as real experiments by changing and altering things until everything works: menus, the way you pack your pack, how you guy your tent. At first you'll carry too much, so pay special attention to those things you never use, and leave them home next time.

As with day tours, it seems more adventurous to ski overnight loops, rather than ski somewhere, camp out, and then follow your own trail back. Making tracks seems closer to the essence of backcountry skiing than following them, even if the tracks are your own. Touring on the flanks of a large range or wilderness region, one can enter the mountains up one watershed, then tour along ridgelines to another watershed, which leads back out to the same side of the range. Long, backbone-like mountain chains, or their spur ranges, can often be crossed perpendicularly in two or three days. In California, there are trans-Sierra tours from a few days to a week or more in length, depending on the point you choose to cross the range. In the Colorado Rockies, there are numerous overnight tours from one inhabited valley to another, over high passes that are crossed by dirt roads in summer but snowed-in six months of the year. In the East, large, contiguous tracks of uninhabited mountain country are rare, but the whole Appalachian–Adirondack region offers great two- and three-day tours across rolling, forested ranges.

When the time comes to think about a one-week ski tour, the large western parks and national forests spring to mind. But you can also enjoy a long, sustained, and remote tour by skiing along the length of a smaller mountain group, rather than skiing from one side to the other—traversing a range, not crossing it. This strategy can yield an amazingly long and adventurous ski trek. Or how would you like to ski for two months in remote country, without having to fly to the ends of the earth, to Greenland or Patagonia, to pull it off? Two of my friends, Bill Nicolai and Pamela Kelly, managed this adventure by skiing the length of the High Sierra on skinny skis in fifty-six days, from north of Carson Pass to south of Mount Whitney. It wasn't an epic struggle, but a relaxed and sustained spring tour, with plenty of time to photograph and enjoy good skiing along the way. What made it possible was placing food and fuel caches at various points along the route. Bill and Pam skied up side canyons to place these caches the week before they started; this served as a kind of warm-up for the long tour. During the tour, they were never more than a couple of days' skiing from inhabited valleys to the east and west, while they followed the Sierra crest from north to south—an important safety factor. Similar trips are possible all over the country, for those who have sufficient free time and the imagination to put them together.

Real ski mountaineering trips in remote high ranges obviously demand a climbing and mountaineering background, as well as skiing experience. By the time you've climbed enough to be ready for such major efforts, you'll probably also know enough about distant ranges to pick and plan your expedition's goals. You'll need an extra measure of determination to cope with all the peripheral problems of traveling to a remote part of the globe to "do your thing."

From the general to the specific: where can you get detailed information about which valley, which peak, which ridge route to select for this weekend's tour? Often from a guidebook. Many, if not most, of the important touring regions in the country now have some kind of written guide. Some ski touring guidebooks focus on only one kind of tour, one kind of skiing (gentle-terrain Nordic skiing, for instance), while others describe just about every type of skiing found in a given region. Some are handsomely printed, bound, and illustrated; others are little more than photocopied pamphlets. Some guides deal only with marked trails, rather than the full spectrum of backcountry skiing.

I had considered compiling a list of ski touring guidebooks as an appendix, but gave up the idea for two reasons. In a couple of years it would be outdated, since more guides are being written all the time. And also, since there are a number of regions of the country where I haven't yet skied or toured, I really couldn't judge and recommend the accuracy of many of these guidebooks. Besides, if a ski touring guidebook *has* been written for a region you're interested in, you can surely find it at your local Nordic ski shop.

The other source of specific information is other skiers: friends, club members, ski shop personnel, touring instructors and guides, and National Park Service or Forest Service rangers. And very specific information about a proposed touring route can be drawn from your own memories of this area in summer. Everything looks different with snow on it, but not *that* different. After moving to Colorado a few years ago, I immediately began climbing, skiing, and rambling through the "new" mountains near my new home. Many of my best tours in the San Juans have been repeat visits to valleys and canyons I had visited the summer before.

Backcountry skiing is still a young sport in America. People have been stomping around in the mountains on skis for over a hundred years—but mostly to deliver mail, carry supplies to a mine, or check snow and water gauges, half of the time muttering and grumbling about the "damn snow on the ground." Things changed after World War II, but somehow the charm of the backcountry got drowned out in our rush to build and enjoy downhill ski areas. The touring skier was definitely an eccentric, if not a nut; and such skiers were few and far between. Today things are changing and I, for one, am delighted. I don't think its new-found popularity threatens the purity and delight of our backcountry ski experience. Skiing is so much harder than walking that I don't see the backcountry ever being overrun by skiers. (Snowmobilers are another question!) But because so few of us have been doing it for so short a time (relatively speaking), the best ski tours are probably still waiting to be discovered.

The best tours! That too is relative. Some touring routes across well-known mountain ranges will surely become classics, for their spectacular scenery or their impressive slopes. Just like the famous *Haute Route*, a six-day ski tour from Chamonix to Zermatt, which is the most famous (but not necessarily the best) high-mountain skiing in the Alps. Other incredible backcountry ski routes will be known among only a handful of friends. Still other, wonderful routes may be skied only once in the next fifty years, and some never.

Rather than focusing too closely on the question of skiing routes, or specific information for specific ski tours, we should come back to our original definition of backcountry skiing—*skiing far from the beaten track*. It doesn't take a packed slope, or a packed Nordic track, to destroy the appealing mystery of backcountry skiing: too much information can do it too. If every traverse and turn, every false step and landmark is memorized before you ski off into the forest, what's left? Often I'll avoid reading a guidebook description of a ski tour or a climbing route, because it's such a pleasure to find my own way.

Already, I think, you know enough. I've gotten you started and worked on your skiing, opened a few doors, shared some hot tips, and hinted at sights and secrets you can only explore for yourself. The backcountry is waiting: endless winter, eternal spring, white horizons. The back of the beyond on skis.

You're on your own.

Backcountry Skiing: a Non-Exhaustive Bibliography

The following is simply a list of my own favorite titles, among many, many more, that deal with ski touring, ski technique, wilderness medicine, and winter survival. They are either books that I have enjoyed, or learned a lot from, or both. Perhaps you will too.

BARNETT, STEVE. *Cross-Country Downhill.* Pacific Search Press, Seattle, Washington, 1979 (second edition, revised). 112 pages.

An enthusiastic, energetic account of downhill techniques for skinny skis. This book made a major contribution to the "telemark renaissance" I have mentioned throughout *Backcountry Skiing.* Many of Barnett's insights on the mysteries of telemarking are real original discoveries. The chapters on parallel and so-called open turns are less exciting and sometimes downright confusing.

BRADY, MICHAEL. *Cross-Country Ski Gear.* The Mountaineers, Seattle, Washington, 1979. 211 pages.

A fascinating small volume that could easily have been entitled, "All You Ever Wanted to Know About

Cross-Country Ski Gear and Much, Much More!"
An almost scientific study of ski equipment
construction, materials, technology, etc. Not light
reading. Invaluable reference work for the fanatic.

GILLETTE, NED. *Cross-Country Skiing.* The
Mountaineers, Seattle, Washington, 1979. 223 pages.

Simply the best, most up-to-date book on the
intricacies of pure Nordic ski technique that I know.
The author is a former Olympic competitor as well
as a backcountry adventure skier of note. He does a
great job in covering that most deceptively simple of
all Nordic techniques, the diagonal stride, including
its modern refinements and variations for cross-
country racing.

HACKETT, PETER H. *Mountain Sickness.* The American
Alpine Club, New York, 1978. 77 pages.

This small, pamphlet-sized book is the last word
on the prevention, recognition, and treatment of
acute mountain sickness in all its forms, including
the dreaded high-altitude pulmonary edema (HAPE).
By a doctor who has practiced extensively at high
altitudes in the Himalaya.

PAINTER, HAL. *The Cross-Country Ski, Cook, Look &
Pleasure Book.* Wilderness Press, Berkeley, California,
1973. 166 pages.

The only really witty book I've ever seen on
cross-country skiing. Irreverent, outrageous, sly,
charming, offbeat, and it even contains a bunch of
useful advice on practical touring. Need I say more?

PERLA, RONALD I. AND M. MARTENELLI JR. *Avalanche
Handbook.* U.S. Department of Agriculture, Forest
Service, Agriculture Handbook 489, 1975. 238 pages.

If you're tempted by steep slopes and midwinter
powder, reading—no, studying—this book is an
important first step to avoid a sad and early end to
your touring career. It's well illustrated, clear, and
remarkably readable for what is basically a scientific/
technical work. A must! Write to the U.S. Government
Printing Office for this one; available in a few stores.

STEELE, PETER. *Medical Care for Mountain Climbers.*
William Heineman Medical Books Ltd., London,
1976. 220 pages.

This book is more immediately practical, if
somewhat less encyclopedic, than Wilkerson's
manual listed further on in this bibliography. Its
twenty-one chapters are divided into six sections: an
introduction to emergency care, danger of immediate
death, serious conditions, common ailments, high
altitudes, and miscellaneous. No-nonsense, commonsense approaches. Hard to find in the U.S. but
available in some mountain shops.

WASHBURN, BRADFORD. *Frostbite.* Museum of Science,
Boston, 1963. 25 pages.

A handy, pamphlet-sized monograph on
frostbite: what it is, how to prevent it, emergency
treatment. Useful reading before an Alaskan ski
expedition or any really cold-weather touring.

WATTERS, RON. *Ski Camping.* Solstice Press/Chronicle
Books, San Francisco, 1979. 154 pages.

A splendid book, which first impresses one with
its dramatic layout and striking photographs. It's also
a treasury of tips for comfortable winter camping,
menu planning, cooking, and coping on ski tours.
Some material on basic ski technique, too.

WILKERSON, JAMES A., EDITOR. *Medicine for
Mountaineering.* The Mountaineers, Seattle,
Washington, 1967. 368 pages.

For years the basic reference work and guide to
treating injuries and illness in a mountain wilderness
setting. Comprehensive, detailed. Twenty-six chapters
divided roughly in four sections: general principles,
traumatic injuries, environmental injuries, non-
traumatic diseases. This book has saved more than
one life, and is commonly available. Get it when you
feel the need to go beyond the basic Red Cross first-
aid manual.

Photo Credits

Index

302